PENGUIN BOOKS
THE OTHER SIDE OF BELIEF

Mukunda Rao teaches English at Dr. Ambedkar Degree College, Bangalore. He is the author of *Confessions of a Sannyasi* (1988), *The Mahatma: A Novel* (1992), *The Death of an Activist* (1997), *Babasaheb Ambedkar: Trials with Truth* (2000), *Rama Revisited and Other Stories* (2002) and *Chinnamani's World* (2003).

He lives with his wife and son in Bangalore.

The Other Side of Belief

Interpreting U.G. Krishnamurti

MUKUNDA RAO

PENGUIN BOOKS

PENGUIN BOOKS
Published by the Penguin Group
Penguin Books India Pvt Ltd, 11 Community Centre, Panchsheel Park, New
Delhi 110 017, India
Penguin Group (USA) Inc., 375 Hudson Street, New York, NY 10014, USA
Penguin Group (Canada), 90 Eglinton Avenue East, Suite 700, Toronto,
Ontario, M4P 2Y3, Canada (a division of Pearson Penguin Canada Inc.)
Penguin Books Ltd, 80 Strand, London WC2R 0RL, England
Penguin Ireland, 25 St Stephen's Green, Dublin 2, Ireland (a division of
Penguin Books Ltd)
Penguin Group (Australia), 250 Camberwell Road, Camberwell, Victoria
3124, Australia (a division of Pearson Australia Group Pty Ltd)
Penguin Group (NZ), cnr Airborne and Rosedale Roads, Albany, Auckland
1310, New Zealand (a division of Pearson New Zealand Ltd)
Penguin Group (South Africa) (Pty) Ltd, 24 Sturdee Avenue, Rosebank,
Johannesburg 2196, South Africa

Penguin Books Ltd, Registered Offices: 80 Strand, London WC2R 0RL,
England

First published by Penguin Books India 2005

Copyright © Mukunda Rao 2005

The views and opinions expressed in this book are the author's own and the
facts are as reported by him which have been verified to the extent possible,
and the publishers are not in any way liable for the same.

Typeset in Sabon by InoSoft Systems, Noida
Printed at Repro India Ltd., Navi Mumbai

For Shruti
who lived like there was no tomorrow

Contents

ACKNOWLEDGEMENTS IX

FOREWORD XI

BOOK ONE: THE WAY IT IS

PRELUDE 3

'NO BOUNDARIES' 17

'CAN YOU TAKE IT?' 29

DOUBT IS THE OTHER SIDE OF
BELIEF 49

A CON GAME 54

'CANCER TREATS SAINTS AND
SINNERS IN THE SAME WAY' 66

'HAVE YOU EVER HAD SEX,
KRISHNAJI?' 79

THE END OF SAMSARA 91

THE DARK NIGHT OF THE
BODY 104

THE MYSTIQUE OF NIRVANA 126

BOOK TWO: INTERPRETING
U.G. KRISHNAMURTI

GOD(S), FEAR AND ULTIMATE
PLEASURE 155

MYSTICISM DEMYSTIFIED 166

viii   Contents

GURUS AND HOLY BUSINESS 173

AVATARS AS ULTIMATE
MODELS 180

RELIGION IN A SECULAR
MODE 189

THEORY AND PRACTICE 203

SUPERMAN DEBUNKED 218

THE TWO KRISHNAMURTIS 227

BODY, MIND AND SOUL—DO
THEY EXIST? 244

THE ENIGMA OF THE NATURAL
STATE 269

THE ETERNAL RECURRENCE 289

BOOK THREE: ANTI-TEACHING

TELLING IT LIKE IT IS
THE VOICE OF UG 301

NOTES 345

Acknowledgements

This has to be said. There is nothing original about this book. It is perhaps different, the difference being in the way I have strung things together and developed a narrative. But there is nothing in there that I can claim as purely my own. I have borrowed ideas, even expressions, from several sources and I have been inspired by many. I am the inheritor of all that has happened before, so to speak. It would be an impossible task, therefore, to enumerate all the help I have received, or mention the names of all those who have been of great help to me in writing this book. However, I remember with gratitude J.S.R.L. Narayana Moorty, a retired professor based in America, who read through the first draft of the book and provided very helpful criticism and suggestions. He is the best any writer could hope to have as his first reader. K Chandrasekhar has been a great friend and support all through this difficult period of writing. He not only offered me access to his notes on UG, but also, despite his busy schedule, over several days answered all my queries concerning UG's past, as well as freely shared his own experiences with UG. I am greatly indebted to him. I am also indebted to Major S. Dakshinamurti for pointing out certain factual errors in the text and for his useful suggestions. I cannot thank Dr Mundra enough for his continuous support and encouragement, and for putting his entire library at my disposal. I am immensely grateful to Mahesh Bhatt for his great help all the way and for writing the foreword to the book. I gratefully acknowledge the critical inputs from both V. K. Karthika and Paromita Mohanchandra and their efforts in publishing the book.

Foreword

The story of man's relentless pursuit to understand the secret of existence is timeless. Trapped between a dead past and an unborn future, the human animal has, since the dawn of time, asked these two questions—'Who am I?' and 'Why am I here?' These are the questions which propelled the author to the doors of the most subversive man in human history—U.G. Krishnamurti. And the outcome of that encounter is this exceptional book.

This book stands alongside others that have dealt with the history of man's search for an enduring truth. However, I would like to venture a word of caution . . . by the time you have flipped through the first few pages of the book you will realize that the author is making you look at the human situation through the eyes of a man who has torn down every sacred institution built by human thought, brick by brick, over the centuries.

We humans are burdened with a kind of consciousness that insists on our having a goal. That is why we yearn for stories which provide us with a sense of eternal meaning. No wonder stories which construct ideas prescribe rules of conduct and specify a social clout have been enshrined in our consciousness. The construction of narrative is a most important business of our species.

In this book, however, the author tells you the story of a 'story-buster', one who mocks, contradicts, rebuts, and has nothing but contempt for our universal stories. Nobody loves a story-buster . . . not unless the old story is replaced with a new one. Much of our ancient history concerns the punishment inflicted on those who challenged the existing narratives. Jesus was nailed to the cross, Socrates was forcibly given hemlock. The great story-busters Darwin, Marx and Freud were anything but lovable to the mass of people whose time-honoured narratives they attacked. There is nothing lovable about the hard-heartedness spouted by UG—it infuriates and stuns the reader.

But strangely, as you read page after page, anecdote after anecdote, this book has a cleansing effect. It challenges the status quo, exploring the lives of individuals through the history of mankind, from Socrates and Nietzsche, to J. Krishnamurthy, who have all played vibrant roles in the continuous evolution of human values and culture.

Ranging from UG's encounter with the sage of Thiruvanamalai, whom UG met at the restless age of twenty-one, to his fierce run-ins with the messiah of the twentieth century, J. Krishnamurthy, who left an indelible mark on world culture— the book is full of intimate anecdotes that enrich you with invaluable wisdom. To me it is indispensable, not because it shows where we have been, and where we are going, but because the author unflinchingly deals with the extreme grief of the loss of his daughter Shruti, who died in a road accident. The dignity with which he climbs out of this bottomless abyss, the way in which he grapples with the irreversibility of death and the question of afterlife, humble you. After the death of his daughter, when the author met UG unexpectedly, UG asked him a simple question with a gentle smile, 'How old was she when she died?'—thereby hurling him into the eye of the storm that was raging inside him. 'She was twenty-one' he replied, and stopped there. But what he wanted to say was that Shruti was a rebel, that she was not in awe of her mother's social activism and feminism or her father's philosophy, which she thought were shams—no different from the stupid conservatives, whom they often criticized.

This book fills you with a sense of reverence and passion for life because of the author's ability to connect with his pain, confront it and have the courage to live through it. It is his pain as well as the universal fear of loss, which we all dread so much, that gives him the ability to connect with the reader. We understand that it is the transient and ephemeral nature of life that makes it so precious. It is death that heightens the experience of life and makes us value it even more. For me, he says it all when he says 'Shruti's life was like UG's smile . . . brief, but warm, very warm, and enigmatic too.'

Mahesh Bhatt

BOOK ONE

THE WAY IT IS

Prelude

After a lapse of nearly twelve years, I finally went to see U.G. Krishnamurti again in January 2002. Every year the news of the arrival of this strange 'bird in constant flight' in Bangalore would somehow reach me, but I wouldn't feel the urge or curiosity to go and see him. There seemed no need to go and greet him or listen to his reproaches. But then, I would also tell myself: hasn't he become a part of me, a vital part of my consciousness? Is there really any way of getting away from him?

Perhaps there was another reason for not having kept in touch with him. Maybe I was afraid! I had had enough of him—enough of these two Krishnamurtis. If J. Krishnamurti had tried to skew my spiritual search and puncture my hope of attaining moksha, UG had destroyed the very ground on which I had still been struggling to carry on my search somehow. There seemed no point to it at all. It was all futile. This search, this yearning, almost literally like searching for a needle in a haystack, or like looking for a black cat in a dark room, or was it more like chasing one's own shadow? It was not just unproductive or uncreative, it seemed positively harmful.

'I can't help you,' UG had warned again and again. 'Nobody can help you, and you can't help yourself either.' In fact, there is nothing there to search for, to attain, he had added. And then finally, destroying all hopes, he had warned yet again: 'Your very attempt to become something which you are not is what makes your life miserable. Your very search for freedom creates its opposite and takes you away from it, that is, if there is such a thing as freedom at all.'

★

Indian spiritual traditions teach that not by wealth, not by progeny, but by renunciation alone is immortality attained, and you are advised that renunciation can be taken up after completing the life of a student and a householder. However, Yagnavalkya says in the *Brihadaranyaka Upanishad* that the very day when one becomes indifferent to the world (samsara) or comes upon a sense of disgust with life and the world, one should leave and become an ascetic.

Even as a student I had felt this disgust. I was not even twenty, but I had already started thinking of myself as a spiritual person born for higher goals. I spent most of my time outside the classroom, in public libraries and at the Ramakrishna Ashram library situated near my college, studying religious texts and the lives of spiritual masters, and again in the evenings, at home, I would immerse myself in reading or making notes from religious books. Since ours was a large family of five brothers and a sister, and there was hardly any quiet corner to meditate, I would sit in the open field in front of our house and meditate as long as I could, or gaze upon the heavens until tears streamed out of my eyes.

Inspired by Gandhiji's life and ideas, I tried to lead a simple life. I wore khadi trousers and shirts, rubber slippers, and avoided sweets, stimulating beverages, and girls. I believed I was spiritually ripe enough to enter into a full-time *adhyatmic* or spiritual life. I had no doubt that I was another Vivekananda in the making, who would soon burst upon the world and deluge it with ennobling spirituality. I believed I was born to understand the secret of existence, understand and experience the ultimate Brahman and with *Brahmajnana* transform the world into a realm of ananda, a new age, the age of transcendental consciousness!

The whole thing sounds like a weird joke or a funny story today. However, it was during that time and in such a frame of mind that I first heard J. Krishnamurti speak. It was in the 1970s, on a summer evening at Lalbagh in Bangalore. I had no clear idea of his teaching, just that he was a spiritual teacher of extraordinary quality.

Silhouetted against the trees, lit up by the setting sun, he sat on a small platform. A fairly large crowd, mostly men, sat still, eager, expectant; the rock behind us still radiated heat, and on top of the rock stood a mini tower like a witness, erected some 465 years ago, to mark the border of Bangalore.

The effect of J. Krishnamurti's (JK) talk on me was devastating, to say the least. I do not remember how I walked the sixteen or eighteen kilometres home. It was past midnight when I lay on my bed. I was on fire and there was this terrible anger, yet a strangely profound expectation. Suddenly mountains were not mountains, rivers were not rivers, the sky was not blue any more than blood was red, and people did not seem to be what they appeared to be. In short, nothing was what it seemed to be. Yet, for the next few years I went through the motions of my academic studies and daily routine like an actor, all the while with this peculiar awareness that all this was but a hugely entertaining yet painful drama, a grand *lila* that Brahman was playing through me.

'Awareness' became my mantra, and I felt a constant burning from my head to my toes. Every object, every face seemed like the centre of the universe. And I walked around in the full glare of the seven worlds, as it were, like some naked Digambara.[1] Friends, relatives, even parents eyed me with awe and respect, yet not without some misgivings.

In the second year of my BA course (with philosophy as one of my optional subjects), I left home and visited Swami Chinmayananda at Trivandrum. I had written to Swamiji, 'I am ready . . . Who can stop the blossoming of the flower, who can stop . . .' and was truly prepared to jump into the sea if he asked me to. Smiling through his handsome beard, Swamiji said that it was absolutely necessary for me to complete the BA course and acquire some worldly knowledge and skills before I embarked upon sanyasa. I was heart-broken. It was like being jilted by the one you loved most. From there I went to Pondicherry. The white skins and the garrulous Bengalis at the Aurobindo Ashram made me feel like a foreigner. Auroville, supposedly an international city, looked incomplete and hopeless, and it seemed to me that any spiritual sadhana in this place, drained of all energy after the death of the Mother, was doomed to fail. And from there the trip to Ramana Ashram at Tiruvannamalai only completed my disillusionment.

However, in the final year of my BA course, I again went to

Sandeepani Sadhanalaya in Bombay. Swami Chinmayananda was then touring the Western world. The second-in-command, a no-nonsense Vedantin, Swami Dayananda, saw that I was deadly serious. He suggested I relax for some days and feel things out before I took the final plunge. But JK wouldn't let me relax before taking the final step. His iconoclastic ideas were playing havoc with my mind, and I began to think that a genuine search for truth could not be transacted within an already established pattern of life and study and sadhana in an ashram; that truth, if it could be found at all, wouldn't be inside a conventional religious order or tradition, however good and profound. For there was no genuine search there, only a trained confirmation of answers to all questions already given by tradition. After ten days of deep contemplation, terrible confusion and misery, I left the ashram, returned home and sat for the final BA examinations.

Soon the disgust with the world changed into disgust with everything spiritual. The post-graduate course in English literature brought me down with a thud. I thought ambivalence in life was only human and natural; conflict was the stuff of dualism, and without dualism there could be no art, no music, no love, no samsara, and no search—so why not play along in this world of maya, and see how it goes!

Literature worked as a catharsis, at once a way out and a way into life. Then came love and marriage, profound discoveries and transformative experiences. To know one person intimately and deeply was to begin to understand oneself and humanity. One learnt also that there was no love without desire, and desire, I realized to my horror, operated always within the domain of power. If there is to be love which is not the way of power, then desire and expectations have to come to an end; perhaps only then would there be true understanding and the blossoming of true love. But is it possible? Wouldn't it be like burning one's boat in the middle of the sea?

The spiritual seeker turned into a man of samsara, and into a helpless writer. Still, to quote from the last part of my first novel: 'With all this, I must admit, I feel this volcanic burst within me: there is this sannyasi still alive, kicking, restless, contemplating; licking moksha cream, insatiable, burning and exploding with fury, and with one sweep whacking the whole universe into one big zero . . .'[2]

The very first meeting with U.G. Krishnamurti shattered me. I realized that JK's 'pathless path' had crystallized into a path in me. It was truly hopeless. The very search for truth seemed absurd and an exercise in futility, for all efforts to reach a goal only took one further away from the goal. As UG would say, it is like the case of a dog and his bone. The hungry dog chews on a lean, dry bone, and doing so hurts his gums and they bleed. But the poor dog imagines that the blood that he is savouring comes from the bone and not from himself. It was fairly simple and clear. The problem lay in the so-called solution! Rather, the solution was the problem. The answer was already there in the question. And the question was *me*, myself.

One day, while sitting in a public library at Cubbon Park, Bangalore, I experienced a great, terrible fear. Everything around me blanked out and I felt engulfed by some great darkness. I could almost touch it. Then I began to descend into some sort of a bottomless pit. It was most frightening. I felt I was going to die, but even in that state of terrible fear, I thought it would be embarrassing to fall dead in a public library. This ridiculous thought seemed to have brought me back to my 'normal' consciousness. I do not remember clearly what happened later. Perhaps it was something brought on by my hunger or mental fatigue, or I don't know if I missed my bus that day!

For the next eight years I met UG every time he came to Bangalore. I wrote two fairly 'comprehensive' articles about UG for newspapers in Karnataka. It was a sort of cathartic exercise, futile though it was, to get him out of my system. I stopped meeting him and then I let myself plunge into life.

I started working on a novel and tried to get on with my married life and teaching at a college. I worked with NGOs and got involved with issues concerning women, the caste problem, communal conflicts, and human rights. Some of my friends had travelled a different path. They had started with radical politics and moved towards spirituality; I had started with spirituality and then come round to politics and uncertainties.

Twelve years. Life was all on the surface. It was all there:

ambivalent, enigmatic, too complex to arrive at any clarity of understanding. Two children. Four books. A play. More than twenty years of teaching. A trip to Cambridge. Greying beard. Ageing parents. Several wars. Communal riots. The demolition of Babri Masjid. Assassinations. Farmers committing suicide. Terrorism. India going nuclear. Pakistan going nuclear. Multinational corporations beginning to take control of the world. The gargantuan wheel of globalization rolling on. The world ruled by politicians and scientists who were out of control. Fear uniting the world. The death of politics. Terror and violence, a seamless whole, connecting religious groups with political parties, secret agencies with fundamentalists, and business industries with the mafia, and all springing from the same source, from the same ideology of control and power over the world. The search for alternatives, for different, peaceful, non-violent and non-exploitative ways of doing and being gained urgency, but there was no conviction or strength. It seemed there could be no new creation without destruction, but there was the terrible lurking fear, that there would be nothing left to create after the destruction. UG arrived in Bangalore. Twelve years had gone by. It was time to go and meet the sage in rage, the cosmic Naxalite.

That's how, that afternoon, along with a doctor friend and a young German who was visiting Bangalore, I went to see UG. Since the doctor was not feeling too well, the German friend drove us through the heavy evening traffic. He drove like an expert BTS bus driver. 'You drive quite well,' I remarked. 'Yes . . . people here respect big vehicles,' he quipped. It was a Tata Sumo, big, heavy and intimidating! Smaller cars quietly gave way, and on seeing the monster coming, pedestrians thought twice before crossing the road. He had read some J. Krishnamurti and was going to see UG for the first time. The air was heavy with pollution and the usual din of the evening. I was not sure what I would feel at seeing UG, nor whether he would even recognize me. I reassured myself that I was just going to meet an old friend. No questions, no interrogations, just a meeting with the most wonderful yet intriguing human being I have ever known. Such were my thoughts.

It was one of those well-planned, government-sponsored layouts, with tarred roads, underground sewage and parks. And it looked like a typical middle-class house with potted plants along the compound wall and just enough space for a car in the drive, but the portico was strewn with slippers and shoes. As we stepped into the brightly lit sitting room, we saw about thirty people sitting, most on mats, a few on chairs and sofas, and there on a long sofa pushed against the wall, sat the figure in white, like a huge, distinctly unique pigeon among birds of varied hues. His hair, grey and flowing, had thinned. The face, fair and lined, surprisingly looked not much older than what I had imagined. He returned our pranams and we sat on a mat. The atmosphere was not like what I had experienced in the past (though in a different neighbourhood and a different house). I was particularly struck by the large number of young men and women ; they looked trim, fresh and relaxed. They smiled, laughed and shot questions at UG with ease. The people I used to be familiar with were sombre, hesitant and profoundly respectful. Indeed they were there even now, all full of concentration or in some deep cogitation. There was a sanyasi too, in ochre, a young one with chubby cheeks, almost a boy, who kept restlessly shuffling from the hall to the room to the portico and back. A few foreigners too, from France, Germany and Israel. A stout Jewish woman seated on a sofa was busy making notes in her scrapbook.

I looked again. UG looked much older now, but certainly not like someone who has lived on this planet for eighty-four years. The incredible charisma was still there, the same grinning lips and unblinking eyes, and that enchanting glow that radiated from the whole of his body. And the voice: unmistakably straightforward, curt, harsh, and at times even abusive. And his humour—tongue-in-cheek, sardonic, acerbic, devastating yet eliciting peals of spontaneous, indulgent, nervous laughter from the small crowd.

The host, Chandrasekhar, asked, 'UG, don't you remember the professor? Twenty years ago, he had written two articles on you!'

UG did not remember. But soon, in response to another question, he started, in lighter vein, recalling his days in America, his wife's little adventures while working in a library there, his eloquent speeches which had been reported with high praise in prominent newspapers. Then the inevitable happened. The free-flowing words fell like soft pebbles and tickled the crowd into giggles and guffaws.

Nobel Prize winners were brought down from their heights, gurus were torn to pieces, shibboleths of all grand and noble ideas were smashed to smithereens.

Was Mother Teresa a lesbian? So what? Hadn't she been a godsend, giving succour to thousands who faced a miserable life and death? And then how could one belittle the extraordinary personality of the Dalai Lama? Isn't he one of our central symbols of peace, non-violence and compassion in a world beleaguered by violence and corruption? I did not open my mouth. Some of my activist friends would have been scandalized and feminists would have been outraged. But then UG has never been either gender-sensitive, nor politically correct. He has been crude, politically scandalous, delightfully wicked and religiously blasphemous. Almost all the central symbols of various religions and cultures, all major ideologies and philosophies were subverted or dismissed as so much garbage. If there was a God and if He were to make the mistake of walking into the room now, even He would have been roundly abused, ridiculed and laughed at, and then mercilessly butchered. There was nothing sacred or sacrosanct, nothing unquestionable and incontestable there. Subversion was the way of thinking. And then subversion too was subverted and demolished.

A little later, maybe because only a few minutes before UG had talked of 'divine thoughts' and 'bouncing breasts' in the same vein, a young man, neatly dressed, his back erect, and much inspired, asked, 'UG, can you have sex?'

A ridiculous question for a man of eighty-four! With an oh-my-god smile, UG held up the tip of his forefinger. 'There is nothing here,' he said quietly, 'that says I am a man, I am a woman, or that I am an Indian . . .'

There was, of course, the irrefutable biological fact of UG having fathered four children. That was in the past, before the 'calamity'. No thought now stayed long enough for any sense of identity to build up and continue, thoughts which were essential for sexual excitement, in fact all thoughts got burnt. That was UG's song. Now, all of a sudden, in the middle of this 'indecent' conversation, he bangs the wooden teapoy with his fist several times. *Thud, thud-thud* . . . the sound fills the now silent space, and he thunders, 'There is no interpretation of the act. There is nothing here that calls it soft or hard or that it's painful . . .'

We look on with stunned silence. How does one understand this act of UG? Who is speaking? How does *he* know? Isn't that an interpretation, too?

Coffee is served in shining steel tumblers. I am a tea man, nevertheless I try to enjoy the hot coffee, wondering how on earth the host could serve coffee and snacks to so many visitors every evening. The next day I learnt that some guest or other would buy packets of milk and snacks and unobtrusively leave them in the kitchen.

More questions. More scandalous and subversive answers, which are actually no answers at all—all questions are just shot down. He is like a machine gun that goes off every time we toss a question at him. UG himself admits: 'The machine gun is not interested in killing. But it is designed to trigger and shoot at the slightest movement anywhere, and this machine gun just shoots.'

In these meetings there are always foreigners who usually look a little pinched and lost, and there are always sannyasis or swamijis who all look like *thrisankus* caught between heaven and earth, and then, determined by some law of life as it were, there is always a joker, a court jester. So then, promptly, the stout and dark man with chubby cheeks and beady eyes comes alive. 'All right, UG,' he shouts from the back row, 'every human being has some weakness, even the great ones. We should understand that. All right, what are we doing here? What are you trying to say? Why are you shooting down everything we say? We can always improve, can't we? We can change, no?'

There is no such thing as improvement or change or psychological transformation in UG's dictionary. There is only calamity, death which could be a rebirth, a new beginning. But you cannot desire it, cannot even talk about it, for when it happens, 'you' are not there.

The Jewish woman burbles something about 'enlightenment'.

UG grins as if something absurd had been said. There is no such thing as enlightenment. He is no messiah. He says: 'Messiahs have only created a mess in the world.'

'Sir, you should come down to our level and speak, otherwise we cannot understand you!' a middle-aged man pleads.

'Sir, I am next to you. Don't you see?'

UG's answers are no answers and yet they seem to be perfect answers that sometimes hit you like thunderbolts. Once, a good friend of the host, K. Chandrasekhar, who was a deeply religious man and something of a scholar, had asked UG: 'Sir, what is the state you are in?'

'Sir,' UG had replied, 'all I know is that I am in Karnataka State. I suppose this is Karnataka State?'

The apparently simple, witty answer stumped him completely, and it was, in fact, a moment of great illumination. He went back home and threw away all the religious books he had treasured as priceless gems till then.

Robert Carr, who has written *God Men, Con Men* on UG and his own spiritual search, knew J. Krishnamurti before he met UG. His meeting with UG was so disturbing and illuminating that he quit his spiritual vocation and started a restaurant in California. Then there is the story of a psychiatrist who quit his practice and never went back to UG. We cannot also forget to mention the man in Switzerland who, after meeting UG, landed up in a mental asylum. There are literally hundreds of such stories of people who

UG in conversation with the author and other admirers

have been tremendously affected by UG in one way or another. Some UG admirers I have met in Bangalore have described UG's influence on them in 'negative' terms: 'He has not given me anything, rather he has only taken away my ideals, my spiritual search, my fond hopes, illusions, crutches . . . he has helped me simplify my life, to put my thinking on a different track that is free of the burden of the tradition, of all these searches for non-existent goals...' Of course there are also people who believe that he is an 'enlightened' person, a 'jivanmukta', whose very presence and touch can change their lives. But ask UG and he would say: 'You come here and throw all these things at me. I am not actually giving you any answers. I am only trying to focus or spotlight the whole thing and say, "This is the way you look at these things; but look at them this [other] way. Then you will be able to find out the solutions for yourself without anyone's help." That is all. My interest is to point out to you that you can walk, and please throw away all those crutches. If you are really handicapped, I wouldn't advise you to do any such thing. But you are made to feel by other people that you are handicapped so that they could sell you those crutches. Throw them away and you can walk. That's all that I can say. "If I fall . . ."—that is your fear. Put the crutches away, and you are not going to fall.'

Comparisons can be misleading, for each individual is unique and different. Yet if one were to risk some comparison, if only to enhance our understanding, one might say that UG at times brings to mind the stories of the Zen masters who give sometimes nasty, sometimes provocative, and at times apparently outrageous answers. UG also might impress one like an arrogant and sneering avadhuta[3], or a totally indifferent pratyekabuddha, or as one simply, furiously mad!

A Zen koan goes like this: Once, a monk approached a Zen master and requested to be enlightened. The master asked the monk to get closer and then whispered in his ear: 'Zen is something that cannot be conveyed by word of mouth.'

Once, a disciple, troubled and confused by the many definitions of Buddhahood, asked his master: 'What is the Buddha?'

The master said, 'He is no other than this corporeal body of ours.'[4]

Now, if one did not read between the lines, this answer could only add to one's confusion, for the Buddha is not generally associated with corporeality. The answer is meant to break the dialectical and dualistic thinking of the disciple and open his eye to the truth.

That is why, when questions about Zen, Enlightenment, or the Buddha-nature are asked, the masters refer to a piece of garbage, to a cat climbing a tree, to the sound of one hand clapping, to waters that do not flow, to the sound not heard by the ear; or the master might just slap or kick the disciple and chase him out.

Attachment, or clinging to knowledge and experience, however profound or insightful, too becomes an obstacle in the realization of Zen or Buddhahood. Hence, seekers are warned: 'If you meet the Buddha on the way, kill him!'

UG's answers too, which are apparently irrational, unreasonable, nasty, and at times even abusive, are aimed at shocking and breaking the questioner, lighting a fuse, opening the inner eye, or just stopping one from going back to him again.

Still, people flock around him. They get hurt, snubbed, insulted; they get mad, angry, hopeless, and yet, they go back like moths that want to be annihilated or incinerated in the fire. And then there are the 'regulars', like the diehard fans of famous filmstars, who show up every time UG is in Bangalore.

One day, UG said to one of them: 'Why do you come here every day? You must really be a low-grade moron to come and sit here and listen to the same crap day in and day out. I say the same words, the same things over and over again, there is nothing different. You'll not get anything from here. There is nothing to give, nothing to take, nothing to know . . . Sorry, you can go to any guru you like. I am not selling anything here. Bye-bye.'

Suddenly, now, someone asks a question that is totally out of tune. 'UG, what is your favourite dish?'

Grinning wickedly, UG says, 'Soup prepared out of the tongues of new-born babies.'

Too repugnant to 'decent' ears. They could now get up and walk out. But nobody moves. There is an awkward silence. Many of them know that UG does not touch meat, and strictly speaking, he is not even a vegetarian, for he hardly eats vegetables or fruit. While in

India, he literally lives on oats with cream, idlis or beaten rice with milk, and an occasional coffee with cream. His total intake of food is less than that of a normal five-year-old. Yet he remains alert and agile throughout the day, exuding tremendous energy. Food is at the bottom of his needs, he says. He sleeps for hardly four hours and is usually up by four or five in the morning, and by six he is ready to take on the visitors who start streaming in from the early hours up to almost nine at night. He can talk for almost twelve to fifteen hours at a stretch and still be as sprightly and absorbed as a child who has not finished with his or her games. He never takes any exercise and yet he is very fit and nimble on his feet, like a cat. He is a marvellous machine. An amazing, miraculous body!

He is no saviour, no god-man; he claims nothing. He defies classifications. He argues that what he says carries no philosophical undertones, no mystical overtones; it is neither enigmatic nor mystifying. His words mean what they say, plainly and simply, as spelt out in any good dictionary. There is nothing profound or spiritual in his utterances, only plain facts and clear descriptions of the simple physiological processes of the body.

But he disagrees with and questions all our assumptions and presumptions, all our ideas and theories, all our pet beliefs and radical notions. He raises his hand in a questioning mudra and deals a deathblow to the very foundations of human culture.

He explodes and declares:

Love is war. Love and hate spring from the same source. Cause and effect is the shibboleth of confused minds. There is no Communism in Russia, no freedom in America, no spirituality in India. Service to mankind is utter selfishness. Jesus was another misguided Jew. Buddha was a crackpot. Man is memory. Charity is vulgar. Thought is bourgeois. Mutual terror, not love will save mankind. Attending Church and going to a bar for a drink are identical. There is nothing inside you but fear. God, Soul, love, happiness, the unconscious, reincarnation and death are non-existent figments of our rich imagination. Freud is the fraud of the twentieth century, while J. Krishnamurti is its greatest phoney . . .

On our way back home, the German friend gushes, 'What UG says is correct.' He has obviously enjoyed UG's attack on the famous personalities, in particular on the Nobel Prize winners. He is young, he has come from Bonn to visit an orphanage and school run by a German woman now separated from her Indian husband. He is a student of psychology. UG has touched a chord in him; he is truly excited.

Back at the doctor's residence, the doctor asks me, 'So, what do you think, meeting UG after so many years?'

The German friend's eyes open wide and he is all ears.

My first thought is that I must write a book on UG, if only for my own clarification. But I only smile like one who has just come back after meeting a long-lost friend!

2

'No Boundaries'

Quite unexpectedly UG was back in Bangalore in September 2002. Three months earlier our daughter Shruti had died in a road accident. It was past midnight when we received the news over the phone. When my wife and I went to the government hospital, at around 2.30 a.m., there was no doctor to tell us how she died. In the mortuary, she lay on a metal stretcher, her hair spread over and trailing down the metal frame; it looked as if she had lain down to relax and dry her hair after a bath. But it was a mortuary, smelling of death and decay.

The boy who had ridden the bike died on the spot but she was still breathing, her friends said. Yet they had only stood there on the blood-splattered road, feeling paralysed, or was it that they were drunk and scared of the police? The 'golden hour' was lost. When the police finally arrived, they did not take her to the private hospital which was hardly a five-minute drive from the spot. It was as if nature, her friends and the police had all conspired not to let Shruti survive.

Words fail to describe the sorrow. They say losing one's child is the greatest sorrow in life. Really, if there is sorrow, this is it. Every other pain or suffering seems trivial compared to this. Two things happen. One, you feel a deep wound in your chest, a gaping hole which never seems to close. Two, you fall into a daze. It lasts for days, perhaps several months for many, but when you come out of it you find yourself in deep pain, struggling to come to terms with the fact of death. If not for that 'daze', maybe one would come to reckon with the fact of death and that would be the end of it, emotionally. It usually doesn't happen, the sorrow lives on.

One astrologer friend said that Shruti had died after twelve in the night, which is the *brahma kala*, meaning that she had completed her span of life on Earth. Another friend said that we should look at her death differently. She had lived the way she wanted, she had lived a full and vibrant life, something most women and even many men would take a lifetime to experience, while many never would. In effect, they were saying it is not how long but how you live that is important.

But words don't console you and you realize they have no meaning, they are empty like the hollow of your hand.

Three days after the funeral I went to the burial ground. It was as if I was seeing the world from afar, very far, yet I could see everything in its minutest detail. There were so many men, women, boys, girls and children everywhere, even cats and dogs and buffaloes and cows, and occasional birds crossing the dismal sky or perched on tree tops or on electric poles; inside the burial ground, a scrawny goat stood stubbornly on a tombstone. And I felt with a stab in my heart that my daughter was nowhere there. The same evening, in the third column of the edit page of a popular newspaper, I chanced upon a familiar quote from Shakespeare's *King Lear*. Upon being told of the death of his most loved daughter Cordelia, King Lear wails inconsolably thus:

Why should a dog, a horse, a rat have life,
And thou no breath at all? Thou'lt come
no more,
Never, never, never, never, never . . .

The next day, when I went out I again confronted the same reality, but there was a strange, and different perception of things this time. 'Look,' I told myself, 'there is life everywhere, it is the same life, it is Shruti everywhere, the same life-energy pulsating in every creature, everything . . .'

Streams of friends come and go, many sit in silence, and when they finally manage to speak, they only say that they don't know what to say. Yes, what can they say? They know that one can never console the parents, it's better to remain silent. But life goes on. Habits take over. There is hardly any break in the routine. Hunger for food never ceases. The tongue never fails to recognize the taste of food, or distinguish between tastes. Life both sustains and survives death. UG is right, I think. The body is indifferent; it is not in the least concerned about your sorrows, it is only interested in its own survival. Joys and sorrows are only a nuisance, an avoidable disturbance in the chemistry of the body, to its otherwise harmonious function. Fortunately, the endocrine glands which control and regulate the vital functions of the body are not affected. The body does not care about death, it goes on.

Before my daughter's death I had started working on this book. I had already referred to a dozen books and made copious notes. I started working again and attending to my duties at the college.

I went to meet UG on the very day of his arrival in Bangalore. The long ride, almost twenty-five kilometres, on my scooter in the hot afternoon, tired me. I was sweating and feeling a little odd about my worn-out demeanour. There were already about twenty people in the room. Most of them looked familiar. Heat or rain they would be there, if only to be in the explosive presence of UG.

UG returned my greeting and said, 'Come, sir.' And I was directed to sit beside UG on the sofa.

'How are you, sir? You look old!' said UG with a smile.

The author with UG

'I have grown old, sir.'

'Old and wise!' he quipped, flashing a smile.

'I'm flattered, sir,' I said. 'You didn't recognize me the last time.'

'I was prepared, sir,' he said, deflating the sense of pride or whatever I had begun to feel.

Just then the lady of the house came out and passed around two plates of sweets. UG offered his plate to me and said, 'Take, sir. You are not sweet enough!'

I did not react. I took a small piece of the milk sweet and looked around, now feeling a little awkward. Chandrasekhar Babu, the host, who was sitting at the other end, mentioned my daughter's sudden death to UG.

Over the years I have seen that people react to news of death in different ways. There are those who find it difficult to speak and then fall silent, those that deliberately start speaking about other things, those that have ready-made words of condolence and then come out with stories of death as if that would somehow console us, and those who think that they are expected to speak about their own experience of death and suddenly become melancholically loquacious.

I have not heard UG speak about (actual) death. UG would, of course, respond to the news of death as he would respond to any other subject, without any show of emotion or sympathy. But more than ten years ago, I was told, UG had made an unexpected remark about the sudden death of one Nagaraj who was the private secretary to the Postmaster General of Karnataka. He never married. 'The cigarette is my beloved,' he used to say. Whenever UG came to Bangalore, Nagaraj would apply for two or three months leave from his office and spend the whole time with UG. 'UG, consider me as part of the furniture here. I have nothing to ask of you. Please let me just hang around here. That's all I want,' he would say. He made notes in shorthand of UG's conversations with the visitors, which were later used in the book *Mind is a Myth*.

Nagaraj retired from his job but not from his smoking habit. When he couldn't control the urge, he would go out, puff away hurriedly at a cigarette and then come back to his spot close to UG. One day, he suddenly decided to quit smoking. When he mentioned it to UG, expecting some encouragement, the latter said,

'Double your quota. Don't stop smoking,' and even assured him that he wouldn't die of lung cancer. But Nagaraj stopped smoking, fell into depression, ignored the withdrawal symptoms and died a year later. Recording the incident in her book, Shanta Kelker writes: '. . . I kept repeating, "UG, I just can't believe Nagaraj is no more. I half expect him to walk in any minute with his loud hellos." UG replied, "What makes you think he is not there? He is very much here now." That jolted me. I turned around to see if I could discern any friendly spectre gracing the scene, but to no avail. Trust UG to see things which the rest of us can't! UG continued, "Even when you thought you were seeing him when he was alive, you were not actually seeing him. Do you think you can *see* anything or anybody?" '[5]

On another occasion, upon hearing about the death of a young man called Papanna who used to come and see UG every time he was in Bangalore, UG had suggested to Chandrasekhar Babu that they should go to see the boy's mother. As soon as she saw UG at the door, she rushed out of the kitchen to receive him. She was about sixty; it was a family of great musicians. Her eyes filled with tears and she soon started talking about her son. UG listened to her tale of woe in utter silence. Only Chandrasekhar interrupted her a couple of times and offered some words of consolation. UG did not, he just listened to her with total attention. After nearly half an hour, when she was exhausted and somewhat calmed down, UG got up, did his pranams to the mother and walked out. The mother probably believed UG to be an enlightened man and expected him to say some consoling words. But UG offered none, nor cared to please the family by accepting their food and drink. However, he had let the mother pour her heart out, let her empty herself of the dead weight.

In 1982, UG's son Vasant died of cancer at the age of thirty-two. Friends and close associates say that during those days they did not see even a trace of sadness in his face. UG was in Bangalore when he received a telegram which stated that Vasant had cancer and had been admitted to Bombay Hospital. His reaction to the news, Bangalore friends say, was not remotely close to that of a father. However, the friends in Bangalore insisted that UG should spend the rest of his time in India with his son in Bombay. Mahesh Bhatt received UG and his companion, Valentine, and made arrangements for their stay in Bombay. It so happened that Valentine fell ill suddenly; she had contracted tuberculosis and she had to be hospitalized. Mahesh Bhatt says that UG and he had to shuffle between the two hospitals at the opposite ends of the city. Friends who believed UG had miraculous powers expected him to cure his son of the cancer. UG laughed the idea off, saying that his touch would only hasten Vasant's death rather than cure him of cancer.

'Why should this happen to the son of someone like you?' asked a friend of UG, meaning how could an 'enlightened' man's son die of cancer.

UG asked, 'Why not my son?'

It seemed a callous, heartless response coming from a father. And yet, every day, UG went to the hospital and sat by the bed of his dying son. And he was there when the end came.

Mahesh Bhatt writes: ' "He is dead," said UG, in a matter-of-fact tone over the telephone. He asked me to meet him at the hospital to make arrangements for the funeral. We had known that Vasant's end was near. One of my friends had hoped that UG would perform a miracle. As we walked to the hospital after hearing the news of Vasant's death, my friend believed even then that UG would bring his son back to life. What actually happened at the hospital took us totally by surprise. UG wanted the body to be removed and cremated immediately without any ceremonies. The hospital would not release the body until all the bills were paid. It was 6 a.m. and our total combined resources were nowhere near the amount needed. Then UG laughed and said, "You can forget about your sentiments and solemnity surrounding death. In the end it all comes down to money." We were shocked. We all found his conduct quite lacking in the decorum that such an occasion demanded. The expected miracle did not occur. We were amazed at UG. There was no trace of emotion in him. He simply attended to the legal formalities that were necessary for the cremation and walked away from the scene.'[6]

While my daughter, Shruti, still lay all wrapped up in white sheets, but adorned with flowers and a huge garland of roses, the first copy of my new book *Rama Revisited and Other Stories* arrived by post. In a story called 'Sanjaya Speaks', which is based on the aftermath of the Kurukshetra war, Sanjaya, thinking of the suffering of Kunti and Draupadi, speaks to himself thus: 'Suffering is a disease, mother. It eats into your vitals and destroys your sanity.'

Later in the story, on seeing her children's bodies cut to pieces by Ashwathama's sword, Draupadi turns hysterical and revengeful. But the ghastly sight snaps something inside Yuddhisthira; he decides to renounce everything and go off to live the life of a hermit. He rejects everything, the bloodstained victory, his wife and brothers, even Krishna whom he calls an unrealized god, an unborn truth. He declares: 'I reject you all . . . I shall leave you all, strip myself of this yet fatal garb of civilization, and wander through the forest and live the life of a hermit. I shall meet cold and heat and illness and hunger and death as they come. I shall live on fruits fallen from trees, never pluck them from trees nor from the ground. I shall totally abjure violence and fear no creature. If a tiger chews off one of my arms, I shall offer him the other arm, nay, my whole body if that should satiate his hunger. I will go on thus, forward and never back, but with no goal in mind, for all goals are delusive . . .'[7]

I agree with Sanjaya; suffering is really a bad habit. I understand Yuddhishthira and feel like him, but I cannot do anything about it any more than Yuddhishthira himself did in his life. And I think I know why UG was unaffected by his son's death and behaved the way he did. But I suffer like every other father who has lost his child. I tell myself: we live and it's a blessing. Human life is a blessing! Or is it a curse? Shruti never walked, she always ran. Even a hundred years would have been insufficient for her energetic soul, I tell my friends. She never got a chance. Some of us have been blessed with a chance or two; I had a miraculous escape once in a road accident; but this girl, this most marvellous piece of work, this spirited life that deserved to live, never got another chance. And I tell my wife: 'She is not the type who'll remain out there for long. She'll return. She'll live again, but not as our daughter.'

But is there life after death? Is there reincarnation? Or is it just a belief sprung from our fear of death, our fear of nothingness; from the sense of void the dead leave behind? On a number of occasions, UG has said that there is no rebirth, but if you believe in it, there is—indeed a very intriguing and paradoxical answer.

I recall here a moving story from J. Krishnamurti's *Commentaries on Living*. It is one of the most insightful and profound dialogues on death one could ever read. In these commentaries, Krishnaji usually starts with a long description of the place, environment and people, before moving on to the dialogue. In this particular section, he starts off with descriptions of a magnificent old tamarind tree, of pilgrims who come from all parts of the country to bathe in the sacred waters, of the moon making a silvery path on the dancing waters, and then offers a brief sketch of a funeral as a prelude to the discussion on death. The precise, simple prose is a marvellous piece of writing that combines most effectively the technique of the essay with story telling. '... Often they would bring a dead body to the edge of the river. Sweeping the ground close to the water, they would first put down heavy logs as a foundation for the pyre, and then build it up with lighter wood; and on the top they would place the body, covered with a new white cloth. The nearest relative would then put a burning torch to the pyre, and huge flames would leap up in the darkness, lighting the water and the silent faces of the mourners and friends who sat around the fire. The tree would gather some of the light, and give its peace to the dancing flames. It took several hours for the body to be consumed, but they would all sit around till there was nothing left except bright embers and little tongues of flame. In the midst of this enormous silence, a baby would suddenly begin to cry, and a new day would have begun.'

The narrative then moves over to the dying man. He is a fairly well-known person. He lies on a cot, surrounded by his wife, children and close relatives. As Krishnaji walks into the room, the old man waves him to a chair and asks his people to leave them alone for awhile. The dying man speaks with difficulty: 'You know, I have thought a great deal for a number of years about living, and even more about dying, for I have had a protracted illness. Death seems such a strange thing. I have read various books dealing with this problem, but they were all rather superficial.'

'Aren't all conclusions superficial?' Krishnaji simply asks.

'I am not sure,' the old man begs to differ. 'If one could arrive at certain conclusions that were deeply satisfying, they would have some significance. What's wrong with arriving at conclusions, so long as they are satisfying?'

With remarkable tact Krishnaji agrees only to point out that the mind has the power to create every form of illusion, and to be caught in it seems so unnecessary and immature.

But the old man persists: 'I have lived a fairly rich life, and have followed what I thought to be my duty; but of course I am human. Anyway, that life is all over now, and here I am, a useless thing; but fortunately my mind has not been affected. I have read much, and I am still as eager as ever to know what happens after death. Do I continue, or is there nothing left when the body dies?'

'Sir,' Krishnaji asks tenderly, 'if one may ask, why are you so concerned to know what happens after death?'

'Doesn't everyone want to know?'

Krishnaji refuses to answer, for there are no answers. But he asks . . . 'If we don't know what living is, can we ever know what death is?' And he goes on to suggest most persuasively that living and dying may be the same thing, and the fact that we have separated them may be the source of great sorrow. Why doesn't one allow the whole ocean of life and death to be? At last the man admits: 'I don't want to die. I have always been afraid of death . . . All my reading about death has been an effort to escape from this fear, to find a way out of it, and it is for the same reason that I am begging to know now . . . You can tell me, and what you say will be true. This truth will liberate me . . .'

'But what is this "me"?' Krishnaji asks. 'The 'me' exists only through identification with property, with a name, with the family, with failures and successes, with all the things you have been and want to be. You are that which you have identified yourself; you are made up of all that, and without it, you are not.'

But the dying man wouldn't give up, he wouldn't let the ocean of life and death be. He wants to know, he grows desperate. He feels he has become the hunter as well as the hunted. He begs Krishnaji to be compassionate, not to be so unyielding. His mind is now like a galloping horse without a rider. He begs Krishnaji for some clue, some solace. He cries and asks, 'Will you help me, or am I beyond all help?'

There is no help. The very need for help is the problem, which prevents one from letting all things go and be. 'Truth is a strange thing,' Krishnaji says and he is magnificent, and his concluding remarks wash over the dying man like the cleansing waters of the Ganges. 'You cannot capture it by any means, however subtle and cunning; you cannot hold it in the net of your thought. Do realize this and let everything go. On the journey of life and death, you must walk alone; on this journey there can be no taking of comfort in knowledge, in experience, in memories. The mind must be purged of all the things it has gathered in its urge to be secure; its gods and virtues must be given back to the society that bred them. There must be complete, uncontaminated aloneness.'[8]

Now, turning to me, not smiling any more, in a rather sombre voice, UG, this other Krishnamurti, only asks, 'How old was she?'

Is it an opening offered to me to speak about my daughter, about death? Is it an invitation to ask questions that had been troubling me all these months? I just say, 'She was twenty-one,' and stop there. But actually I want to tell him that Shruti was a rebel, that she was a great critic of all our much-talked-about social values and beliefs, that she thought her mother's social activism and feminism, her father's philosophy and writings were all so much sham, or that we were not too different from the 'stupid' conservatives or traditionalists we often like to criticize. She would have been an apt disciple of UG. Three years before her death, when she had just turned eighteen, she had written in her diary that being a prince the Buddha had everything at his disposal, probably more than what he desired, and so could afford to say that desires and worldly pleasures are the beginning of sorrow. If he had been born in a poor family, he would have probably wanted to be a prince, or sought all kinds of comforts and luxuries. If the Buddha, who declared 'Desire is the cause of all suffering', was alive today, he would get no followers. For today's life is all about desires. 'I have desires,' she declares. And she goes on to say that she wants to fulfil all her desires. Be a contented human being. And then, she concludes: '. . . of course die when the time comes.'

I want to tell UG that eight months ago, when I had taken a couple of friends to see him, Shruti had complained to her mother that I had not cared to invite her. She would have surely enjoyed, like the German friend, UG's irreverent remarks, his demolition acts, his total dismissal of all authority, in particular the religious. She detested authority, parental authority in particular. She was a free spirit, a wild bird that loved to fly aimlessly in the untrammelled air. Shruti lived intensely, almost feverishly as if there was no tomorrow. I imagine her riding pillion on the 800cc sport bike, her hair flying in the cool midnight breeze, screaming in joy, before the lorry pulled out on to the middle of the road and stopped her and her friend in their tracks.

In one of her college assignments, 'Clocks', beside clocks of different designs embedded in strange settings, Shruti had written:

> Time is merciless
> Yet heals,
> Brutal
> Yet binding,
> Irreversible
> Yet changing.
> Time is a bitch . . .
> It is like fate
> Lines on your palms,
> All decided
> Much before you arrive . . .

Elsewhere, next to a picture of a girl with large wings, she had scribbled:

> Free spirited
> No boundaries
> No limits
> No questions.

After the milk sweets, there is some *khara*, salty and crispy munchies to kill the sweet taste so that the coffee will not go bland on the tongue. Soon, the discussion picks up. Actually it is no discussion. It is a monologue—or, rather, only talking. It seems pointless to ask who is talking to whom. There is only talking, either loudly and outwardly, or silently and inwardly, and both are a single unitary movement. Hilarious, scandalous, ironical, sardonic and paradoxical. At one point during this freewheeling blather and what seemed uproarious yet obscene and repulsive laughter, the subject of death pops up. UG declares: 'There is no way you can experience death, least of all your own. You only experience void. And the void is nothing but a break in the continuity of memory, of knowledge. Relationship is nothing but memory, knowledge. So, what is death without memory?'

A crack in the delusion, a chink of insight, a seed sown, and I realized I could not pull it up, push it open, there was no magical, mystical way for him. An involuntary sigh escaped me. It was time to leave. The sun had gone sneakily, the heat was down, and one could feel a cool breeze playing in the trees outside. I got up and made my pranams. UG looked up and brought his palms together and smiled briefly, fleetingly, a little enigmatically, I imagined.

I really do not know how I can possibly capture or interpret that smile in my story. It has surely to be a 'memorable' task! Is there really anything beyond memory?

Shruti's life was like UG's smile, brief but warm, very warm, and enigmatic, too!

3

'Can You Take It?'

Uppaluri Gopala Krishnamurti was born on 9 July 1918 in Masulipatnam, a small town in the state of Andhra Pradesh. Three years earlier Gandhiji had returned from South Africa with a huge reputation as a mass leader of unique qualities. His non-violent struggle against the British rule in India, which was to be in many ways a cultural and a philosophical battle against the colonial ideologies as well, was still in the making. The First World War was drawing to a close, but the almost-four-year war had ravaged Central Europe, an estimated ten million people had lost their lives and twice that number had been wounded. In the month of March, Russia had signed a treaty with Germany, ending its participation in the war, but inside Russia another war for freedom led by the Bolsheviks was gaining ground throughout the land.

At that time, the Theosophical Society, started by the Ukraine-born Helena Petrovna Blavatsky, was nearly forty-three years old; and the Brotherhood of Theosophists had caught the imagination of people and in a war-torn era, Theosophy was increasingly seen as one of the religious alternatives in the Western world. On a sprawling, verdant, twenty-seven acre plot at Adyar, the headquarters of the Theosophical Society had already been established. And with Annie Besant as the high priestess of the Society, the search for the World Teacher had ended on the Adyar beach with Leadbeater spotting a fourteen-year-old boy, lean, morose-looking, but with rather vacant eyes, squatting on the sand. But when UG was born, Jiddu Krishnamurti was already twenty-three years old and was looked upon as the Christ come back, as Lord Maitreya, as the Kaliyuga Avatar who would establish a new religious order or dharma in the world.

There are strange, interesting parallels in the lives of JK and UG, just as there are radical differences between their teachings. JK's mother died when he was ten-and-a-half. UG's mother died seven days after he was born, just as Queen Maya, the story goes, had died seven days after giving birth to Siddhartha. It is an intriguing parallel, and it is said that there are many such parallels between the lives of the Buddha and U.G. Krishnamurti as well. But this narrative is more about the differences rather than the similarities between the two great masters.

It is said that mothers have tremendous influence on the growth of their children. Their nursing and suckling and warm touches and embraces leave a lasting effect. She is the first teacher and the child begins to see and experience the world first through her eyes and words. But in both UG's case and the Buddha's, it seems that mothers were an anathema. From the traditional Hindu point of view, it is said that at their death, these mothers are bestowed with deliverance or moksha by their to-be-enlightened sons. But according to psychologists, without a mother's love a child may grow up to be unbalanced. The theory doesn't hold much water in this story. In fact, this whole theory is problematic. The belief or idea that 'mother's love' cannot but be creative, right and good for a child is at best a cultural assumption, or even wishful thinking.

Anyway, UG did not enjoy the benefit of a father's love either. A few days after the mother's death, UG's father returned the jewellery and the five thousand rupees he had received as dowry of his deceased wife to his father-in-law. And he married again and left his son to be brought up by UG's maternal grandmother and grandfather. However, as the years passed, UG's stepmother is believed to have taken a liking to UG and all his stepbrothers and stepsisters are believed to have had cordial relationships with him. So, it was not as if his father abandoned him or that he was unloved.

Still, psychologically speaking, one might say that a sense of betrayal, loss, separation and painful reconciliation seem to play a markedly poignant role in UG's life. In reality, however, one is not too sure if separation from his father had any telling impact on his personality. Interestingly, according to Freudian psychology, the father is seen as the first 'enemy'. In fact, during the growth of the boy into an adult, all the obstacles to his growth, all 'enemies', are supposed to get associated with the father figure. In other words, the father figure gets associated with the social order into which the son either tries to fit or rebel against.

In occidental myths, too, the father figure is a recurring theme, a major symbol. In the story of Odysseus, as Joseph Campbell points out, the father-quest is a major adventure. 'Go find your father,' says Athena to her son, Telemachus. Eventually it seems that this symbol of the father was transfigured into the symbol of God in Christianity. Jesus is born of a virgin mother. His true father is the Father in heaven. And it is said that when Jesus goes to the cross, he is on the way to the Father, who is the ultimate transcendental source.[9]

Evidently the symbol of the father doesn't work the same way in the Eastern mythologies. Fathers are irrelevant. They are there, apparently very important, but ultimately insignificant, or rather often shown as a great burden to be cast aside or transcended. At least that is what we see happen in the lives of the two Krishnamurtis. After a separation of nearly twenty-two years, when JK, now proclaimed as a vehicle for the World Teacher, meets his father at his house at Adyar, it is the father who tries desperately to come to terms with his son's new avatar. Almost similarly, after nearly sixty years, in 1977, UG's father, Uppaluri Sitaramayya, asked to see him on his deathbed. UG was not keen on meeting the old man, for he thought it wouldn't do him any good, but only hasten his death. But upon the urgings of Valentine and other friends, he went to see his father in his stepbrother's house. It is a tearful reconciliation—tears, remorseful and pathetic, on the part of only the father. In the stories of Indian mysticism, there are no fathers and mothers and brothers and sisters. And it is usually the fathers who get kicked, not the mothers, that is, if they are still alive. Blood relations carry no weight, no value whatsoever. In fact, they are seen as a burden to be cast aside in one's journey towards freedom.

★

UG's grandfather, Tummalapalli Gopala Krishnamurti, was a prosperous lawyer and quite an influential person in the town of Gudivada. Before her death, UG's mother is believed to have told her father that her son was born for a high spiritual destiny and he should do everything necessary for that destiny to be fulfilled. It is said that the old man took his daughter's prediction seriously and gave up his flourishing law practice in order to devote himself entirely to the upbringing and education of his only grandson.

T.G. Krishnamurti was, in the words of his grandson, a 'mixed-up man'. He was a great believer in the Theosophical Movement, in Annie Besant and Leadbeater, and in Jiddu Krishnamurti as the future World Teacher. At the same time, he believed deeply in the Brahminical tradition or *parampara*. Steel Olcott and other leading Theosophists would visit him at his home. The walls of his drawing room were adorned with pictures of Blavatsky and Olcott, to which were later added photographs of Annie Besant, Leadbeater and the young J. Krishnamurti. So UG grew up in a peculiar milieu of Theosophy and orthodox Hindu religious practices. Hindu swamijis, sants and gurus frequented the house. The old man enjoyed having long discussions on religious matters with them, and he gladly and religiously offered them the hospitality of his big house. Chanting and readings from religious scriptures were held frequently. There would be days when readings from the Upanishads, *Panchadasi*, *Naishkarmya Siddhi* and such texts would start in the early hours and go on till the end of the day. By the age of eight, UG knew some of these texts by heart.

Despite growing up in such a religious atmosphere—or perhaps because of it—UG says that God became somewhat irrelevant to him, even before he became a teenager. The hypocrisy and double standards of his elders did affect him deeply. The young mind could see through them and observe that what they preached did not operate in their own lives. Generally, parents believe that they know their children quite well, the truth actually is the other way round. Children not only know more about their parents and elders, they often see through them. Speaking about these upsetting experiences, UG particularly recalls the day when his grandfather had rushed out of his room in great fury and thrashed his crying granddaughter because her weeping had disturbed his meditation. The child almost turned blue. It was a sort of traumatic experience for the small boy too, and he couldn't help thinking: 'There must be something funny about the whole business of meditation. They talk marvellously, express things in a very beautiful way, but what about their lives?'

In December 1925, the Theosophical Society observed its golden jubilee at its headquarters in Adyar, Madras. Since they had not reserved a room in Adyar, UG's grandparents dropped their plan of going to the celebration. But the seven-year-old UG was very keen to go and fervently prayed to his favourite god, Lord Ganesha, to make his grandfather change his decision. To his huge surprise, T.G. Krishnamurti did change his mind and decided in favour of the trip. It seemed UG's intense wish had had an effect on his grandfather's sudden decision to attend the golden jubilee.

It was at once a gala event, and an event of great expectation and promise. J. Krishnamurti had already started giving his discourses as the World Teacher, though some within the Theosophical Society were not sure if JK himself was the World Teacher in the flesh, or merely a mouthpiece of Lord Maitreya. By then, tremors of rebellion within the citadel of the Society had cracked its solidarity. Four years ago, in the same premises at Adyar, JK had warned: 'True spirituality is hard and cruel, and the World Teacher . . . is not going to be lenient to our weaknesses and our failings . . . He is not going to preach what we want, nor say what we wish, nor give us the sop to our feelings which we all like . . .' And these warnings had gone almost hand in hand with apparently profound observations such as: 'Nothing could ever be the same. I have drunk at the clear and pure waters at the source of the fountain of life and my thirst was appeased. Never more could I be thirsty, never more could I be in utter darkness. I have seen the light. I have touched compassion which heals all sorrow and suffering; it is not for myself, but for the world . . .' And a year later, he declared: 'I am the love and the very love itself. I am the saint, the adorer, the worshipper and the follower. I am God.'

But now, on the way to Adyar to attend the golden jubilee celebration, this World Teacher, who had said 'never more could I be in utter darkness', this man who had called himself 'God', was shattered by the news of the death of his brother, Nityananda. A year ago his father had died, but JK had not attended the funeral. Now thousands of miles away from his brother (at Ojai), after having passed through a heavy storm, he had received the day-old news of his death. For ten days he was 'completely disoriented and dazed with disbelief'. In his book *Star in the East—Krishnamurti: The Invention of a Messiah* Roland Vernon says that JK felt let down by the Masters. They had promised to protect Nityananda against all danger and let him work shoulder to shoulder with him in his career as the World Teacher. It seemed nothing short of a terrible betrayal, and 'the ideological edifice in which he had come to believe, now began to crumble'.

In point of fact, by then, JK had already been frustrated and disgusted with the infighting in the Society and he had begun to move away from the likes of Leadbeater, Arundale and their coterie. Now the death of his beloved brother further impelled him to question and re-examine the ideology and practices of the Theosophical Society. And in 1927, he was to declare: 'I hold that doubt is essential for the discovery and the understanding of the Truth...' And he reprimanded his followers for their blind beliefs and invited them to reject all spiritual authorities, including his own, and practise doubt as a method of inquiry, and 'scrutinize the very knowledge which you are supposed to have gained. For I tell you that orthodoxy is set up when the mind and the heart are in decay . . .' And two years later, on 3 August 1929, he was to dissolve the Order of the Star, sever all his connections with the Theosophical Society, and declare: 'Truth is a pathless land, and you cannot approach it by any path whatsoever, by any religion, by any sect. Truth, being limitless, unconditioned, unapproachable by any path whatsoever, cannot be organized; nor should any organization be formed to lead or to coerce people along any particular path . . . My only concern is to set men absolutely, unconditionally free.'[10]

But in 1925, J. Krishnamurti was still a part of the Theosophical Society. On 29 December 1925, UG for the first time heard his namesake speak during the golden jubilee function. UG, of course, already knew about JK and Annie Besant from the pictures that adorned the wall of their house in Gudivada.

The day after the talk, when the December sun shone brightly on Elliot Beach at Adyar, UG met J. Krishnamurti. UG was seven years old then and the World Teacher twenty-seven years his senior. It was a silent encounter, though. Along with his admirers, JK came out for his usual walk by the beach. Briefly he disengaged himself from the others and moved over to the spot where UG and some other boys were collecting seashells. What might have transpired between the two, one just a little boy and the other a giant of a man, is hard to conjecture. But years later, they were to meet as teacher and disciple, as teacher and seeker, the seeker soon turning into a rebel, and the rebel into a colossus. They were to cross each other's path on several occasions. For some years, their lives were to run like parallel lines, or like two gods crossing each other, one quiet and profound, the other fierce, explosive yet pure and cleansing. And this most intriguing, almost fifty-year relationship between them was to end in yet another silent but mysterious encounter just minutes before JK's death.

Even as a boy, UG was not merely mischievous and restless as most boys are, he was also most irreverent, belligerent and brutally frank. A quality which continues to operate in UG even today, the only difference being that now he can be more devastating, and scandalously outrageous, particularly when he cuts down even his close associates and blasts the most revered and celebrated personalities, when he refuses to please anyone high or low, rich or poor, a prime minister or a chauffeur, with sweet talk.

Two particular incidents stand out from the many reports of his mischief and belligerence. Once, when he was hardly five years old, the grandfather, infuriated by his misbehaviour, had belted him. Livid with anger, the boy had grabbed the belt from his grandfather and had hit him back, shouting, 'Who do you think you are? How can you beat me?' The grandfather never again dared to raise his hand against the boy. The second incident happened when UG was twelve years old. Just before the final examinations, UG and his *chela*s planned to steal the question papers. UG bribed the attendant, acquired the original stencil cuts of the question papers, and with excited, democratic zeal, distributed the papers to several of his classmates. When the authorities came to know what had happened, they dismissed the attendant and re-conducted the exams. UG would have been expelled from the school but for his uncle who happened to be on the governing committee.

A sense of disgust with religious rituals came early to UG. This happened when he was fourteen, during the death anniversary of his mother. He was in a rage at the hypocrisy of the priests who performed the rituals. He was expected to fast the whole day, as

were the Brahmin priests who performed the death rituals. After
the first round of chanting and rituals, UG saw the priests go out
and followed them. From the morning he had not eaten anything
nor even drunk a glass of water, but he saw the priests, who were
also expected to fast, enter a restaurant. Rushing back home, UG
says that he removed his sacred thread and threw it away, then
went and announced to his grandfather that he was leaving home
and needed some money.

'You are a minor. You cannot have the money,' replied the
grandfather harshly.

'I don't want your money. I want my mother's money,' demanded
the grandson.

'If you go on this way, I'll disown you,' the old man tried to
scare the little boy.

The little boy, whose mind had grown much beyond that of boys
of his age, said coolly, 'You don't own me. So how can you disown
me?'

If UG was difficult for his grandparents to handle, he was kind
and affectionate to his school friends and to the servants at home.
As a boy he detested the caste discrimination practised at home.
He observed that the domestic workers, who came from a lower
caste, were fed with the leftovers of the food cooked the previous
day. When his protest against such a practice had no effect on his
grandmother, he went and sat with the workers one mealtime and
insisted upon being served the same cold food. He was also sensitive
to the problems of those of his school friends who came from poor
families. With the pocket money he received or the money he
occasionally stole from his grandfather, he would pay their tuition
fees, and at times even buy their textbooks and shoes.

Perhaps the grandparents put up with his eccentricities because
they knew he was precocious and believed that he was destined for
higher things. In fact, UG says that he used to be constantly
reminded about his great spiritual destiny by his grandfather. It is
quite possible that UG too took his mother's prediction quite
seriously and looked upon himself as a great guru in the making.

When he was about fourteen, a well-known Sankaracharya of
the famous Sivaganga Math visited T.G. Krishnamurti's house. The
acharya, with his large retinue of disciples and attendants, was

received with great pomp and fitting religious ceremony. The old man did not mind the heavy expense, it was for a noble cause, and he believed it could only have a positive effect on his grandson, for the spiritual quest had already begun in him. The young boy was, of course, fascinated by the pomp and glory that surrounded the acharya, and the great reverence he commanded from his disciples and admirers. UG says that he wanted to be like the acharya when he grew up. He was ready to throw away all his little desires, quit his studies, bid goodbye to his grandparents and follow in the footsteps of the pontiff, and hopefully become the head of the famous Math. He even dared to express his wish to join the acharya. The acharya only smiled and politely turned down his request. He was too young for the hard life of a sannyasi, and leaving home at his tender age would only cause unnecessary unhappiness to his grandparents, he said. However, he gave UG a Shiva mantra. UG recalls that he took the acharya's advice seriously and chanted the mantra 3000 times every day for the next seven years. Keen on achieving spiritual greatness, the boy chanted the mantra everywhere, even in the classroom. What spiritual benefit the chanting did to him is not known, but it certainly did affect his studies and in the final exams of his SSLC he failed in the Telugu language paper.

★

After a long gap, in the year 1932, the convention of the Theosophical Society was once again held at Adyar. The organization was in a mess, if not in total disarray. Sexual scandals, defection of splinter groups, and a grave uncertainty about the Society's goal after JK had severed his connections with it, had reduced it to the state of an exclusive cult with farcical rituals, and vague and unclear, if not unconvincing ideas and objectives. The Theosophical Movement, which was once seen as the way, combining the best from the Eastern and Western religious traditions, to lead a much-confused and beleaguered humanity out of the *Kali Yuga*, the Dark Age, had lost its centre. Still, old horses such as George Arundale and others, with the reluctant approval and participation of their ageing and frustrated president, Annie Besant, were desperately trying to prop up the image of the Society and bring its disenchanted members together under the new, apparently revolutionary notion of 'World Mother'. It was in such a state of affairs that the convention was held at Adyar.

The old man was there with his grandson. He was one of the seniormost members of the Theosophical Society and a privileged member of the Esoteric Group. He had contributed thousands of rupees and supported several of the Society's programmes and projects. That day, along with his grandfather, UG too stood in a long line of people to pay his respects to Annie Besant, with flowers in hand. The old lady, looking ill, shrunken and pale, sat in a chair, receiving and accepting greetings and obeisance from admirers. She was still revered but also had her critics within the society. But she was no longer the revolutionary visionary, the energetic soul and extraordinary force that she had been in the 1920s. When T.G. Krishnamurti stepped forward and offered her the flowers, she did not respond nor showed any sign of recognition, but was absorbed in looking at the young boy who stood by his side. And then suddenly she asked the youngster: 'You are going to work for the Theosophical Society, aren't you?'

Later in the evening, the vice-president of the Theosophical Society, Jinarajadasa, who had heard Annie Besant's remark, sent word to the old man and gave UG an autographed copy of the book *I Promise*. It was a small tract on the spiritual entities called the Masters who were supposed to be guiding the Theosophical Movement, and about what was required to become a disciple of the Masters. UG was thrilled at the turn of the day's events. It is said that on days when his grandfather was not around, UG would sneak into the 'esoteric room' to meditate sitting in front of the pictures of the Masters, and he is believed to have had visions of the Master Kuthumi. Once, when I sought to verify this matter with UG, he brushed it aside, saying they were all 'thought-induced' states of no great consequence.

In the 1880s, Blavatsky had propounded the philosophy of the Great Brotherhood of Masters. There are many who believe today that these Masters were entirely Blavatsky's creation, and that they were modelled after real people. However, in the years following Blavatsky, the controversial Leadbeater, through his prolific writings and incredible announcements of his meetings with these Masters (such as Master Kuthumi, Master Morya, the Mahachohan, and even the World Teacher, Lord Maitreya) on the astral plane, had further strengthened the almost unquestioned belief in the great role of these Masters in the spiritual advancement of humanity.

In 1929, with the dissolution of the Order of the Star, J. Krishnamurti had openly raised doubts and questions regarding the spiritual importance of these Masters, if not their existence. A year later, despite his dismissal of the Masters (although during his Theosophical years he had both talked and written about his meetings with these spiritual entities), when he was pinned down to answer categorically whether or not the Masters existed, he had responded rather ambiguously thus: 'I will explain. In the search for truth, you have in the background of your being a realization that you are seeking something fundamental, lasting, real . . . and you attribute that reality to types—to highly evolved types (Masters). But the moment you approach that type and have yourself adjusted to it, reality is not in that type any longer, and you go further on . . . You are all the time seeking this thing and attributing it to persons whom you may happen to come across. But gradually you will eliminate these imagined types until at last you arrive at your goal. Because I have found reality, I say to everybody who is willing to listen: Do not attribute the totality of truth to individual types. Seek the ultimate, which is of no person, of no sect, of no path . . . You must be empty as a desert to understand. All these questions of types arise when there is still this clinging to the illusion of personal aid from outside.'[11]

Being a member of the Esoteric Group and a firm believer in Theosophy, it seems that T.G. Krishnamurti was not fundamentally affected by JK's dismissal of the Masters, nor his breaking away from the Theosophical Society. He had tremendous faith in Annie Besant, and until his last days, remained a believer in Theosophy. We do not know how seriously or deeply UG took to Theosophy and its Masters. However, he did visit Adyar now and then with his grandfather, and when he moved to Madras for his higher studies, Adyar did become his second home. Later, going by the records, he maintained an active relationship with Arundale, and in particular with Jinarajadasa whom he liked very much. He corresponded with them occasionally and even discussed his practical problems and spiritual dilemmas. And when he started working for the Theosophical Society, he was to adopt Master Kuthumi as his spiritual guide, who, incidentally, had been the spiritual guide of JK as well during his Theosophical years.

'Then so many things happened,' says UG. And there is a leapfrogging of almost seven years in the story. We do not have any details as to what happened between him and his grandparents during these years. We do not know much about his high school days, about his friends and his relatives and their feelings towards him. One can only imagine the difficulties the grandparents must have faced in bringing up a little monster such as UG, who must really have been at once the bane and joy of their existence.

UG's grandmother, Durgamma, played as important a role as the grandfather in his upbringing, although she remains on the margins of UG's story. She was a woman of strong feelings, and made no secrets of her likes and dislikes. She was an 'illiterate', but a repository of mythical stories and 'native' intelligence. Giving an instance of this, UG says that it was from her he learnt the 'original' or etymological meaning of the concept of maya and other such Hindu concepts. But as a boy, it seems that he often used to be quite irritated and angry with her. He never called her 'grandma'. The more she pleaded with him to at least once call her 'Ammamma-Grandma', the more stubborn he would become and even refuse to speak to her. Exasperated, once she is believed to have said that he had 'the heart of a butcher'. True enough, one day, he got so irritated with her begging and cajoling that he had screamed at her, letting fly a string of abusive words in English he had picked at school. A stunned grandfather had later sighed with relief: 'Thank god she doesn't understand English!'

In the story of UG's childhood, it is the grandfather who stands out as an imposing, formidable figure, who had to be demolished and reduced to nothing. But actually he must have been a man of great strength and understanding. If he had not taken his daughter's prediction seriously, if he had not loved his grandson, he couldn't have abandoned his lucrative career and devoted himself to the upbringing of this little maverick. He threw open his house to holy people not merely for his own satisfaction or spiritual pleasure, but because he must have believed that an early exposure to things spiritual would have a positive effect on the boy. Further, he not only took UG along with him every time he visited the Theosophical Society at Adyar, he also took young UG to various holy places, ashrams and centres of learning in India. He was a wealthy man all right, but he was no miser and spent generously on his grandson. It was surely because of his encouragement and support that for seven summers and a few more times in-between, UG could travel to the Himalayas to learn classical yoga from the famous guru Swami Sivananda of Rishikesh. Ultimately, the old man's efforts might not have led to the result he expected. That is a different matter. But in hindsight, one could say that he did play an important role in the life of his grandson, providing him with the necessary financial support and social security so that the young UG could pursue his interests without any encumbrance.

It is not through the study of religious texts, not through contemplation, but through a series of 'shocks' that UG, as a young man, developed a disgust for rituals and philosophies, and decided to strike out on his own and find things out for himself. The words or teachings of the religious masters he had met, including those of his grandfather, did not correspond with their actions. Their beliefs and philosophies did not operate in their lives. They all spoke well, but theirs were all empty words. Still, the boy wanted to test the validity or otherwise of these ideas and beliefs before rejecting them. He had to find out, to use UG's own words, 'to myself and for myself, if there was anything to these teachings'. Talking about that period and his own search and struggles, UG says quite candidly: 'I did not know how to go about, I did not know then that wanting to be free of everything was also a want, a desire.'

So he went probing, testing, trying to put everything into 'practice'. After UG completed his schooling in Gudivada, he moved to Madras so that he could pursue his higher studies without any bother. By then UG had developed a fairly cordial relationship with Arundale and Jinarajadasa, and had no difficulty in finding a place to live in the headquarters of the Theosophical Society. He lived there until his marriage in 1944.

UG as a young man

UG took up a course of study in philosophy and psychology at Madras University. The noted T.M.P. Mahadevan was his philosophy teacher. But the study of the various philosophical systems and of Freud, Jung and Adler made very little impression on him. In fact, it didn't seem to have much bearing on the way he experienced life, or on the way he was 'functioning'. 'Where is this mind these chaps have been talking about?' he asked himself. And one day, he asked his psychology teacher, 'We are talking about the mind all the time. Do you know for yourself what the mind is? All the stuff I know about the mind is from these books of Freud, Jung, Adler and so on that I have studied. Apart from these descriptions and definitions that are there in the books, do you know anything about the mind?' It was an extraordinary and original question from a boy hardly twenty years old. The professor was naturally taken aback and perhaps a little intimidated too; nevertheless, he is reported to have advised UG to take his exams and just write the answers he had been taught if he wanted a degree. 'At least he was honest,' recalls UG. Somehow UG completed two years of his BA Honours course. In the final year, however, he did not take the exams and did not complete the course.

It was during this three-year degree course at the university that UG made several trips to Sivananda's ashram at Rishikesh, both to learn yoga and perform his *tapas* in the caves there. Spiritual seekers or sadhakas would live in the cave near Rishikesh to perform rigorous *tapas* for years. UG had a little cave to himself where, sitting cross-legged, he would meditate, at times for ten to seventeen hours at a stretch. At that time, young though he was, UG says he experimented with his body by going without food or water for several days, pushing the body to the limits of its endurance. Once, he even tried to live on grass. This was the time he also came upon certain mystical states. These mystical experiences came and went, says UG, but deep within him there was no transformation; they did not touch the core of his being. It was indeed a period of great learning, excitement, and frustration too.

At that time, Swami Sivananda had a wide following both in India and abroad. By birth he was a Tamil Brahmin, by profession a physician. The story goes that after his 'religious experiences', he abandoned his medical practice and went to Rishikesh to pursue a monastic career. Soon he became a swamiji of great popularity and power but remained a shrewd physician at heart. Today his teachings might be viewed as somewhat naive, quite reactionary and brazenly patriarchal. He urged women not to compete with men but become good mothers, and if they pursued a career at all, take up nursing or medicine. He exhorted his disciples not to eat rich and spicy food, not to eat meat, and to avoid sex totally if possible; if not, to keep it to the minimum; and if they couldn't help using their hands for pleasure, he advised them to record it in their spiritual diaries and see if the *japa* and *pranayama*, as taught by him, helped them to overcome the urge. He was a practical man and quite pragmatic too. It was under this extraordinary swamiji that UG learnt classical yoga. But one day, as fate would have it, UG caught the swamiji eating hot pickles, and that marked the end of his yoga training at Rishikesh.

By then UG was in his twenties, a period of extreme restlessness and change. The study of philosophy and psychology had only added to his confusion and he had quit the university in great frustration. The training in yoga had left him high and dry. He had found that Swami Sivananda was no different from the many other yogis he had met. To make matters worse, he became aware that he was in no way different from others either. He had meditated and performed tapas to no avail. He had come upon several mystical states, but to his horror he found himself still caught up in conflict, in greed. He found himself burning with anger all the time, and sex remained a nagging problem. UG's own description of his situation at the time is telling. 'I arrived at a point when I was twenty-one where I felt very strongly that all teachers— Buddha, Jesus, Sri Ramakrishna, everybody—kidded themselves, deluded themselves and deluded everybody. This, you see, could not be the thing at all—where is the state that these people talk about and describe? That description seems to have no relation to me, to the way I am functioning. Everybody says "Don't get angry"—I am angry all the time. I am full of brutal activities inside, so that is false. What these people are telling me I should be is something false, and because it is false it will falsify me. I don't want to live the life of a false person. I am greedy, and non-greed is what they are talking about. There is something wrong somewhere. This greed is something real, something natural to me; what they are talking about is unnatural. So, something is wrong somewhere. But I am not ready to change myself, to falsify myself, for the sake of being in a state of non-greed; my greed is a reality to me . . . I lived in the midst of people who talked of these things everlastingly—everybody was false, I can tell you. So, somehow, what you call "existentialist nausea" (I didn't use those words at the time, but now I happen to know these terms), revulsion against everything sacred and everything holy, crept into my system and threw everything out: No more slokas, no more religion, no more practices—there isn't anything there; but what is here is something natural. I am a brute, I am a monster, I am full of violence—this is reality. I am full of desire. Desirelessness, non-greed, non-anger— those things have no meaning to me; they are false, and they are not only false, they are falsifying me. So I said to myself I'm finished with the whole business.'[12]

UG did not 'shop' around much, but he did shop around seriously though briefly. He was not only frustrated with swamijis such as Sivananda Saraswati, he was disgusted with himself too. His own sadhana and mystical experiences had led him nowhere. There seemed truly no way out and he became 'sceptical of everything, heretical to my boots'. Studying UG's cynical state of mind and his intense agony, a chance acquaintance (who later became a friend), Swami Ramanapadananda, suggested that he should go and see Sri Ramana Maharshi who was then considered to be an enlightened soul, and an embodiment of the Hindu mystical tradition.

UG was not sure if it would be of any help to him. He thought he was finished with holy men; they only said, 'Do more and more and you will get it.' He believed he had performed the required sadhana; whatever he had done was enough. In fact, there was nothing to these sadhanas, for they left you only in greater conflict and confusion. He was finished. For he had realized that the solutions offered were no solutions, and that the solutions themselves were the problem. Still, on Ramanapadananda's suggestion, he read Paul Brunton's *Search in Secret India*, particularly the chapters related to Sri Ramana Maharshi. He was not convinced, yet, 'reluctantly, hesitatingly, unwillingly', he agreed to go and meet the great sage.

In 1939, when UG went to see him, Ramana was already well known throughout the country as an enlightened master and a great guru in the long tradition of Indian spirituality. Paul Brunton's book had made him known in the religious world of the West, too. Scholars, writers and spiritual seekers sat at his feet and conversed on the means and ways of self-realization. And many had been struck by his serene face, his tranquil eyes, his simplicity, and the simple idiom in which he talked of the path to self-realization.

At the age of sixteen, Ramana, then called Venkataraman, underwent a 'death experience'. One day, sitting in the first floor of his uncle's house, the young boy was seized with fear of death. Strange as it may sound, the boy lay down on the floor, stretched out his limbs, held his breath and waited. 'Am I dead?' he asked himself. Evidently he was not. The experience lasted for about half an hour; there was no loss of consciousness, rather there was an

awareness of what was happening. There was some great change
taking place inside of him! What was it? Who is it that is conscious
of what was happening? That was the beginning of his intense self-
inquiry which was to become the core of his teaching in later years,
and the beginning of an awakening that eventually took him to the
hills of Arunachalam.

The 'death experience' was to occur again and again but in short
spells over the next sixteen years. The last one happened in 1912,
at Tortoise Rock in Thiruvanamalai; he had to be lifted out of a
cave in a state of samadhi.

'Who or what is this *I* that is asking the question?' used to be
Ramana's general response to almost all the questions asked by
seekers. Ramana was well-acquainted with the Hindu scriptures
and generally used well-known spiritual terms in his talks with the
spiritual aspirants, so much so that scholars and spiritual seekers
tend to see similarities between Ramana and the ancient spiritual
texts, rather than differences.

Ramana was sixty years old when UG, all of twenty-one and
restless, went to see him. It was a large hall with a red-tiled floor.
In one corner, close to a large window, sat the half-naked sage on
a long, white divan, reading a comic strip; sometimes, during the
morning hours, sitting in the same spot, he would be cutting
vegetables, like a sculptor chiselling away at a stone, with total
attention. Some distance away, from the burning joss sticks in an
incense burner, threads of bluish-grey smoke rose and floated in the
quiet air. Devotees and truth-seekers sat at a respectful distance,
drinking in the beatific visage of the sage of Arunachalam.

He sat with feet folded beneath, naked except for a narrow
loincloth. His head was covered with closely cropped grey hair,
and his moustache and stubbly beard looked equally grey. His
copper-coloured skin glistened in the light that poured in from the
large window. Now and then he would pause, looking up intently
with a blank gaze, or with a slight tilt of his head, at the green
landscape outside the window. There was utter silence, pregnant
and profound, and nobody as much as stirred a limb let alone ask
questions. It was enough to sit there bathed in the enveloping
silence, and feel the presence of the Master in one's heart. Many
people had reported having experienced tremendous peace, and

their anxiety and questions drop away in his overwhelming presence.

UG sat there on the tiled floor and wondered: 'How can he help me?' Ramanapadananda had told him that like hundreds of truth-seekers before, he too would experience a penetrating silence and all his questions would drop away, and a mere look from the Master would change him completely. There was, of course, a great silence, only the fan hanging from a wooden beam above whirred quietly, but to UG the whole thing was disconcerting.

At last the sage looked up and their eyes met briefly. But nothing happened. The clock on the wall registered the passage of time. An hour had passed. The questions had remained and there was no sign of UG's trouble coming to an end. Two hours passed, and then UG thought: 'All right, let me ask him some questions.' He wanted nothing less than the ultimate freedom, nothing less than moksha. But he asked, 'Is there anything like moksha?'

The sage answered in the affirmative.

'Can one be free sometimes and not free sometimes?'

'Either you are free, or you are not free at all.'

'Are there any levels to it?'

'No, no levels are possible, it is all one thing. Either you are there or not there at all.'

All right, thought UG to himself and then shot his final question. 'This thing called moksha, can you give it to me?'

Ramana answered with a counter-question: 'I can give it, but can you take it?'

We do not know if this is the order in which the dialogue took place. UG is not sure, and there is no record of it among the published talks or dialogues of Ramana during that period. UG says he asked the questions in English, and Ramana answered both in Tamil and English. Ramana's mother tongue was Tamil, but he knew two other south Indian languages well, Telugu and Malayalam, and had a working knowledge of English. UG, of course, knew Tamil. During his stay in Madras, he had picked Tamil at the university and also by watching Tamil films. During his unexpected second visit to Bangalore in September 2002, one evening, when I wanted to clarify the language in which he spoke to Ramana, as if to answer my as-yet-unasked question, UG spoke a few words

of Tamil to a Tamil-speaking astrologer who was sitting by his side
on the sofa. He spoke in the perfect intonation of a born Tamilian.

'Can you take it?'

No guru before had given such an answer. They had only advised
him to do more sadhana, more of what he had already done and
finished with. But here was a guru, who was supposed to have been
an enlightened man, asking, 'Can you take it?'

The counter-question struck UG like a thunderbolt. It also seemed
an extremely arrogant question. But UG's own arrogance was of
Himalayan proportions: 'If there is any individual in this world who
can take it, it is me . . . If I can't take it, who else can take it?'
Such was his frame of mind. However, the absolute conviction with
which Ramana had fired the question at UG had its effect. He had
more or less asked similar questions to many gurus during his seven
years of sadhana, and he knew all the traditional answers. He had
even stumbled upon certain mystical states, yet the questions had
remained unanswered. What was that state that all those people—
Buddha, Jesus and the whole gang—were in? Ramana was supposed
to be in that state! But then Ramana was like any other man, born
of woman, he couldn't be very different, could he? But people said
that something had happened to him. What was that? What is there?
He had to find out. And he knew in the very marrow of his bones,
as it were, that nobody could give that state to him. 'I am on my
own,' he told himself. 'I have to go on this uncharted sea without
a compass, without a boat, with not even a raft to take me. I am
going to find out for myself what that state is . . .'

4

Doubt Is the Other Side of Belief

Germany's invasion of Poland in September 1939, which soon led both Britain and France together to declare war against Germany, plunged the world into yet another bloody war. The Congress Party of India expressed its strong objection to Britain for taking this unilateral decision to enter the war with Germany without taking into confidence the provisional governments and the Congress Party. And the party issued a statement to the effect that the issue of war and peace for India must be decided by the people of India, and cooperation must be between equals by mutual consent for a cause which both considered to be worthy. It was sheer rhetoric, and too late to prevent the war. However, the Muslim League led by Jinnah found the situation ripe for pressing their demand for an independent state for Muslims. Meanwhile, in view of the growing crisis, Gandhi advised suspension of satyagraha, and wrote an open letter to Hitler, appealing to him to desist from plunging the world into war.

When almost the whole of Europe was reeling under the war, in 1942, UG says that a friend, Duncan Greenlays, took him along to see Gandhiji when he was in Madras on the occasion of the Silver Jubilee Celebration of Dakshin Bharat Hindi Prachar Sabha. There is no record of the conversation UG had with Gandhiji. UG doesn't remember any details of the meeting either, except that he said to Gandhiji, quoting J. Krishnamurti's words: 'Both violence and non-violence spring from the same source.' And the apostle of non-violence, UG says, was stunned into silence. Further, UG is believed to have said to the Mahatma, quite brutally, that through his fasting he was seeking martyrdom, and who knows, one day somebody might put 'a teeny-weeny bullet' into him and that would be the end of him.

UG's (JK's?) criticism of Gandhiji's belief in non-violence sounds preposterous, and from a political perspective one might say that to state that both violence and non-violence spring from the same source is to indirectly support violence, to side with fascism, with brutalities perpetrated in the name of some imagined god or ideology. From a Gandhian perspective, though, violence means termination of dialogue, of relationship, of the possibilities of creative change. In other words, non-violence is a creative means of conducting a dialogue for the possible resolution of conflicts; it is to keep a relationship, a space alive for understanding and change.

But that is not how non-violence has worked in history. Nevertheless, in a deeper analysis, several questions arise as to the creative possibilities of non-violence as an approach to conflict resolution. Both JK and UG obviously have never either supported or approved of violence and killing. Still, they would probably argue that non-violence, in the sense of compassion, is not a result of the self or will; it is always spontaneous or non-volitional. Compassion, therefore, cannot be converted into or used as a method to solve a problem, much less employed as a political weapon. In other words, the 'ego' or the self which is the ground and source of division or separative consciousness is in operation in both violent and non-violent approaches and, therefore, ultimately destructive. Non-violence may not lead to physical violence; non-violence may eschew causing physical injury or death, but eventually it could and would cause subtler forms of violence which in turn could soon become a source of tremendous frustration and violence that could finally lead to greater destruction and suffering. One wonders if that is what happened during the partition of India. This, of course, needs to be examined.

However, the violence of the Second World War took a heavy toll, the like of which the world had not experienced before. The *war to end all wars* killed about fifty-five million people, including six to seven million Jews. In Nagasaki and Hiroshima, which were devastated by the atom bombs dropped on them by the USA, more than 2,00,000 people lost their lives and about 1,00,000 died later, not to speak of the long-term victims of radiation.

While the bloody war raged in several parts of Europe, JK was entrenched in the beautiful Arya Vihara, at Ojai. All his travel plans and public talks were cancelled. Although he felt lonely and isolated during the war years, there was some positive effect too, in that his relationship with Rosalind Rajagopal Sloss grew stronger and more intimate, and he also had the benefit of meeting and talking to distinguished writers and intellectuals, which appears to have had some influence in shaping the language of his future discourses. He met and held long conversations with British writers such as Aldous Huxley, Christopher Isherwood and Gerald Heard, who all had fled London for the safe environs of California. JK was to later encounter other luminaries such as Stravinsky, Bertolt Brecht, Thomas Mann and Bertrand Russell.

Despite the devastating effect of the First World War, the post-First World War generation had not lost hope in the possibilities of achieving great changes in the world. There was indeed an intense inquiry and search for alternatives. The Theosophical Society was seen as one of the great alternatives which had the potential to usher in a new world of peace and creative living. But with JK breaking away in 1929, with the death of Annie Besant in 1933, with internal rivalry and conflicting leadership, and now with the Second World War sweeping across the whole of Europe, the Theosophical Society's mission of World Brotherhood was in the doldrums. A few senior Theosophists, who had maintained their friendship with JK, were dismayed by his strange passivity with regard to the disastrous effect the war could have on people. JK's close associate, Lady Emily Lutyens, voicing the opinion of several others, criticized JK for escaping from the tremendous reality of the war that threatened to destroy all that was good in the world.

But JK thought otherwise. He remained detached, yet deeply critical of both Germany and the Allied Forces. There was no moral high ground to be held in this conflict by either side.[13] Actually, according to JK, the root of the crisis lay in the individual. The war was only an extension of the conflicts that raged in the hearts of individuals.

In point of fact, his 'passivity' marked a period of deep introspection and re-examination of his teaching, which had hitherto carried the flavour and thrust of Theosophy. This introspection, combined with meetings with some of the sharp minds of the period, seemed to have helped JK develop a new language of discourse: less baroque, more practical and immediate, and more conversational in style. Like a writer brutally chopping off all decorative words, all expressions that mystified things, he ejected from his repertoire words that were loaded with traditional and religious meanings. Simultaneously, he was to come up with new words and phrases such as *choiceless awareness*, *total action*, *seeing is ending*, *the observer is the observed* and so on. He also used simple psychological terms and charged them with new meanings. This change in the style and language of his discourse was to ably accommodate the needs and aspirations of the new generation.

The war to end all wars was a pure deception. An absurdity. Suddenly all utopias were suspect. Universal Brotherhood was a mirage. World unity and peace could not be achieved through any ideology whatsoever. All spiritual teachings, whether of the East or of the West, were at best second-hand, to be discarded, for they

prevented the individual from his or her genuine search for truth, from coming upon insights and intelligence that could make living whole and beautiful. So, then, when JK started giving talks again, he was to address not so much the so-called world problems but the crisis within each individual's psyche. For the individual was the world, and the world problem was basically an individual problem.

UG's students and admirers might find it difficult to accept, but in many ways, I think JK's teaching anticipated UG's *anti-teaching* that was to explode on the world in the 1970s. UG rejected JK's idea of psychological transformation by declaring that there was no such thing as mind, therefore all idea of psychological transformation was hogwash. This might remind one of Heraclitus's teaching which was shown to be false by his disciple. You cannot step twice into the same stream, declared Heraclitus, to which his disciple is believed to have answered thus: you cannot step into the same stream even once. UG's anti-teaching not only pulled the carpet from under one's feet, but destroyed the very ground on which one stood.

The post-Second World War era also saw the emergence of new ideas, new ways of seeing and being in the world. 'Doubt', which was central to JK's teachings, was central to most of these new philosophies as well. It was, to use Albert Camus's words, a great metaphysical rebellion against all ideologies, particularly directed against religious teachings and practices. But soon even the metaphysical revolution was to be questioned, which eventually lead to the very rejection of metaphysics. This was again, in some ways, analogous to UG rejecting 'doubt' as a method of inquiry, for doubt too was only the other side of belief, and all inquiries, all searches for truth were bound to fail. For any search contained within itself some idea of what was to be found at the end of the journey. It was, therefore, no search at all. It was just one grand, extended delusion. It was like the case of the dog chasing its own tail!

A Con Game

The war years were an extremely restless period for U.G. Krishnamurti. After quitting his BA course at the Madras University, he was without a sense of direction. The meeting with Ramana had only deepened his anguish. The search, of course, did not end there, but he was going nowhere. The Theosophical Society seemed to be the way out, if only for want of a better option.

UG wrote to Jinarajadasa, who was then the Head of the Esoteric Section of the Theosophical Society, for advice. Jinarajadasa's reply from London gives one the impression that UG had written about his failure to complete his degree, and his many doubts and conflicts, and sought his guidance. UG also wrote to the then president of the Theosophical Society for guidance. The letters written to UG by both Jinarajadasa and Arundale give the impression, contrary to popular opinion, that both the Theosophical Society leaders were open-minded and sensitive to the doubts and questions of a young mind in search of truth. The following letters written by Dr George Arundale are quite revealing.

10 July 1939
Thank you for your letter dated 8 July. I quite realize that examinations are a very great nuisance, and are indeed of extremely little worth. But one has to go through them for the sake of equipment from the standpoint of the outer world.

We were very glad to have you here in the Office and hope to see you again when you are next in Madras.

10 February 1940
I myself certainly have high hopes for you, and I am always glad to see you at Adyar. I do hope you will pass your examinations successfully.

20 May 1940
I am so sorry you have failed in your examination again. Some of us are not really fit for examinations. We can do other and better things, and if you have an income which will suffice, then why should you not follow your own inclinations and study along your own lines. For my own part, I should not think it is necessary for you to have a university career.

And Jinarajadasa wrote from London on 12 July 1940:

Dear Brother,
I can only reply briefly to your letter of appreciation and inquiries.

It is excellent that you should have the ideals which you have of being of service, but you can work out a great part of the problem before you in the light of the many teachings which you find in Theosophy. Regarding the matter of your desiring to find a Teacher, I might here quote the answer which the Master K.H. gave to the late Bro.C.W.L., who asked that question of the Master in 1883:

'To accept any man as a chela does not depend on my personal will. It can only be the result of one's personal merit and exertions in that direction. Force any one of the "Masters" you may happen to choose. Do good works in his name and for the love of mankind; be pure and resolute in the path of righteousness (as laid out in our rules); be honest and unselfish; forget yourself but do remember the good of other people—and you will have forced that "Master" to accept you.

The hymn of Frances Havergel is often used by me to explain to my hearers certain aspects of the great ideal. When I return to India and I can meet you, I can give you further advice. In the meantime, look within yourself for the guidance which you think you need. You will find that if you are in a quiet state of meditation, with a feeling of aspiration, some suggestion will come in the matter of helping others. Put it into operation even if the result seems not noticeable.

'But remember the teaching of the Gita that you must have no thought of fruit or reward, but act righteously because that is a law of your being, or because it is an offering from your heart to God.

Yours sincerely,
C. Jinarajadasa.[14]

★

Even after leaving the university, UG continued to live in Adyar, at the headquarters of the Theosophical Society. But now he worked as one of Dr Arundale's personal assistants. More specifically, he worked as a press secretary to the president. He would read newspapers, magazines and journals that came to the library from all over the world, and choose articles of importance to be read by Arundale later. It was during this time, UG says, that he discovered *Time* magazine and later it became quite a habit with him to read it wherever he was. It was by listening to the BBC radio and through these magazines and newspapers—which reached them sometimes six months behind schedule—that UG and others at Adyar kept themselves informed of the course of events of the war. For three months, UG also worked in the Adyar library, during which time he had the opportunity to look at the great variety of books collected by Leadbeater. Many Theosophists, including Annie Besant, believed that Leadbeater was gifted with powers of clairvoyance. When he had picked the young JK as the vehicle of Lord Maitreya, everyone at the Theosophical Society had implicitly accepted the infallibility of his choice. Given his brilliance and vast reading, UG thinks, it must not have been that difficult for Leadbeater to invent stories of the past lives of JK, Annie Besant and other members of the Esoteric Society.

With a twinkle in his eyes, and a mischievous grin to go with it, one day, during a chat on Leadbeater, UG quipped: 'As a boy I sat in front of Leadbeater every day, expecting him to see some spiritual potential in me.' To the huge guffaws all round the room, UG added, 'But he never saw any spiritual aura around me.'

UG continued to work at Adyar. He was nearly twenty-five. Sex had remained a nagging problem. Despite the urge, he had not rushed into marriage. It was a natural biological urge, but most religious traditions taught one either to deny it or suppress it. Sex was seen as spiritually debilitating, and ultimately an obstacle on the path to moksha; and by implication, Woman, who was seen as the very paradigm of sex, was a danger to be somehow avoided. UG, of course, did not believe in the denial of sex. Yet he had practised celibacy. He wanted to see what happened to the urge if he did not do anything about it. All this only made his situation more difficult, and he was troubled with guilt. He never consciously entertained any thoughts about girls, yet sexual images persisted. Meditating on gods and goddesses only gave him wet dreams. Study of holy books and avoidance of aphrodisiacs were of absolutely no help. The so-called mystical experiences he had had in the caves of Rishikesh had failed to dissolve his sexual urge.

Physical chastity can only increase the desire for sex. Desire cannot be denied but only conquered, say the wise ones. The myths show how even Shiva is troubled by this eternal dilemma. The following quotation expresses most tellingly the classic or religious conflict between the so-called flesh and the spirit.

> I dwell ever in asceticism.
> How is it then that I am enchanted
> by Parvati?[15]

The following verse of Bhartrhari, a mystic poet of the seventh century, captures the dilemma and its possible resolution both humorously and ironically thus:

> In this vain fleeting universe, a man
> Of wisdom has two courses: first he can
> Direct his time to pray, to save his soul,
> And wallow in religious nectar bowl.
> But, if he cannot, it is surely best
> To touch and hold a lovely woman's breast
> And caress her warm round hips, and thighs,
> And to possess that which between them lies.[16]

UG was already twenty-five, it was time to stop fooling himself and reckon with the fact of sex, to come to terms with his body's urge which can never be false. And he thought: 'If it is a question of satisfying your sexual urge, why not marry? That is what society is there for. Why should you go and have sex with some woman? You can have a natural expression of sex in marriage.'

And so, in 1943, he married a beautiful Brahmin girl chosen for him by his grandmother. But UG was a tough customer, indeed a weird and wonderful bridegroom for his time. To the great disappointment of his grandfather, he rejected a dowry of twenty thousand rupees. Five days of a traditional marriage? Nothing doing, he said. Marriage invitations? He saw no reason for inviting and feeding hundreds of his relatives and friends. What for? He himself prepared a wedding card which was no invitation but only an intimation of his wedding with Kusuma Kumari. He insisted on having his way, it was after all *his* wedding, and he threatened to cancel the wedding if they tried to impose any of their ideas. Even the numerous saris and clothes and silver cups and vessels that had been bought to give away as gifts were returned to the shops and the money reclaimed. He gave the money to his wife and told her that from now on she should have her own money and be economically independent.

The very next day after the wedding, however, he realized that he had blundered. In his words: 'I awoke the morning after my wedding night and knew without doubt that I had made the biggest mistake of my life.'

But there was no way he could undo the mistake now. He remained married for seventeen years, and fathered four children.

'Is that all?' I asked him during one of our conversations in Bangalore. 'Is Woman there just for sex?'

'It is mutual. True of both the sexes. What else?' he asked. 'You tell me.'

'Isn't there such a thing as love?'

UG smiled and said that he had told his wife precisely that, that there was no such thing as love between them.

One might wonder about the feelings of UG's wife, Kusuma Kumari, when she married the handsome, young UG, fairly rich, but with a rather strange background. What was her reaction when he spoke in such a brutally matter-of-fact way about their relationship? Going by the reports of her close relatives and friends, and by UG's own admission, she was a woman of extraordinary courage and strength. She loved him for what he was, and could never think of living without him by her side. She managed the family with great diligence and care. But when, after seventeen years, UG finally left her and the children, she could not go on without him.

After his marriage, UG moved out of the Theosophical Society headquarters and took a house on a street close to the Theosophical Society and Elliot Beach at Adyar. He continued to work for the Theosophical Society. In 1946, Jinarajadasa was elected its president, and for three years, UG worked under him as the Joint Secretary of the Indian Section. Later, given his oratorical gift, he was made a national lecturer. For nearly seven years, he travelled extensively in India and Europe on lecture tours. He spoke on Theosophy at practically every college and university in India. Then he went on a long tour to Europe and North America. Going through the lectures he gave in Europe and India, one is surprised to see how a man who had been so thoroughly frustrated with his own religious search and experiences, who had grown cynical of all religious endeavours and goals, had adapted himself to the philosophy and activities of the Theosophical Society. Did he really take up this work for want of a 'better occupation', as he had said once? Was it like his marriage, with no heart in what he was doing? Was it all inevitable: that he had to go through the whole process, that there was very little to choose from, or that it really did not matter one way or another?

UG with wife Kusuma and daughter Bharati

But a consideration of his life during the 1940s up to 1953 gives one the impression that he took his job as a lecturer quite seriously and led a hectic life. Probably he saw himself as a teacher whose job it was to point out the way of truth and urge individuals to experiment and experience truth for themselves. It seems that he also saw himself as a watchdog and critic of society. The letter he wrote to Gandhiji on 10 March 1946 bears this out:

Dear Mahatmaji,
May I invite your attention to the enclosed cutting from *The Hindu* of 10 March 1946, which perhaps, you have noticed already. I am not averse to idolatry. I believe that every citizen in the world must have freedom of conscience and the right to worship his or her ideas in any manner or form that appeal to that individual. But when an institution like a temple or shrine is created for a living person to which an ordinary individual is drawn because of the sanctity attached to it by a large number of devotees, does it not stifle independent thought and thus perpetuate blind adoration and attachment to form? Even in temples where idols are worshipped, our ancestors have made it very clear that it is the spirit behind the form that is worshipped. And the forms depicted by the images in the temple are said to be purely symbolic representations of some cosmic idea or principle or ideal of perfection. As such, do you approve of and encourage such endeavours on the part of the admirers to perpetuate your form and ideals for which you stand, however admirable and attractive they may be?[17]

Respectfully yours,
U.G. Krishnamurti.

It was a period of great political upheavals. The transfer of power from the British was round the corner. After desperate and futile negotiations with the British, the Congress Party had come round to accept the inevitability of the partition of the country. Gandhiji, who was against the partition, had been marginalized in this political process. In fact, at that time, he was touring the length and breadth of the country, talking to people about the bane of the caste system, in particular, untouchability, about his brand of socialism as radically different from Marxism, about famine in Madras and other parts of north India and about ways of overcoming the food crisis. On receiving UG's letter, he wrote an open reply in the *Harijan* stating that he was much pained to know that a temple had been erected where his image was being worshipped. He called it a gross form of idolatry and an insult to him in the sense that the whole of his life had been caricatured in the temple. 'A man is worshipped,' he wrote, 'only to the extent that he is followed, not in his weakness, but in his strength. Hinduism is degraded when it is brought down to the level of the worship of a living being. No man can be said to be good before his death. After death too, he is good for the person who believes him to have possessed certain qualities attributed to him . . . As a matter of fact, God alone knows a man's heart. And hence, the safest thing is not to worship any person, living or dead, but to worship perfection which resides in God, known as Truth . . .'[18]

At that time, UG too was touring the country, giving talks on Theosophy and its significance in the context of world problems and the human condition. Here, one needs to ask: how much of a Theosophist was UG really? Was he playing some sort of game with himself? Was his involvement a sort of experimental affair for a period of time? His lecture at a German school in Rendsberg, however, gives one the impression of a thoroughgoing Theosophist. It is interesting to note that he made absolutely no reference to JK in his talks; it was as if JK did not exist, although he was very much there in the background. He talked of Madame Blavatsky's occultism, of C.W. Leadbeater's investigations into the occult world, and of Annie Besant's philosophy of service. Yet, in all these talks one recognizes his emphasis on the supreme importance of the individual's search and discovery of truth in the context of his or her own experiments and experiences. The following excerpts from the lecture given at Rendsberg is quite revealing of things to come.

The history of Theosophical thought is the history of the evolution of modern thought. As of all others, the survey of Theosophical thought in successive periods of the Society's history is the general evolution and progress of human thought. The leaders of the Society have a place not only in the Theosophical Movement, but also in the history of world thought itself, in the whole intellectual advance that has been registered these seventy-seven years. Every leader has contributed to this onward and forward movement some small fresh fragment to the Temple of Theosophical Wisdom. Progress always appears in different lights to different people. The Society is not simply a working institution; it is a spiritual organization. It is different from the ordinary human societies or clubs that men form for ordinary purposes of human association; but it is still a Society composed of people of various nationalities, and therefore, not something that you can talk about in the abstract. It is like any other organization made up of members. Sometimes in the life of any spiritual movement, we seem to be just jogging along; nothing very much appears to be happening and we do not seem to be getting anywhere in particular; it is only when we pause to look back and to take our bearings, that we realize what a long way we have, in fact, come from where we started, and what tremendous advances we are really making.

There is bound to be loss as well as gain but the leaders have, during these seventy-seven years, made significant contributions in and through the Theosophical Society, to the religious life of the community as a whole. Each of them had something new to say and that is why we revere them, but each of them in a different fashion proclaimed a different facet of Theosophy and they carried the Society forward with them because they journeyed with their faces towards the light. They have left their mark upon its outlook and activities and have also helped to set the general tone.

Let us look at the different stages of growth and the gradual objectivization of the ideals of Theosophy. Let me very briefly survey the background of the Theosophical Movement and the conditions of the world before its advent.

The world was then divided into two camps, that of rigid materialism and that of a narrow and bigoted form of religion. It was an age of conquering science, when religion was on the defensive. The increase of 'valid knowledge' called Science was having a disturbing effect on the religious traditions. Religion had become bankrupt, for it had no real life in it. The mechanistic theory of man and the Universe grew in clarity and prestige. The philosophy that emanated was a materialistic philosophy which sought in matter the solution of all mysteries. Into this maelstrom of opposing and conflicting forces was heralded the Theosophical Society.

Thus what was wanted, the Theosophical Society supplied. So the work of H P Blavatsky is of great consequence, as she supplied a philosophy of life which was broad enough to include both spirit and matter. The great Theosophical treatise, *The Secret Doctrine*, by Madame Blavatsky, brought together all sorts of facts in the domain of mysticism, religion, philosophy and science to prove that quite apart from science and religion, dogma and worship, there is one step beyond mind touching spirit, which may be called the transcendental aspect of Theosophy . . .

But when Dr Annie Besant came on the scene she tried to contact that spirit and to make that Transcendental into Immanent. And her method of achieving this was the service of mankind. What is the motive for service? Each one of us has to try and delve as deeply as possible within himself to see what really is the propelling force or hidden motive behind his activities . . .

Dr Besant taught us that life is only for service. She stressed the central truth as distinct from dogmatic and institutional forms. This appealed to the modern mind, which was becoming increasingly rationalistic in temper and outlook. She made the evolving universe intelligible to millions of people and from the heights of her idealism she set in motion thought currents which spiritualized them more than any other single influence . . .

'Government of the world', 'The Ideas of Manu, the Bodhisattva and the Logos'. These were all later revelations. These were elaborated by the investigations of Annie Besant and C.W. Leadbeater from whom we also heard of the Monad, the Group Soul, etc.

But the cycle is not complete; if we want to complete this cycle we must be able to see the immanence as well as transcendence. It is really the summation, the integration, the climax of the group of thought-forms, the thought processes and evolution...

And in the words of an American philosopher, adapted slightly, even the Truths of Theosophy may dust the mind by their dryness unless they are effaced each morning and rendered fertile by the dews of fresh and living truth. Otherwise, our love of Theosophy has no reality behind it. The vital principles and truths that operate in any spiritual movement are likely to become a dogma or creed when the movement settles down.

Each one of us must discover his own mystery, what *Light on the Path* calls 'final secret'. To do this is to discover something in terms of our own experience, a vital transforming experience. Until we have discovered that centre in ourselves, whatever may be the magnitude of our contribution, all that activity, all that contribution, is bound to be devoid of the unique and vitalizing factor, namely, individual inspiration.

In the ultimate analysis, it is the individual that matters. Only to the extent that an individual is inspired from within himself can he contribute to the common work and thus energize what we call group activity. This process of inwardness, if I may say so, is not morbid isolationism or an ivory-tower outlook. Now we cannot go deep down into ourselves except in a state of relationship with others. To the extent that we are periodically able to go deep down into ourselves can we find that inspiration which is necessary . . .

The world needs Theosophy. The forces of the world are with us, the times and the spirit of the age are with us and I have no doubt the truths of Theosophy which insist on a quest more than on a creed would enable us to join the pursuit of the ideal.[19]

It was as if the little boy had never forgotten Annie Besant's query: 'You are going to work for the Theosophical Society, aren't you?' And it seems for seven years he tried to fulfil her wish. But he couldn't hang on for longer; there was nothing that sustained his deeper interests. What he had been doling out in his lectures was just 'second-hand information'. Anybody with some brains could do this work. It was not something true to his experience, true to his real self. It was all just a profoundly entertaining con game, and he had become a very efficient con man!

He met Jinarajadasa in England in May 1953, and expressed his frustration and disillusionment, and his intention to quit the Theosophical Society. By now UG had grown in stature, and was recognized as a thinker to be reckoned with. His no-nonsense attitude, and his at times brutally harsh criticism of things had made people sit up and listen to him. In response to his criticism, Jinarajadasa wrote: 'I have heard about your reactions with reference to the Theosophical Society and Krishnaji—how critical you have become of everything and everybody! I should like to know your exact viewpoint and would certainly like to discuss it with you. I suggest that you contribute a series of articles in the *Theosophist*. You can very freely criticize anybody—the President, the General Secretaries, and anybody else, in support of your position. Such articles would be welcome in order to maintain absolute freedom on the platform of the Theosophical Society. It is only by such frank and free expression of opinions that organizations can retain their vigour and vitality. If you feel that the Theosophical Society should be closed down, say so in the articles. Let the members know it and let them begin to think. I feel that I at any rate will be greatly benefited.'[20]

UG was quite keen on leaving. Yet reluctantly it seems, upon the request of the president, he continued with his lecture tour. Jinarajadasa wanted him to hang on until they discussed the matter in detail. But the planned meeting never took place as Jinarajadasa died in America the same year. And eventually, his good friend and adviser gone, UG left the Theosophical Society.

6

'Cancer Treats Saints and Sinners in the Same Way'

J. Krishnamurti, now generally referred to as Krishnaji, returned to India in 1947. Many of his close associates and friends from the Theosophical Society came to listen to his talks. After a break of nearly eight years, he gave eleven talks at Adyar. George Arundale had died recently, and the new president, Jinarajadasa, was most sympathetic to Krishnaji. To most of the old guard, JK at last, seemed to be fulfilling his mission as the World Teacher.

Krishnaji was nearing fifty, but looked much younger, still handsome and flushed with youth. In his kurta and dhoti he looked dignified yet charming. His talks now carried a strange authority and a quiet spiritual depth. Though the core of his teaching had not changed, his lectures were stripped of all messianic expressions. All the old, traditionally devotional terms, poetic metaphors and references to Theosophy had been excised out of his discourses.

He had come at a time when the nation thrashed about in its birth pangs. Partition had led to the carnage of thousands of Hindus, Sikhs and Muslims across the borders of the two new nations. Gandhiji was still alive, struggling to prevent the blood-bath that threatened to destroy all that he had worked for. It was a bloody time and any sensible, let alone critical, conversation seemed impossible. But Krishnaji struck a deep chord in the hearts and minds of the intellectuals, writers, activists, and all those sensitive, forward-looking men and women who came to listen to him. They saw in him a new, yet radical, guru, a truly emancipated spiritual leader, a pure 'Vedantin' that a new, resurgent India badly needed.

But what was this new, radical teaching? In 1980, while writing the second volume of JK's biography, Mary Lutyens prepared a short statement on the 'revolutionary core of Krishnamurti's teaching', and sent it to Krishnaji for his approval. Krishnaji, of course, rewrote the entire statement, retaining just one word: 'core'. The entire statement is quoted here to give a sense of his teaching, which UG was to have trouble accepting, both when he went to listen to JK's talks and in his conversations with JK.

The core of Krishnamurti's teaching is contained in the statement he made in 1929 when he said 'Truth is a pathless land'. Man cannot come to it through any organization, through any creed, through any dogma, priest or ritual, not through any philosophical knowledge or psychological technique. He has to find it through the mirror of relationship, through the understanding of the contents of his own mind, through observation and not through intellectual analysis or introspective dissection. Man has built in himself images as a fence of security—religious, political, personal. These manifest as symbols, ideas, beliefs. The burden of these dominates man's thinking, relationship and daily life. These are the causes of our problems for they divide man from man in every relationship. His perception of life is shaped by the concepts already established in his mind. The content of his consciousness *is* this consciousness. This content is common to all humanity. The individuality is the name, the form and superficial culture he acquires from his environment. The uniqueness of the individual does not lie in the superficial but in the total freedom from the content of consciousness.

Freedom is not a reaction; freedom is not choice. It is man's pretence that because he has choice he is free. Freedom is pure observation without direction, without fear of punishment and reward. Freedom is without motive; freedom is not the end of the evolution of man but lies in the first step of his existence. In observation one begins to discover the lack of freedom. Freedom is found in the choiceless awareness of our daily existence.

Thought is time. Thought is born of experience, of knowledge, which is inseparable from time. Time is the psychological enemy of man. Our action is based on knowledge and therefore time, so man is always a slave to the past.

When man becomes aware of the movement of his own consciousness he will see the division between the thinker and the thought, the observer and the observed, the experiencer and the experienced. He will discover that this division is an illusion. Then only is there pure observation which is insight without any shadow of the past. This timeless insight brings about a deep radical change in the mind.

Total negation is the essence of the positive. When there is negation of all those things which are not love—desire, pleasure—then love is, with all its compassion and intelligence.[21]

UG was present when JK gave his first talk after the war years, at Adyar. By his own admission, UG listened to JK's talks between 1947 and 1953, and from 1953, interacted with JK at a personal level, holding long conversations with him on several occasions. During that time, JK also met UG's wife and their children, and took a particular interest in the health of UG's eldest son, Vasant, who had been struck with polio.

The relationship between UG and Krishnaji cannot exactly be categorized as one between a guru and a disciple, nor as one between two antagonists or rival gurus. What comes through is that right from the beginning, UG seemed to have had problems with JK's image as the World Teacher and his teachings. Often UG would react critically, harshly and scathingly against Krishnaji, exploding with fury like the mythical Shiva in a state of wrath, while Krishnaji would always behave like an English gentleman. But there is no denying the fact that Krishnaji and his teaching had had a great impact on UG, even if, gradually and progressively, he was to reject it all at the end. In some ways, their relationship may be compared to the one between Basavanna and Allama, the two revolutionary, twelfth-century mystic-poets of Karnataka. Incidentally, what is most remarkable about that period is that it produced literally hundreds of mystic-poets who all laid great emphasis not on reading of texts and acquisition of knowledge, however profound or spiritual, but on what A.K. Ramanujan calls *anubhava*: 'The

Experience, the unmediated vision, the unconditioned act, the unpredictable experience'.[22]

Basavanna was born to Brahmin parents and was brought up by his grandmother. He rejected his Brahminhood and was against the hegemony of Brahmins and their caste practices. He was not a mystic of the order of Allama, but a saint–reformer. His *Vachanas*, prose–poems, dramatize themes such as spiritual conflicts and dilemmas, the saint's agony over his sense of separation from his god, and the mystical yearning to be always one with the lord. This was combined with criticism of bigotry, superstitions, caste practices, and an assertion of the need for kindness, love, and of the oneness of humanity that is characteristic of social reformers.

But Allama was like a butterfly with 'no memory of the caterpillar'. His Vachanas are littered with explosive images and bewildering metaphors that always break and leap over and against the limitation of language. The mind is stunned reading about 'the toad that swallowed the sky', or a 'black koil that eats up the sun' and the eye turns within itself as it were seeing a 'blind man catch a snake'. Both the hunter and the hunted die, and the seeker realizes that there is nothing to seek, to know, truth is neither here, nor there, and the one who knows 'gets no results'. Allama was like 'space that goes naked'. He was the guru of gurus. Though respectful, he was caustically critical of Basavanna, Akka Mahadevi and several other vachanakaras of the period for their imperfect rejection[23] of the false, for not being true to themselves and to what they preached. Allama's rebuke of his contemporary gurus is analogous to UG's blasting fury against religious teachers, in particular, his criticism of Krishnaji: 'You are still a Theosophist. You have never freed yourself from the World Teacher role. There is a story in the *Avadhuta Gita* which talks of the avadhuta who stopped at a wayside inn and was asked by the innkeeper, "What is your teaching?" He replied, "There is no teacher, no teaching and no one taught." And then he walked away. You too repeat these phrases and yet you are so concerned with preserving your teaching for posterity in its pristine purity.'

Yet, every year for seven years, UG listened to Krishnaji, despite his doubts and troubles with Krishnaji's ideas and 'insights'. There was really something to JK's teaching, yet he felt that they were somehow not true to his own experience, that they were falsifying him. But he was not sure of himself, he was not certain if what he had come upon by and for himself was true either. He lacked clarity and conviction, and was beset by doubts and questions, all of which were to dissolve and disappear in the heat of the explosive experience, or what UG would call the 'calamity', in 1967.

On 30 January 1948, Gandhiji was assassinated. The then prime minister, Jawaharlal Nehru, in his emotionally charged speech, said: 'The light has gone out of our lives . . . Yet I am wrong, for the light that shone in this country was no ordinary light . . . and a thousand years later that light will still be seen in this country and the world will see it. For that light represented the living truth.'

In response to the gesture of obeisance, the assassin had fired three bullets into the frail body of the old man. Two bullets had passed right through the chest, the third bullet remained embedded in the lung. The hands of the Mahatma, which had been raised in the gesture of greeting, namaskar, dropped, and he had collapsed.

The whole country, already devastated by the Partition riots, sighed in relief on knowing that the killer was not a Muslim, but a Hindu fanatic. Days before the tragedy, Krishnaji had arrived in India to give his public talks. A day after Gandhiji's death, a person asked Krishnaji during his public talk in Bombay, 'Sir, what are the real causes of Mahatma Gandhi's untimely death?'

Krishnaji said, 'Sir, what are the causes that have brought about this assassination? Don't you think each one is responsible for what is happening in the world at the present time? The various incidents that are taking place at the present time are not unrelated incidents but related. The real cause of this murder lies in *you* (emphasis mine). The real cause is you. Because you are communalistic, you encourage the spirit of violence, of division, of caste, of ideology. Obviously, you are responsible and it is foolish merely to blame the murderer. You have all contributed to the murder.

'It is inevitable when a so-called nation is made up of separate groups, each seeking power, position, and authority; then, it is bound to produce not one man's death but thousands. Similarly, organized religion with its dogma and belief will inevitably produce conflict and confusion. When belief becomes stronger than affection, then there is antagonism between man and man—belief in ideology, in patriotism, and so on . . .'[24]

Two other great masters, who had made a huge impact on the religious consciousness of modern India, Sri Aurobindo and Sri Ramana Maharshi, were to pass away in the next three years. Aurobindo died in his sleep on 5 December 1950. He had been a great experimenter in spirituality, a unique teacher among the sages of India's long spiritual tradition.

Four months later, Ramana died of cancer. Rheumatism had crippled his legs and weakened his back and shoulders. The negligence of the body had taken its toll. In 1949, a small nodule appeared below the elbow of his left arm, and very soon it flared up and turned into a tumour, which was diagnosed as a sarcoma. Radium treatment and three surgeries only aggravated the disease. Within a month of the operation, the tumour would return, causing great discomfort and pain. Ramana turned down the doctors' advice to amputate the diseased arm. 'There is no cause for alarm,' he said. 'The body itself is a disease; let it have its natural end. Why mutilate it?'[25]

People were amazed at his indifference to pain, even during the operations. Ramana, of course, felt the pain, but not as others would in such a situation. 'If the hand of a Jnani were cut with a knife,' Ramana said, 'there would be pain as with anyone else, but because his mind is in bliss he does not feel the pain as acutely as others do.' On another occasion he was to say: 'They take this body for Bhagavan and attribute suffering to him. What a pity! . . . Where is pain if there is no mind?'

The distinction between pain and suffering is a crucial one here. Suffering is a mental experience, while pain is purely a physical one. However, the devotees believed that their Bhagavan would not, rather could not, die of cancer. But Ramana himself was indifferent, and he knew! In any case, death was a problem to the devotees, not to Ramana. 'Have I ever asked for any treatment?' he asked. 'It is you who want this and that for me, so it is for you to agree about it among yourselves. If I were asked I should always say, as I have said from the beginning, that no treatment is necessary. Let things take their course.' Two days before his passing away, he refused all medicines. He sat, not in the usual larger hall from where he had given darshan and talked to thousands of his devotees, truth-seekers and admirers, but in a room (called the 'nirvana room', constructed for his convenience); he sat, all shrunken, the ribs protruding, the skin blackened as a result of the radiation therapy, as hundreds of his devotees passed slowly by the room, taking in the beatific smile of their dying master. Next evening, although it was quite late, the devotees still clustered outside the room, and began singing 'Arunachala-Siva'. Minutes later, outside the hall, from the hill, even down from the streets of the town, hundreds of people later reported seeing a bright light move across the sky and disappear behind the peak of Arunachala.

Once, to a question as to why an enlightened man like Ramana had to suffer and die of cancer, UG had apparently coldly observed: '. . . cancer treats saints and sinners in the same way.'

UG has more or less made the same kind of comment on Sri Nisargadatta Maharaj's death by throat cancer. Nisargadatta Maharaj was a remarkable mystic. He was also a bidi smoker. Perhaps it was smoking or tobacco chewing that eventually caused his cancer, but we cannot be sure. If it was so, couldn't it have been prevented? And the question has to be asked again: 'Why should the ones who are supposed to have touched the source of life, die of cancer?'

Incidentally, Sri Ramakrishna too died of throat cancer. He ate a lot of sweets, and chewed tobacco occasionally. The frequency with which he went into trance or samadhi, his strange visions and experiences, make the most bewildering reading in the annals of mystical literature. Undoubtedly the most peculiar among the sages of modern India!

His throat trouble started only a year before his death. It was diagnosed as 'clergyman's sore throat', and the doctors thought that it was caused by bad weather and his constant talking, singing and frequent recurrence of 'Bhava-Samadhi'. Medicines and 'proper' diet were prescribed, and the Master was asked to rest his vocal organs, none of which Sri Ramakrishna could or did follow consistently. When the discomfort and pain became acute, a further diagnosis revealed that it was a case of cancer, called 'Rohini' according to one school of Ayurveda. All sorts of medicines, including homoeopathy, were tried. But Sri Ramakrishna being what he was, he could never give rest to his vocal chords. And the recurrences of his samadhi seemed to aggravate the disease. It was as if the rush of energy, instead of destroying the cancer cells, only added to its life and fast multiplication. The way twelve of his close, young disciples—who all became famous swamijis, Swami Vivekananda being the foremost—took care of their master makes a moving story. Ramakrishna was not a rich people's guru. The only money he came by was a paltry sum he drew as a 'retired' priest at the Dakshineswar temple. Every time Ramakrishna and his disciples moved to a new place, in order to pay the rent and meet other household expenses, the disciples had to raise funds, sometimes pledging their belongings.

But why should their master suffer from such a deadly ailment? Couldn't the power of Mother Durga cure him? Couldn't he do it himself with his spiritual powers which could send people into trance in no time? Or, was it all a divine play, a divine *lila*? One group of his close disciples felt it was all a lila, to test the devotion of the disciples, to strengthen their character and lead them to the path of renunciation. The other group thought it was all the doings of the Divine Mother, the purpose or mystery of which the Master himself could not fathom. The third group took a rational view of the whole matter and reasoned that Sri Ramakrishna, like all other human beings, had a physical body that was naturally subject to the laws of nature, so that it was idle and futile to ascribe some esoteric meaning or mystical reasons for his illness. Despite this difference of opinion they all believed that the Master had probably taken the 'sins' or disease of some devotee upon himself, or that the 'impure' bodies of people who came and touched him had affected him adversely. This belief was partly strengthened by Ramakrishna himself who had once chided Mother Durga thus: 'Why dost Thou bring here these worthless people who are like milk adulterated with five times its quantity of water? My eyes are almost gone by blowing into the fire to dry up the water, and my health is shattered. This is beyond my power to do. Go and do it thyself . . .. I find no time even to bathe or eat. This (his own body) is but a perforated drum, and if you beat it day and night, how long will it last?'

For some time, the disciples tried in vain to prevent strangers from touching the feet of the Master. But the Master himself was not cooperative. He talked and talked, even when he was in pain. He did not stop giving spiritual instruction, he even sang and danced with the disciples, and almost every day as a rule, fell into samadhi.

When the disciples pleaded, 'You must cure yourself, for our sake at least,' he replied: 'Do you think that I have been undergoing this suffering voluntarily? I do wish to recover. But how is that possible? It all depends upon Her will.'

'Your will is at one with Hers!'

'It won't do any good. How can I ask Her for anything when my will is entirely merged in Hers?'

The flow of old associates, devotees and admirers only increased tenfold. He did not stop speaking. The recurrence of his samadhi and mystical visions amazed and humbled the disciples. He was once heard saying to himself: 'Had this body been allowed to last longer, many more people would have been spiritually awakened.' Then after a pause: 'But Mother has ordained otherwise. Lest people should take advantage of my simplicity and illiteracy, and prevail upon me to bestow the rare gifts of spirituality, She will take me away. And this is an age when devotional exercises are at a sad discount.'[26]

As days passed into weeks and weeks into months, his body shrank, the pain grew acute, and internal bleeding aggravated the condition. But he refused to be bedridden. One day he made Narendra sit in front of him, and gazing at him Ramakrishna fell into samadhi. Narendra, who later became Vivekananda, reported that he felt a subtle force like an electric current penetrate his body, and he lost consciousness. When he came back to a normal state, he saw the Master in tears. 'Today I have given you my all and have become a faquir!' whispered the Master. 'Through this power you will do immense good to the world, and then only shall you go back.'

The day before his passing away, the pain became unbearable and his breathing difficult. In the early hours of Monday, 16 August 1886, Sri Ramakrishna fell unconscious and his body turned stiff. The stiffness was something unusual and some of the disciples thought that the Master had only entered into a state of deep samadhi. They massaged his back and limbs, hoping against hope that he would return to consciousness. Almost fifteen hours later, at about noon, Dr Mahendra Lal Sarkar, who had attended on the Master before and had become his great admirer, declared Sri Ramakrishna Paramahamsa dead.

J. Krishnamurti's epic career as a teacher came to a dramatic end with his last three talks in January 1986 at Adyar, from where he had begun his life as the World Teacher. Despite high fever, he had managed to speak for three days. When the discomfort and fatigue increased, all the programmes, including the talks at Bombay, were cancelled and he was flown to California. Back in Ojai, at Arya Vihar, his home for several decades now, he could not relax. He sat under the pepper tree in the same place where he had first experienced the beginnings of his 'awakening'. It was noon, the landscape was swathed in soft light. He sat gazing upon the hills beyond. He looked a picture of a dead leaf, all wrinkled and ashen. He was dying. And it seems his condition was not exactly what he had described two years ago in the last entry of his last journal (25 February 1983–30 March 1984). It went thus: 'As one looked at that dead leaf with all its beauty and colour, maybe one would very deeply comprehend, be aware of, what one's own death must be, not at the very end but at the very beginning. Death isn't some horrific thing, something to be avoided, something to be postponed, but rather something to be with day in and day out. And out of that comes an extraordinary sense of immensity.'

The next morning, he experienced intense pain. Nobody suspected, that death lingered just round the corner, waiting. He was rushed to Santa Paula Hospital. For eight days he suffered through X-rays, intravenous feeding, morphine injections, CAT scans and liver biopsy. His condition was diagnosed as cancer of the pancreas, it had spread to his liver and there was no hope of recovery.

Some of his close associates, of course, expected a miraculous recovery. After all, the clairvoyant Leadbeater had picked him as the perfect vehicle for the Lord Maitreya to descend on earth. And then JK himself had undergone 'the process', considered to be both a cleansing and awakening process. How could such a person be afflicted by such a deadly disease?

It is said that Krishnaji himself was shocked, and a couple of

times he did break down in tears either out of pain or shock or
both. He is also reported to have said that 'the condition' might
have been caused by some wrong he might have committed in the
past, or could have been due to some vestiges of psychological
impurity (which reminds one of Gandhi's intense and agonizing self-
introspection during the Naokhali days just before the partition of
India).

Actually, it was not as if JK had not suffered from any illness
before. Over the years, he had had bronchial complaints, kidney
problems, urinary tract infections, prostrate gland trouble and
hernia. Yet, with extraordinary discipline of body and mind, with
great resilience and indefatigable energy, for almost seventy long
years, he had travelled round the world, giving talks, meeting
people, trying in his own inimitable style to light a fuse, to urge
and inspire his listeners to boldly tread the 'pathless land' and
become a light unto themselves.

In less than thirty days after the deadly diagnosis, his condition
deteriorated rapidly. He suffered excruciating pain and had to seek
relief with the use of morphine. Almost ten years ago, in a meeting
with his close associates at Ojai, Krishnaji himself had asked: 'If
people come here and ask, "What was it like to live with this man?"
would you be able to convey it to them? If any of the Buddha's
disciples were alive would not one travel to the ends of the earth
to see them, to find out from them what it had been like to live
in his presence?' Now, just ten days before Krishnaji breathed his
last, gazing at the wasted and shrunken body of the teacher, when
one of the Trustees of the Krishnamurti Foundation asked: 'What
really happens to that extraordinary focus of understanding and
energy that is K after his death?'

Krishnaji replied: 'It is gone. If you only knew what you had
missed—that vast emptiness.'[27]

Krishnaji was ninety-one years old when he died on 17 February
1986. Exactly a year before, Krishnaji, hale and healthy, had just
returned from India. The German-born Michael Krohnen, one of
the main protégés of the legendary restaurateur and chef Alan
Hooker, the grandfather of 'California Cuisine', was at Ojai at that
time. A great admirer of Krishnaji and a truth-seeker in his own
right, Krohnen had cooked lunch for Krishnaji and his guests. That

day, he had prepared a meal of corn and olive salad, guacamole, green bean soup, cumin potatoes with a three-cheese spinach quiche, broccoli with sauce olivos, and fruit salad and yogurt for desert. Krishnaji, along with eleven guests including Mary Zimbalist, had the lunch at Arya Vihar, talking about 'the tumultuous events surrounding Indira Gandhi's assassination'.

After the sumptuous lunch, while clearing the table, Krohnen commented on the enormous amount of travelling Krishnaji had done recently. Krishnaji had looked up at him with kind eyes and had said: 'You know, sir, all this travelling by air, ship and car is not very good for the organism. We have done it for seventy years, or more. It unsettles the body, upsets it. It always needs time to quieten down again and to adjust. If it wasn't constantly on the move, the body might live a lot longer—maybe a hundred years, or maybe a hundred and twenty. So stay settled and lead a quiet life.'[28]

But JK lived for ninety-one years. Gandhiji lived for seventy-nine years. He wanted to live for 125 years to complete his mission on earth, but became a victim of Hindu fanaticism. There have, of

A fairly recent photograph of UG

course, been people who have lived beyond a hundred. Incidentally, UG also believes that if the body is not abused, one might go on to live for 120 years, provided the body is genetically programmed to live that long. UG is eighty-five at the time of writing this. He has travelled to almost every country, including China, meeting and speaking to people for at least ten hours on an average every day for more than fifty years. Sometime in the 1970s, on hearing about UG from Maurice Frydman, Nisargadatta Maharaj had said, 'Now he knows what he knows. All else is over. At least he still talks. Soon he may cease talking.' That was said more than thirty years ago. UG continues to travel and talk to whoever cares to listen to him. But some day, chuckles UG at times, he has to stop travelling, and even stop speaking. And in response to the Maharaj's comment, he says, rather playfully, 'Maybe I will develop throat cancer or something. It is the privilege of only a saint to die of cancer. I told Mahesh to see that in my death certificate the cause is put down as cancer and not anything else. Otherwise I won't be recognized by the world.' And then he adds a little seriously, 'Anyway it is only when I stop travelling that I will drop dead.'

7

'Have You Ever Had Sex, Krishnaji?'

JK came back to India in 1953 and gave several talks in Madras, Banaras and Bombay. He talked of the art of listening, the art of looking at one's problems without conclusions, of conditioning and men's conditioned responses as communists, Hindus, Christians, of the tremendous discontent in society, of the mind that always compares, of the futility of our becoming, of desperately trying to change from 'what is' to 'what should be' without understanding, and so on. His fourth talk in Madras was concluded thus: '. . . So our problem is the change to the unknown, not to the known, and that is the only revolution, the change which comes about when the unknown comes into being in my mind. Please follow this. When the unknown comes into being, the unknown cannot be with the 'me' when the 'me' is pursuing consciously some end. Until that unknown, that truth, comes into being all labour is in vain. So, for that unknown to come into being, the mind must cast away all knowledge of the thing which it has learned in its self-protection; the mind must completely, totally, empty to receive the unknown; the mind itself must be in a state of the unknown. Then from that unknown we shall build, and then that which we build is everlasting. But without that, they who labour to build, labour in vain, which only creates more misery and more chaos in the world.'

After the talk, JK would answer a few questions from the audience. That evening many questions were sent in. JK said that he would not give answers, but would try to investigate the problem together with the questioner and find the truth of the problem. The first question he picked to answer happened to be the one sent in by U.G. Krishnamurti.

Question: Sir, what kick exactly do you get out of these talks and discussions? Obviously you would not go on for more than twenty years if you did not enjoy them. Or is it only by force of habit?

J. Krishnamurti: This is a natural question to put, is it not? Because the questioner only knows or is aware that generally a speaker gets a kick out of it, some kind of personal benefit. Or is it merely old age? Or, whether one is young or old, is it the habit? That is all he is accustomed to, so he puts the question.

What is the truth of this? Am I speaking out of habit? What do you mean by habit, force of habit? Because I have talked for twenty years, am I going to talk for twenty more years until I die? Is the understanding of anything habitual? The use of the words is habitual; but the contents of the words vary according to the perception of truth from moment to moment. If a speaker gets a kick out of it, then he is exploiting you. That is what most of us are used to. The speaker is then using you as a means of fulfilment, and surely it would destroy that which is real. As we are concerned to find the truth and *what is* from moment to moment, in it there can be no continuity; all habit, all certainty, all desire for fulfilment, all personal aggrandizement must have come to an end, must it not? Otherwise, it is another way of exploiting, another way of deluding people, and with that surely we are not concerned.[29]

The next day, UG attended a discussion with JK, to which only selected people were invited. Since UG was now a prominent member of the Theosophical Society, he had easy access to these meetings. After a brief discourse on the question of death and the death experience, JK looked at UG and asked, 'What do you have to say, sir?'

A heated discussion ensued, and JK did not allow anyone to intervene, saying that it was something the two of them needed to thrash out between them. In a sense it was the beginning of their long quarrel for many years. In these quarrels or arguments, JK was, of course, always a gentleman, always restrained and reticent, even at times when the situation seemed impossible, just coldly polite; while almost as a rule, UG would be direct, harsh, sometimes even crude. If this hurt people he was not too bothered, for he believed that if one got so easily hurt the relationship was not worth anything. So then, at the next day's meeting, when JK talked about subconscious and unconscious states of mind, UG interrupted rather brusquely, 'Sir, I don't see any mind in me, let alone a subconscious or unconscious mind. So why are you talking to me about these states?'

This was totally unexpected and shocking. Nobody spoke to a world teacher that way. Nevertheless, JK answered quietly, 'Sir, for you and me there is no such thing as a subconscious or unconscious mind. But I am using these terms for those people . . .' He obviously meant the others in the gathering.

From that day, UG stopped going to the discussion meetings. But two days later, Mr L.V. Bhave, their mutual friend, urged UG to meet with JK personally. It is quite possible that JK himself was interested in meeting his namesake and so had requested Bhave to bring him over. Whatever the case may be, apparently the first meeting went off very well. UG had no questions to ask, rather he talked briefly about himself, about his background and his grandfather's long and close association with the Theosophical Society and its leaders, and then about his own work with the Theosophical Society as a lecturer for the past seven years.

Surely by then, JK must already have had some information about UG. UG was well known in certain circles as an extraordinary speaker and as a sort of spiritual rebel. True enough, now JK responded saying that he had heard of UG's visits to Norway, Sweden and Denmark. And with a little smile he continued, saying that in fact people in those countries had become confused because of his and UG's common names, and that in order to clear the confusion, he had to write to them.

A time would come when the confusion would cease and UG would be referred to as the 'Other Krishnamurti', sometimes as 'anti-Krishnamurti' or 'antidote to Jiddu'.

These interesting palavers, often ending in fierce discussions, continued for two years, whenever JK visited India and gave talks. UG says that JK used him as a sounding board, as a mirror to see himself. In any case, we cannot overlook the fact that UG needed to confront JK. He may not have looked upon JK as a guru, but the need and urge to meet the guru was certainly there. There is no third party record of their conversations or arguments. What we know is from what UG has shared with people whenever he had been pressed to speak about his encounters with JK. Over the years, the answers have been the same, almost word for word. It is as if every time the question is asked, the answer comes out exactly the way it had been recorded on a cassette. The following dialogues are constructed out of the several conversations UG has had over the years with his close associates and from his answers to people's questions about JK.

One morning in Madras, UG asked JK, 'Yesterday, in answer to a question on the Masters, you said, "As for the Masters, I have never denied their existence." My question to you, Krishnaji, is: Do they or do they not exist? And I want a straight answer.'

JK said, 'Anything I say becomes authoritative.'

UG replied, 'I am not impressed by your diplomatic answers which neither confirm nor deny. Why do you give all these ambiguous answers? Why not hang the whole thing on a tree for everyone to see?'

JK did not give any straight answer, instead he deflected the conversation on to other subjects. Interestingly, this question has fascinated many seekers. Towards the end of his life, JK has gone on record to say that indeed he has been a vehicle or medium for some unnameable, mysterious spiritual forces, if not the Masters.[30]

However, on another occasion, apparently in a blasting mood, UG asked, 'Do you mean to say, Krishnaji, that the state you are in happened through the method you are indicating to your listeners?' When no answer was forthcoming, UG remarked sharply, 'Before the war you were using utterly mystifying language. Now, after the war, you have come up with what I could call the *Krishnamurti lingo*. Your teaching is nothing but Freudian-Jungian-Rankian-Adlerian stuff with a religious slant. Is this just to give people a new toy? Children in my time used to play with dolls made of deodar wood. Now you are providing them with walking, dancing and talking dolls.'

UG never tires of repeating these barbs even now, particularly to Krishnamurtiites, teasingly referred to as 'widows of J. Krishnamurti'.

UG in a playful mood

On that day, however, JK is believed to have laughed and said, 'If it works, it works. If it doesn't, it doesn't.'

On yet another occasion, in response to JK's idea of changing the world, UG said plainly, 'I am not called upon to save the world.'

Aghast at UG's barefaced apathy and heartlessness, JK said, 'But, sir, the house is on fire—what will you do?'

'Pour more gasoline on it and maybe something will rise from the ashes.'

'Ah! You are absolutely impossible!'

One day, the subject of the education of UG's children came up and JK is believed to have suggested that he send his children to Rishi Valley School.

UG's two daughters were attending Besant Theosophical School which was close to their house, so UG said that the arrangement was convenient and the school was good enough for the children.

Pulling a face, JK said, 'They teach religion, sir.'

As if stung by a scorpion, UG retorted, 'What do they teach in Rishi Valley School? Instead of having them attend a prayer meeting, you drag those poor unwilling students to watch sunsets from the hilltop. How is that different? You like sunsets. So the children have to watch them too. You know, I spent three-and-a-half days in that Guindy National School. You will recall that you gave talks to us during that time. There is nothing marvellous about those schools. As for myself, I attended a street-side school. And what's wrong with me!'

It seems that there was hardly any subject that was not discussed by the two Krishnamurtis. JK was fifty-eight years old then, and UG thirty-five. It's a pity that these conversations were not recorded, or perhaps they were considered to be too damaging to be put in the JK archives. Anyway, one day quite inevitably as it were, the subject of sex too came up. UG, as he was and is wont to, offered his direct, clinical opinion of the subject.

'It's only sex,' he said.

'There must be so much more to it, sir,' JK suggested.

'What, for example?' asked UG.

'Love,' JK replied.

'What has love got to do with it?' UG asked, rather irritatingly.

UG's wife, Kusuma Kumari, happened to be present during this discussion, perhaps wondering what these two bulls were fighting over. When the subject of sex came up, stung by some curiosity, she suddenly asked JK: 'I am not going to ask questions about sex, except one. Have you ever had sex, Krishnaji?'

It was too bold a question to ask a world teacher nearing sixty.

It was, in some way, like a scene replayed from the story of Sankara, the great philosopher–poet, mystic-religious reformer of the sixth century. The episode is fairly well known to all those who are familiar with the life and teachings of Sankara.

After winning many intellectual and philosophical battles in favour of his formulation of Vedanta, it is said, Sankara decided to take on Mandana Misra, an authority on Vedic rituals or what is called *karmakanda*.

The great debate takes place in Mandana Misra's house; his wife, Ubhaya Bharati, known for her learning, agrees to be the referee. Just as the debate begins, she goes off to attend to the unfinished household chores and cook the meal for the two great debaters and their guests.

After hours of arguments and counter-arguments, Sankara comes through victorious, thus establishing the supremacy of Vedantic knowledge. Ubhaya Bharati gives her verdict, and Mandana Misra accepts defeat and willingly becomes Sankara's disciple.

After consuming the meal prepared by Ubhaya Bharati, Sankara, in his pride and silly arrogance, commits the error most philosophers are prone to. Sankara wishes to defeat Ubhaya Bharati, the judge, and proclaim his absolute superiority.

Ubhaya Bharati accepts the challenge. The debate goes on for seventeen days, and at last, Ubhaya Bharati silences Sankara by opening the subject of sex. She says: 'Discuss the science and the art of love between the sexes. Enumerate its forms and expressions. What is its nature and what are its centres . . .'

In short, what does he know about sex? Has he had sex with a woman? Does he know his body and the body of a woman?

Sankara is obviously stumped. But he was not a master of logic and philosophy for nothing! He asks for a month's time to answer her questions and then goes away with his disciples.

The story takes on a metaphysical twist here. With his yogic powers he leaves his gross body behind in a cave (to be taken care of by his disciples) and with his subtle body or prana enters the dead body of King Amruka. The ministers and the many wives of the king are, of course, overjoyed to see their king come back to life. Now Sankara goes about his task of acquiring the knowledge and experience of sex; in short, to know himself in the body. Interestingly and strangely, in this new life brimming over with pleasure and joy, Sankara forgets all about his unfinished debate with Ubhaya Bharati. As days pass into weeks, the poor disciples get worried about their master and the future of Vedanta. And so, disguised as dancers, they come to the royal court and remind their master of his unfinished task. Sankara leaves the court, re-enters his body, meets with Ubhaya Bharati and wins the debate with his newly acquired knowledge of sexuality.[31]

The message of the story, despite the metaphysical twists and flights, is very clear for any discerning mind. The problem, however, one might say, is not with Sankara, but with his followers, who interpret the episode in purely metaphysical terms and render Sankara into a hollow, rather bodiless spirit.

However, JK's response to Kusuma Kumari's question that day, to say the least, was quite disappointing. Unlike Sankara, in order to answer the question, he didn't need to ask for time. He was no stranger to sexual experience. But at that time, there was great curiosity about his sexual life. Kusuma Kumari was aware that during JK's early years with the Theosophical Society, in the 1920s, a number of young girls had fallen in love with the handsome would-be world teacher, but nothing had come of it. Perhaps she wanted to know if there was anything to these stories. So why not directly ask the man himself?

However, in the 1930s, JK developed an intimate relationship with Rosalind, the wife of his close associate and editor, Rajagopal. During the war years they lived almost like husband and wife. In the 1950s, the relationship began to sour, and then completely fell apart when JK filed a case against Rajagopal in the 1980s. Only after JK's death in 1986 did the world come to know about his physical relationship with Rosalind, through her daughter's book, *Lives in the Shadow with J. Krishnamurti*.

At that time, Kusuma Kumari had no clue about Rosalind or his other affairs, nor did UG. They say women have a sixth sense regarding these things. Perhaps this is true and Kusuma Kumari felt that JK couldn't have been innocent of sex given the way he spoke about it. But UG was stunned by his wife's apparent audacity.

JK too was stunned for a moment. Then he said quietly, 'Amma, that's an impertinent question.'

Obviously it was not. That is why Ubhaya Bharati had to ask the question of Sankara and Kusuma Kumari of JK.

However, the meetings between UG and JK did not stop there. They continued to lock horns over some issue or other.

One Sunday morning, UG took his entire family, including his son Vasant, who had been stricken with polio, to see JK. UG had already talked to JK about his son's physical handicap, in connection with his planned trip to the USA to get medical treatment for the boy. Hearing about it, JK had expressed his wish to see the boy. When JK had to give public talks in the evenings, he did not normally see anyone in the morning, but he made an exception for UG and his family.

That morning, the subject naturally turned to the boy's medical treatment. UG's wife, Kusuma Kumari, became an eager participant in the conversation since it concerned her son's health. UG discussed his financial situation frankly with JK. Of the money he had received from his grandfather, he had been left with about ninety thousand dollars, which would be more or less the amount he might have to spend for the medical treatment of the boy.

'Ninety thousand dollars is a lot of money!' JK exclaimed, and then he suggested: 'You know I used to heal people. Why don't you let me try?'

On quite a few occasions, JK had cured people of what were then considered to be almost incurable ailments. Vimala Thakar, who became a spiritual guru in her own right, has written about JK curing her of ear trouble which the doctors were unable to diagnose or offer any treatment for. Rohit Mehta, a spiritual seeker and thinker, had heard JK speak during the convention of the Theosophical Society in 1925, 1926 and 1927 and become his admirer. Rohit Mehta was also a political worker and was jailed several times. In the1930s, while in prison, he fell seriously ill. Upon Gandhiji's advice, he was released on parole and hospitalized. The doctors diagnosed his condition as spinal paralysis and beyond recovery. He was bedridden for nearly eighteen months. A common friend, Jamnadas Dwarkadas, persuaded Krishnaji to visit Rohit Mehta at the hospital. The patient and the teacher talked for some time, then, Mehta says Krishnaji touched his spine with his fingers for a minute or two and went away. Within a week he was able to sit up in bed, within two months he could walk, and after a few more days he felt completely restored to normal. 'The doctors attending on me were astonished to see my recovery and told me that my cure was not due to their treatment,' says Mehta.[32]

But on that day, in response to JK himself offering to try his hand in curing Vasant, UG said, 'I am a sceptical man. I did hear a lot about your healing work. It doesn't work in this case. The cells in the boy's legs are dead. You cannot put life into them. If you can make him walk, then I will believe you. Jesus walked on water probably because he did not know how to swim. Fortunately for him and unfortunately for others the water was only knee-deep. And in the story of the multiplication of the loaves of bread and the fishes, he probably cut the bread into many smaller pieces.'

JK burst into laughter.

Kusuma Kumari glared at UG and said, 'Why are you standing in the way of Krishnaji's wanting to help the boy?'

UG acquiesced and the healing process began the next day. Every morning, until the day he left Madras, JK tried his healing technique by massaging the boy's legs. But there was no improvement in the condition of the boy. Then JK told UG and his wife to postpone their planned journey to America by one more year, so that when he came back to Madras the next year, he could try his hand again to heal the boy. The second experiment also proved to be a failure. As UG had said before, the cells in the boy's legs were dead, and no power on earth could revive them.

The final meeting in India between UG and JK took place in Bombay. UG asked him, 'Where are you? Are you *there*? Or are you actually taking a journey with us? You pick a subject and ask us to proceed step by step, logically, rationally, sanely and intelligently. There comes a point when you exclaim, "I got it! Somebody got it?" It is theatrics. It's a performance. To put it crudely, it is burlesque. You take off and talk of love, bliss, beatitude, immensity and so on. But *we* are left high and dry. You are offering us bogus chartered flights.'

One does not know how JK reacted to UG's attack. But UG continued, as if it was now or never. He said, 'What is there behind all those abstractions you are throwing at me? Is there anything at all? I am not interested in your poetic and romantic descriptions. As for your abstractions, you are no match to the mighty thinkers that India has produced—you can't hold a candle to them. The way you describe things gives me the feeling that you have at least *seen the sugar*—to use a familiar traditional metaphor—but I am not sure that you have *tasted the sugar*.'

But JK, as he was wont to, never gave a direct or satisfactory answer. This was going to be UG's last meeting with JK for a long time. Again he asked, 'Come clean for once. Don't throw these abstractions at me.'

This was too much, even for a gentleman. Still, JK did not get angry, and he reacted in a way that was typical of him by then: 'You have no way of knowing it!'

Suddenly the whole thing seemed ridiculous to UG, and he burst out in anger: 'If I have no way of knowing it and you have no way of communicating it, what the hell have we been doing here? I have wasted seven years listening to you. You can give your precious time to somebody else. I am leaving for New York tomorrow.'

Now, cool as a cucumber, JK said, 'Pleasant journey and safe landing!'

An extraordinary incident took place during one of these conversations, which has to be recorded here. On the third day of his conversations with JK in 1953, while speaking of 'death' to him, UG could not complete the sentence: '. . . apart from all that, I . . .' Suddenly he slumped back as an overwhelming fear of coming to an end seized him. He gasped for breath, felt as if 'a vacuum pump was sucking the life out of me', and then felt invaded by an overpowering current of energy. Next day, when he talked about the experience to JK, he is believed to have said that if there was anything to the experience, it would express itself, if not it would fade away. The experience had thrown UG somewhat out of gear, and by his own admission, from then on his perception of things underwent a radical change. Nothing seemed as it used to be. Was it a mystical experience? Or some kind of physiological tremor that would again surface, explode and settle down in years to come? However, all these experiences or mystical states, including the ones he had had in the caves of Rishikesh, UG would often say, are 'thought-induced' and of no great importance. They all fall within the realm of time and space, of opposites, they are of no significant consequence, and they fade over a period of time. If he wanted, if he had fallen into the illusion that it was the highest state a human being could attain to, that it was indeed the state of enlightenment, as most mystics have done before and continue to do, he could have founded a religious order and become a guru. But that would have been the end of UG. He says he had to 'brush it all aside', free himself, and move on.

★

UG left for America with his family in 1955. Before that, a careful consideration of his letters indicates that he and his wife went on a six-week tour to Europe in 1953. After visiting Norway and Germany, he was back in London in May. In a letter written from London to one of his friends in India, he mentions meeting Bertrand Russell at Richmond. The details of their conversation are not available. UG too does not remember the details of the discussion he had with Russell, except that he told the great pacifist that it was futile to wish or talk of peace without disbanding the other subtler structures of violence which sustain and perpetuate violence on a larger scale in the world. He is believed to have said, 'The H-bomb is an extension of the policeman! Are you prepared to do away with the policeman?'

Bertrand Russell replied: 'One has to draw a line somewhere.'

UG told him, 'If we settle for lesser evil, we'll end up with only evil.'

8

The End of Samsara

It was an era of growth and expansion for America when UG landed in Chicago. Dwight D. Eisenhower, the then President of the USA, pursued a policy of 'progressive conservatism' that supported and encouraged business enterprises throughout the land. The infamous McCarthy era, the witch-hunting of communists, had just ended. But the condition of black Americans had remained dismal, although blacks from the South were migrating to the northern industrial cities and contributing to the rapid economic growth and expansion of America. In the southern states, where racial discrimination and segregation of blacks were openly practised, a civil rights movement had developed under the leadership of Martin Luther King Jr, which played an instrumental role in the Civil Rights legislation of 1954 that ended the segregation of the blacks in public schools, and later in passing the Civil Rights Bill in 1957.

It was, indeed, both politically and culturally, an interesting period to be in America. But to UG, America was like a transit camp, a sort of preparatory ground before he would strip himself of everything and go adrift in Europe. Meanwhile, he tried to be a good father and make himself useful!

The money he had taken with him to the USA was just enough to meet the expenses of his son's medical treatment. But it was worth it, thought UG, for his son couldn't have received better treatment anywhere else. The doctors assured him that Vasant should be able to walk in a year's time. It meant they had to stay in the USA for another year, perhaps longer, so with his resources diminishing fast, UG had to do something to earn some money. He took up what he was best at—lecturing. Unlike in India where his lectures had been for free, here he was paid a hundred dollars per lecture. He now even had a manager to arrange his lectures: Erma Kramli, nearing eighty, who had at one time arranged talks for Annie Besant and Vijayalakshmi Pandit. UG gave about sixty lectures at various clubs, institutions and even universities. He came to be recognized as an orator, and as 'a noted thinker from India'. His talks were reported in newspapers and critical appreciation of his ideas came from every quarter. The lectures were not only on religion and philosophy but on wide-ranging subjects touching upon politics, education, economic affairs, American aid to India, Nehru's politics and statesmanship and so on. His fame as an extraordinary speaker and noted thinker from India earned him the friendship of the then mayor of Chicago, the famous economist Paul Douglas (who later became a Congressman), Senator Everatt and many other noted personalities from public life.

Despite his many quarrels with JK over several issues, UG kept in contact with JK through letters. The following letters by JK show his interest in UG and his concern regarding the medical treatment and progress of UG's son.

13 January 1956

My dear Krishnamurti,
Thank you very much for your letter of 4 January. I had heard that you were in America lecturing. I am so glad to have heard from you about your son that there is every possibility of his being able to walk in a few years. If you are going to Ojai, you will be able to meet Mr Rajagopal who will be there. As you say, I hope we shall be able to meet in March in Bombay. Please give my best regards to your wife.
With best wishes,
Yours very sincerely,
J. Krishnamurti.

11 December 1956
Dear Mrs Krishnamurti,
Thank you very much for your letter of 14 November. It is very good of you to have written at some length about your family and I am very glad that your son is so very much better and I hope

before he comes back, he will have completely recovered and will be able to use his legs.

I am very glad indeed that the two interviews that you had have been of some help. I do not know when I shall be coming to America and when it will be possible for us to meet. I hope everything will be well with you both and your son.

With best wishes,

Yours affectionately,
J. Krishnamurti.[33]

Vasant's condition did improve considerably with the medical treatment, and he was able to walk, dragging his diseased foot, but without using crutches. UG continued to lecture in different parts of America, including four notable lectures on the major religions of the world, at the university at Washington. During those days, he did once visit Rajagopal at Ojai. Rajagopal is believed to have taken an instant liking to UG and talked quite freely and critically of his relationship with JK. That was the time Rajagopal's relationship with JK had begun to sour. In point of fact, by then Rajagopal had already learnt all about his wife's (Rosalind's) sexual relationship with JK, but apparently he did not wish to talk to UG about it. UG came to know about the affair, with utter shock of course, only when Rosalind's daughter, Radha Sloss published her book on JK in 1991. Recalling one day in Bangalore the meeting with Rajagopal in 1956, UG said that he found Rajagopal to be quite brilliant, but that despite his criticism of and strained relationship with JK, he lacked the courage to break away from JK and live on his own.

On UG's home front at that time, however, there was no major change, and his relationship with his wife was as good as it could be between the likes of him and Kusuma Kumari. With all his eccentricities, his spiritual quest, UG was not that 'bad' a husband and father. Kusuma Kumari, of course, as always, remained a devoted wife and mother. If at all, the only major problem that erupted now and then in the family was the problem regarding money. UG was never good at managing his financial affairs or handling money.

The following letter by UG to his uncle in 1956 gives us an idea of his life in America, his concerns and anxieties about the family, his frustrations, and of things to come.

58, South Michigan Avenue, Chicago-5
23 February 1956
Sri T. Jagannadham Garu,
Vijayawada-2

My dear Uncle,
I have just received a letter from Mr K. Subba Rao of Adyar, saying that Bezwada site appeal has been dismissed. He says that my absence from India is responsible for it. Well, whatever it is, my feeling in these matters is: 'The Lord hath given it to me and the Lord hath taken it away. Blessed be the name of the Lord.' I am glad in a way because I am now free to do what I have been wanting to do all these days, that is to say, I want to pass on to my children all that I have received from my grandfather. I want to do it right away. Out of the properties which I got by the partition deed between myself and Mr Narashima Rao, this is what I have done. 7½ acres bit has been sold and the sale proceeds have been utilized to pay Rs 60,000 to Mr Narashima Rao (to equalize the share), Rs 4000 to clear my grandfather's debts and the balance of Rs 10,000 to my wife as gift for purchasing a house at a later date. Gudivada godowns have been sold for Rs 30,000 and the amount is in the form of Govt. Securities. I wish I could sell off the remaining bit of Bezwada site, subject to lease, and invest that also in Govt. Securities and hand over the whole lot. It may not be possible to do it now. I have with me the draft prepared by you, with the clause that my grandmother's demands have the first charge. I do not know how to register the document here . . .
I have decided to stay on here for another year, possibly two or three years. My lecturing has been a tremendous success. They have received the headlines and editorial comments in all the leading papers. You know lecturing in America is not the unpaid labour that it is in India. Work in this country suits me very well indeed. One can be a true brahmin (meaning one in pursuit of and realization of brahman) here in America. It may sound very strange

but that's what I am going to do till I fall dead.

I do not want to own anything. America can keep me busy all the five days in the week . . . as long as I choose to remain here, paying me 100 dollars for each lecture. You have no idea how many clubs there are in the US. Rotary alone has 70,000 clubs. Every club wants to hear me. Kiwanis, Lion, Elkas, Executives, and Women's clubs . . . and every club has extended an invitation . . .

It is quite a strain. I am now taking rest and I am scheduled to give a series of lectures at the University of Southern California, Los Angeles, early April. We are all moving to California for a six-month stay on the Pacific Coast to fulfil lecture engagements. We will get back to Chicago next October as my son is attending a school for handicapped children. I do not feel sorry for having brought him here and spending an enormous amount. Where in the world can he get such facilities—all free! The doctors have assured me that he will be all right after five or six years. My wife expects to take her MA Degree before I leave America next March (1957) for a brief visit to India. It wouldn't be difficult for me to educate all my children here with my own earnings. But what is the point. They have to be in India and the type of education here in America is unsuitable for Indian conditions. It will only give them false sense of values . . . I wouldn't care to live in this country . . .

I have promised to give Philosophical Library, New York, all my radio and television talks for publications before the end of April. It was not for nothing that Mr Jiddu Krishnamurti gave so much of time. I am now speaking with great certitude. By the way, I have asked Mr Subba Rao to wind up my show at Madras and pack all things to Pulla. But my library is the real headache. I do not know what to do with it. I have no use for them. I do not read books these days. I have no interest in any authority. I do not read anything except TIME . . . to keep myself in touch with what is happening in the world. Daily paper has 125 pages and who reads that stuff, I do not know. Well, there are papers with three to four million circulation. I do not think India can ever dream of this standard of living. (But) are people happy with all the wealth? Eighty per cent of people here go to a psychiatrist. My wife is now completely disillusioned about the glamour that is America . . .

Weatherman threatened worst winter in living memory. Contrary
to his forecast, winter this year has been very mild. Anything
around zero or one or two below zero . . . Strangest of all, we
haven't had much snow this year . . .

Affectionately,
U.G. Krishnamurti.[34]

The letter reveals both an eagerness to do things and finish with
everything. In the same breath he says, 'America can keep me busy'
and yet, his search for truth, Brahman, would not cease 'till I drop
dead'.

'I have no interest in any authority' had been his mantra from
a young age. Yet he would meet and discuss things with gurus if
only to probe and test them and reject them all later. As he himself
would confess on a number of occasions, he lacked clarity and
conviction, and he wanted to give these gurus the benefit of doubt,
for who knows, 'perhaps the chap knows something I do not know'.

And then the declaration in the letter, 'I do not want to own
anything,' was an indication of things to come.

He gave around sixty lectures a year and at the end of the second
year, he felt not only exhausted but also quite depressed with the
whole lecturing business. Two incidents stand out during this
period. A couple of days after his lecture on 'Meaning and Mystery
of Pain', he was laid up with mumps. The discomfort was almost
unbearable and the pain too excruciating, yet he refused to see a
doctor. As always, he was overcome by a terrific curiosity to see
into the structure of pain, as it were; after all, just a couple of days
ago, he had given a lecture on the meaning and mystery of pain.
This sort of curiosity would, again and again, drive him to probe
and experiment with himself, to find things out for himself, the same
curiosity that had years ago made him eat grass during his tapas
in the caves of Rishikesh, if only to find out whether he could
survive on it. The pain, however, became unbearable and he lost
consciousness. The story goes that he was rushed to a nearby
hospital, but the doctors were not too sure as to the type of treatment
he required. He lay there on the hospital bed, his body turning cold,
and it seemed he was on the verge of death. Half an hour passed,

and then suddenly he regained consciousness. He felt no pain or discomfort now, the body had cured itself of the illness!

A year after this, he began to lose interest in lecturing and started to wonder if there could be some other way of earning his livelihood. His manager, Erma, was shocked. He had become a celebrity of sorts and was in demand everywhere, and there was, of course, good money to take home after every lecture. But UG refused; suddenly, he had no longer the 'will' to work.

However, it seems there were mysterious forces at work here, not letting him collapse, or fall into total despair and drift into nothingness. That was to happen later; it was not yet the time for it. One day, he called his wife and told her that he was finished with his lecturing work. He handed the last hundred dollars to her and told her that from now on she should somehow manage the family; she had two post-graduate degrees and it was time she took up a job. It seems, in anticipation of such an event, he had prepared her well. In fact, from the day of their marriage, he wanted her to be independent, in particular, economically independent. But Kusuma Kumari was at a loss, she did not know what she was capable of, she did not know where to look for a job even if she wanted to. To make things worse, American culture was not exactly to her liking.

The Krishnamurtis lived in a flat on West Cromwell Road, close to the Chicago Theosophical Society building. After the pitiless conversation with his wife, UG had walked out of the house, leaving Kusuma Kumari in a deep quandary. Just as he was walking up the road in a blank state of mind, he ran into a stranger, who had just then come out of the Theosophical Society building. The stranger was Dixon, a retired auditor general, and a staunch, first-generation Theosophist.

The story takes on a mysterious turn here. It may be unsurprising for those who believe in 'fate', in the workings of mysterious powers in our lives—which may not be comprehensible to a rational mind. Some, on the contrary, may think it was just a case of 'coincidence'.

Be that as it may, Dixon stopped UG and asked, 'Are you from Adyar?' and then, upon knowing that UG was indeed from Adyar, he proceeded to narrate his extraordinary dream. He said that just the previous night Master Kuthumi had appeared to him in a dream and told him that he would soon meet a man from India who was in great trouble, and that he should do whatever possible to help him tide over his difficulties. The same Master Kuthumi, UG's spiritual guide during his years with the Theosophical Society in the 1940s and then later abandoned, had come back to reclaim his disciple as it were.

As a retired Auditor General, Dixon received a pension of 500 dollars every month. On learning about UG's financial problems, Dixon then and there offered to pay UG 200 dollars every month in perpetuity. Did UG accept the offer wholeheartedly, or helplessly? We do not know. But accept he did. What we do know is that UG had blown all his money and not saved a penny, and he could not have gone on living in America without Dixon's help. His son, Vasant, attended a school now, and the treatment for his polio was not yet over. And UG too was not yet finished with America.

Again it was through the help and influence of Dixon that Kusuma Kumari found a job as a research assistant with the World Book Encyclopaedia. Since she had degrees both in English and Sanskrit, Marshal Field, the concerned official, placed her in the Sanskrit/Indian section of the research wing.

At that time, Kusuma Kumari was pregnant with their fourth child, and she was not exactly happy going out to work for a living. Somehow her initial fascination for the American lifestyle was gone. In fact, coming from a traditional Indian background, despite her degree in English, she found it difficult to relate to Americans, who to her seemed distant, queer and somewhat intimidating. Now working with them only added to her misery, yet she carried on stoically, and sometimes she would bring her work home. She was required to make notes and answer queries, at times quite ridiculous queries, on several aspects of Indian cultural and religious practices. UG, although not a 'good husband' in a traditional way, did help her out in her research work, reading the necessary books and answering these queries for her.

UG now stayed home. He attended to the household chores and the needs of their handicapped son, Vasant. Dixon became more than a friend to UG, dropping in for long discussions on Theosophy and Indian philosophy. After the birth of their fourth child, Kumar (1958), when Kusuma Kumari started going back to work, Dixon

UG in the late 1960s

too, along with UG, would do the babysitting. This strange
relationship lasted for about two years, and when finally UG left
America at the end of 1959, Dixon died soon afterwards.

In those days, friends would drop in and UG ran what he calls
a 'Philosophers' Corner', and even gave cooking lessons for a fee.
Taking care of the baby was not much of a problem. In fact, it
became an extensive lesson in self-discovery. The child became a
'mirror' to see into and study the functioning of his own self and
body. One evening, on returning home, Kusuma Kumari saw the
kid crawling towards the fireplace and was naturally seized with
terror, but UG did not let her intervene. The child moved close to
the fireplace and stopped. UG smiled as if he had discovered one
of the great truths of existence.

Kusuma Kumari worked as a research fellow for about two
years, earning 500 dollars a month, but she was quite tense and
frustrated. The thought of her two daughters, who had been left
in the care of her elder sister in India, troubled her all the time.
Now, with her fourth child growing up in an 'alien country',
without the benefit of the love and care of the elders and family

members, and with no great change in Vasant's condition, she worried about her two sons' future too, and yearned to go back to India.

To make things worse, UG was changing and she was afraid of losing him. He did go out occasionally to meet friends, and friends too regularly dropped in to have long chats with him. Among these friends she liked John Pietras, a Pole, who had become a good friend of the family. Pietras taught in a university and was greatly interested in spirituality. A year later, after UG's departure from America, he was to become a good friend of Krishnaji as well. Strangely, during the five years when UG and his family lived in the USA, Krishnaji did not visit America. However, it was through Pietras that JK learnt about UG's condition in America, and according to one of the letters Pietras wrote to one of UG's associates, JK is believed to have shed tears, crying 'poor chap, poor chap', upon hearing about UG's problems.

By the end of 1959, things at home came to a head and the relationship between husband and wife began to crumble. There were offers of jobs for UG from the UN and the New York Press Association, but he showed no interest. It seems that he gave a few more talks, perhaps under some pressure or due to some old commitments. The one he gave at Texas (the exact period is unknown), probably the last one, led to a calamitous event. In a manner it changed the course of his life. The talk at Texas had been arranged by a rich and influential woman, who was probably an admirer of UG. After the talk, UG accompanied the woman to her house and slept with her.

UG calls it a 'one night stand', and speaks about it as plainly as he would about his 'mystical experiences', or any other incident in his life. Talking of various incidents in his life, he says there is nothing either to gain or lose, he is not in the 'holy business'. It is just a fact, plain and simple, and it pops up like data from his 'memory bank' every time there is a question regarding it. But when the incident happened, he admits in a matter-of-fact tone, with no trace of guilt or remorse, that he was sort of devastated. He felt he had 'used' a woman for his own pleasure, or sexual satisfaction. That was the end of sex for him, UG says. And he was never to have sex again, even with his wife.

On a few occasions, after UG had become the 'famous speaker from India', Kusuma Kumari had teased him about the rich and beautiful women who generally flocked around him after the talks. She had even asked him if he was not attracted to some of them, and what prevented him from having 'fun with them'. Now, perhaps the news of his 'infidelity' did not shock her, but it surely must have depressed her to know that even her 'lord' had clay feet. The story goes that the rich lady, after being cold-shouldered by UG later on, had even come home to ask Kusuma Kumari if something had gone wrong with UG.

Suddenly nothing was going right for Kusuma Kumari. She was now determined to leave America. The financial position at home was not exactly bad, but the situation was loaded with risk. In the first place, she hadn't been keen on coming to America, and now there was hardly anything that held her interest. More than anything else, her husband was no longer the man she had married seventeen years ago. He had changed, and changed drastically, and now lived like a stranger at home. The children became her priority, and one day she suddenly quit her job for an apparently trivial reason. She was the only sari-clad woman in the entire office of the World Book Encyclopaedia. Every time she walked in, clad in her silk sari, she naturally attracted the attention of the men and women in the office. Her boss thought of it as an avoidable distraction and so suggested that she should switch to something more American. He did not, of course, insist, nor did he make it a condition for her to continue to work there. It was only a suggestion, but she flew into a rage and resigned.

The inevitable happened at the end of 1959. Kusuma Kumari decided to leave America with her children, even if it meant leaving without her husband. Her imploring that he too must return with them to India had no impact on UG. He bought her the tickets and handed over whatever money had been left with him. Kusuma Kumari and her two sons flew to Madras, and then, somewhere on the way to Pulla, in the train, she lost the box that contained UG's books, documents and almost all the letters he had received from important people. It was as if all of UG's past was being systematically erased, and his return made impossible.

For five years, the family had lived in America on visitor's visas.

Although UG had quit lecturing, his wife's job with the World Book Encyclopaedia had enabled their stay in the country. Now, with his wife gone back to India, if he wanted to stay on, he needed sponsorship. The problem was solved when the World University offered him a job. He had been recognized not only as an outstanding speaker, but also as one with a brilliant and well-informed mind. His talents were found to be useful by the university, which planned to open hostels for its students in several parts of the world. UG had no choice; he accepted the offer and made his first trip to India. But he first came to Madras to wind up his 'show' at Adyar.

He stayed at the famous Das Prakash Hotel in Madras. Hearing of his arrival, Kusuma Kumari came there and tried to persuade him to join the family. It was to be UG's last meeting with his wife. She had brought all her children with her, in the hope that UG would, at least for the sake of his children, change his mind. In tears she begged and fell at his feet. He was hard as stone; there was no going back. He was finished with his past. He drew back his legs to prevent her from touching his feet, but in the process the big toe of his right leg hit her nose and blood spurted out of her nostrils. Terrified at the sight of the blood, the eldest daughter, fifteen-year-old Bharati, started screaming. It was like a scene from a tragi-comedy.

The close relatives of Kusuma Kumari, in particular her two brothers, were naturally in a rage at UG's apparently callous attitude and response. But, twenty years later, the eldest brother, Dr T.R. Seshagiri Rao, was to change his mind on reading the book *Mystique of Enlightenment*; and, as a man of science and as one interested in spirituality, go on to write an important paper entitled 'A Response to Science and Spirituality'. But her younger brother would never forgive UG for the pain and suffering he had caused to his sister. The same could be said of UG's eldest daughter, Bharati, who, incidentally believed in J. Krishnamurti as the World Teacher.

UG never went back, never saw his wife again. She was to die in pain two years later. Strangely, in all these years, to this day, UG has not set foot in the place of his birth.

At Madras, UG was met by some of his old Theosophical Society friends and was talked into accompanying them to go and meet Dr S. Radhakrishnan, the then Indian ambassador to Russia, who was in Delhi convalescing after a long illness. After meeting the philosopher–politician, UG is believed to have met the prime minister, Pandit Jawaharlal Nehru, in connection with his work for the World University. At that time, a delegation of industrialists and prominent persons were scheduled to visit Russia in connection with trade and cultural exchange between the two countries. UG was advised to go with the team so that he would have easy access to the authorities he wanted to meet with regard to his work. UG joined them and recalls that he was even invited to give a talk at the Bolshevik Theatre. He, of course, declined the invitation, he says, and chided the Russians for suppressing and almost destroying their native art and culture. He conceded that the one good thing about communism, was that it took good care of the basic necessities of its people, but sadly the country had become totalitarian with *Das Kapital* as their Bible, Lenin as their high priest, and the politburo as their diehard, incurable missionaries.

A month later, UG flew out of Russia to some of the central European countries he had not visited before. Not much is known of his stay, for instance, in countries like Hungary and Romania. It seems he was getting fed up with his work, and visited various cities in central Europe, not to do 'business', but as a tourist, as one eager to touch and know every important place on the world map. Actually, he had begun to drift. And when finally he landed in London, he was almost finished!

9

The Dark Night of the Body

Some of UG's close associates use the Christian mystic's phrase 'the dark night of the soul' to describe UG's aimless wanderings in London. UG disagrees. Most vehemently he says that there was 'no heroic struggle with temptation and worldliness, no soul-wrestling with urges, no poetic climaxes, but just a simple withering away of the will'.

His 'will' beginning to crack, UG arrived in England when the winter had set in. By late afternoon, night descended and enveloped the island like a dark, wet blanket. With whatever money he had been left with, UG managed to find a place in Kedagin Square Apartments in Knightsbridge. During the day, to escape from the shivering cold and the boredom of staring at the four walls of his room, he would slip into the British Museum and spend the whole day sitting at the table next to the one where Marx had done his research for *Das Kapital*. UG was, of course, not interested in doing any research or reading books. He had, in fact, stopped reading books on philosophy and religion some years ago. Yet, to pretend that he was there to read something, he would pick up a Thesaurus of 'Underground Slang' and immerse himself in it for several hours. In the evenings, he would aimlessly wander the streets of London, reading signboards and the names and telephone numbers of London call girls written or pasted on the walls, on telephone booths and even on trees.

Krishnaji had arrived in London in May 1961, and was staying in a small but well-appointed house at Wimbledon. He gave several talks and held discussion meetings at Wimbledon till the end of the first half of June. The year before, he had been down with a kidney infection and had looked washed out. Now he looked sprightly and his usual nimble self. But the 'mysterious attacks', or what is often referred to as 'the process' continued. According to Mary Lutyens, it recurred at Wimbledon. Another distressing occurrence was unfolding within the citadel of Krishnamurti Writings Incorporated (KWINC). Rajagopal ran KWINC like his own little empire and wouldn't let anyone, including Krishnamurti, question his authority. He felt justified because over the years through his hard work, he had developed KWINC into a multimillion-dollar corporation. But when things came to a head, friends advised Krishnaji to assert his control over the affairs of KWINC, even if it meant going to the courts.

Through a common friend, Mr Bhave, Krishnamurti came to know that UG was in London and sent him a message to visit him at his Wimbledon residence. UG was not keen to go, but he had no choice when the great man himself called and said, 'You may come over. We shall go for a walk in Richmond Park.'

The evening was cold but not severely so. London being what it is, it suddenly started raining heavily and the two Krishnamurtis sat by the fireplace in the drawing room and talked. Krishnaji was keen on knowing all about UG's family, and in particular about Vasant's recovery from polio. UG answered the queries as best he could. Now, studying UG's face, which probably looked haggard and lost, Krishnaji said, 'You don't look well. Why don't you go back to India?'

UG smiled tiredly and said, 'I am adrift here in London. I have nothing to do and I don't want to go back to India. My family will try to reconnect with me, which I don't want. I am finished with them.'

An awkward silence fell upon them, only the quiet hissing of the fire floated about like a benign spirit. The teacher in Krishnaji came alive and asked, 'Why are you trying to detach yourself from your family?'

It seemed a ridiculous question from a man who had no experience of family life. UG was not consciously trying to detach himself from anybody or anything, but all attachments were breaking like so many dry twigs, and everything was falling apart, for there was no centre to hold on to. Krishnaji did not seem to understand his condition. And he persisted, the way he would in his public talks and dialogues. 'Shall we go into the subject of why you are not attached to your family, sir?'

It was absurd! Krishnaji seemed to have only one rigid approach to every issue, every problem, like a doctor who had the same medicine for one struck by lightning as well as for one choked by rice.

For the next three days, UG attended Krishnamurti's public talks at Wimbledon, because Krishnamurti asked him to. UG sat there among the nearly 300 people, waiting for the talk to be over, so that he could go and see a movie. But, after every talk, Krishnaji would send for UG and then ask him, 'Old chap, how was it? Has it helped you?'

Nothing helped UG. Nothing changed. Rather, the only change UG felt was the change in the London weather. Winter receded; the air grew warm and the day bright. Summer began and suddenly London had come alive. The streets buzzed with people, mostly tourists; shops went into a frenzy of discount sales; in the evenings, foot-tapping music burst from everywhere, and people, mostly young, sat on rough, wooden benches outside pubs, drinking pint after pint of beer. Suddenly, London seemed like heaven on earth. But there was no such joyful change for UG. Days passed into weeks and weeks into months, as they had to. In September, UG received a letter from his wife. It was depressing, but he took nearly a month to answer her. Sitting in the London Library, he wrote:

It's quite obvious that I have failed to open your eyes and make you understand the reality of the situation. It hurts me to hear, from time to time, the suicide attempts of yours. But my detachment from you and my passive acceptance of your actions is a solid piece of fact. It is not apathy. There isn't a whiff of apathy in me. The bond of family relationships has simply fallen away from me.

I have thought long and hard about this matter. You know I am not the sort of person to be persuaded in these matters and I do not act on impulse. Let the marriage wither on the vine. Neither of us can bear to see the ravages of pain in the other. Let us prefer to cling to the memory of the past. You have not, perhaps, much of a sweet memory to live with or cling to. Maybe you have a lot of things to cry over. Yes,

I am quite as mentally broken down as you are, but it manifests itself in a different way in me. In the past, I may have beaten you and used insulting language toward you. All that is over and done with now. If you feel the agony about me which you say in your letters you feel, I can well understand your feelings. I know you love me deeply. And I loved you dearly too in spite of our many bickerings and constant battles. But this 'broken wing fixation' will destroy you. You can't base your life on sentiment alone and that cannot be the basis of any marriage.

We have known each other for eighteen years. It is impossible to forget the ties of those eighteen years. Old habits and memories have a strange way of surviving. I can never forget you, and I know nothing else will ever equal my feelings for you in intensity. When we first met I liked you very much. That impression will continue, unchanged by anything that has happened since then. In the nature of things, it cannot be otherwise. The bond between us is a 'subtle inner force', which the Sanskrit poet says is the essence of love. It is not 'erotic sentiment'. What happened to 'the feeling that you feel when you have a feeling you never felt before'? I wouldn't know. But we are now at the end of our tether. Tears and torments may have been your lot, but continued angry words, bitterness and rancour, however justified they may be, do not take us anywhere. This sustained nastiness for long periods is neither desirable nor useful. Anger is a terrible corrosive. It may seem advantageous to use 'blackmailing weapons', which is the chief ammunition in the arsenal of your family, and it may bring temporary relief to you, but in the long run it is our children who will suffer.

We cannot blame anybody for the mess we have made in the lives of the young ones. I may have laid a harvest of woe for our children, and I know that it will be laid up at my door that I have left my own children bewildered, with nothing in life to look forward to but sadness. I do not see any reason why things should be any more difficult than they have been. Your stubborn unwillingness to admit the facts of our situation is also responsible for the anguish of our situation.

Why is it, with all the will in the world, I cannot understand what is so obvious to you? Well, anyway, I would rather let things go to the devil in their own way than try to go back to the past. Since we get exactly what we ask for, no more and no less, there is no question of any atonement on my part for the way things have turned out. Everyone weaves his own destiny. If our children take beatings at the cruel hand of fate, I feel that I am not wholly responsible. They are as much your children as they are mine. Let not the idea that I have left you destitute overwhelm you. You have your own name, your degrees and your own properties. Why I acted the way I did and still act is difficult to grasp. But if they are held up against the mirror of my own peculiar interpretation, my actions show a logic of their own. For all I know, life may not run on logic. Whether it is right or wrong, it in no way changes the pain of the situation. But there is nothing that I can do to change the course of events.

One more thought. Postponing a problem of course does not solve it. There is a way out of an unhappy marriage. When one partner breaks the law of commitment, the right accrues to the other of breaking the bond. The woman is not the husband's bond slave but his companion, and as an equal partner is as free as the husband to choose her own way of life. Since the new Hindu Code Bill provides for divorce, why don't you find some grounds either for divorce or legal separation? That would save a lot of mental anguish for us both. Do not for a moment think that I am asking you to do anything I would not do myself. But, personally, it does not matter to me one way or the other.

There is no reason for me to return to India. Be happy and stay happy. I wish you the best and the finest.[35]
U.G. Krishnamurti.

Years later, his hostess in Bangalore, Mrs Suguna, asked him once, 'UG, have you cried at any time of your life?'

UG is believed to have admitted that it was during his aimless wanderings in England that he had cried for the first and last time.

It was the time when, back in India, his wife was dying and he had started to drift. To make things worse he was running out of money. Still, if only to somehow keep himself going, he had to do something. So, whenever an opportunity came his way, he started doing palm-reading for immigrants (mostly from India and Pakistan), and at times even giving cooking lessons for a fee. He could have, of course, managed to live on the unemployment dole, but he didn't. It was a desperate situation. And he couldn't help asking himself why he had become 'a bum living on the charity of people'. It was quite insane! But he seemed to lack the will even to think of an alternative. He just let himself be blown like a leaf 'here, there and everywhere'.

One might recall here more or less similar episodes or experiences in the lives of some mystics or spiritual masters of the past, before they came upon 'enlightenment' or 'illumination'.

In a manner, the anguished cry of Jesus: 'Father, why has thou forsaken me?' might be seen to echo through the lives of many mystics before the separative consciousness dissolved or burned itself out. Interestingly, 'darkness' is the central motif or metaphor for most mystics when they express their agony of separation. The sixteenth-century mystic-poet, Nanak, for instance, would relate his feelings thus:

I have become perplexed in my search,
In the darkness I find no way,
Devoted to pride I keep in sorrow.
Alas, how shall peace be found?

The twelfth-century mystic, Allama Prabhu, expresses his anguish thus:

It's dark above the clutching hand,
It's dark over the seeing eye,
It's dark over the remembering heart,
It's dark here
With the Lord of the Cave
Out there.

Elsewhere, for Allama, this anguish is transformed into wonder:

What's this darkness
On the eyes?
This death on the heart,
This battlefield within,
This coquetry without,
This path familiar to the feet?[36]

UG would probably dismiss these mystical yearnings as 'thought-induced' states. As states still caught up in 'becoming', in spiritual dilemma or conflict, which is rooted in memory, knowledge, while what happened to him was a simple yet explosive physiological process.

Interestingly, in the life of the Buddha too, the period before the 'Awakening' is presented as one of intense struggle and conflict. All the traditional narratives depict the event as the victory of the Buddha over the 'evil forces' of Mara. When the Buddha had seated himself under the Bodhi tree with a vow to seek release from all bondage and attain Nirvana, he is supposed to have been confronted by Mara, who is incidentally also referred to as the God of Love. Mara's army—supposed to consist of his three sons: Flurry, Gaiety and Pride, and three daughters: Discontent, Delight and Thirst—try to break the Buddha's solemn purpose, throwing itself against the would-be Tathagata, like 'the rush of a swollen river breaking against the embankment'. Eventually, the army is defeated and Mara and his progeny flee the mind of the Buddha. Now, the great Tathagata's face, free from the dust of passion, is lit up with a gentle smile, as sweet-scented flowers rain down on the earth from above.

Given their Christian background, some European scholars have interpreted the Buddha's struggle as a battle between 'good and evil'. It is not. If at all, it is only an overcoming of 'evil', which is not something external (neither is it internal). Perhaps it would be more appropriate to say that it is the burning away of what may simply be called 'passion', or the extinction of 'I' which is only the other name of passion, and we cannot speak of 'passion' as 'evil'.

Again, UG would probably say, 'No-no-no,' in his typical, emphatic style. For comparisons are unnecessary, irrelevant, even misleading. And UG would say that in his case it was not some poetic, romantic nonsense—the usage of the apparently poetic phrase 'like a leaf blown here, there and everywhere' is only suggestive of the withering away of choice, of will, and there is nothing more to it.

Even so, what comes to mind now is not the image of some mystic or 'enlightened' master, but that of Shiva, separated from Parvati, wandering in the pine forest, naked, singing, dancing, babbling and laughing himself silly!

In actual fact, while UG was adrift in London, his wife Kusuma was dying in India. For the sake of her children she had come back to India, but the separation from her husband proved to be impossible to bear. She would grow angry, sad, burst into tears, and at times, go berserk. However, when she heard anyone blame or criticize UG for her pathetic condition, no matter how close a friend or relative the person was, she would turn mad with anger. Despite her intense suffering, she refused to write to UG, arguing that it would cause him great pain to know that she and the children were going through such hardship. Even so, till her last day, she did not stop dreaming of UG's return. Not a day passed without her thinking and talking about UG and their married life. 'Sister, he will come,' she would tell her sister or friend or whoever was at her side. 'He'll certainly come. You know, sister, with his fair skin, long hair, and in his white shirt and dhoti, he used to look like Nagayya (a famous Telugu film star at the time) . . . He truly looked like a prince! And didn't he treat me like a princess? Oh, you wait and see, my prince will come on the seven horses.' And sometimes, reminiscing about her past she would burst into tears, saying: 'He used to bring me anything I wanted. He used to send me a sari wherever I was. When he asked me what I wanted for my birthday, I told him I wanted a sari. I was so foolish. Oh, why did I ask for a sari? Instead why didn't I ask him to stay with us?'

When her condition turned from bad to worse, she was admitted to a hospital. After three weeks of medical and electric-shock treatment, she returned home. But as fate would have it, just when she appeared to be recovering from the illness, one day, she slipped, broke her neck, and died.

Only six months later did UG get to know about his wife's death. The friend who managed to track him down and hand him the letter that contained the sad news, was shocked to note that UG expressed no feelings. He only said, 'The letter says my wife died six months ago.' There was, of course, nothing he could do, though he did write to his children expressing his sympathy over the irreparable loss of their mother.

And he drifted along, seeing and not seeing, hearing and not hearing, rather as one who has lost his head. At times, he felt tired, but no hunger. One day, he realized he had only five pence left in his pocket. He was finished. There was no place to go and there seemed nothing he could do. He sat on a bench in Hyde Park, wondering what was happening to him. It was like any other night; a cool breeze played about among the trees, but there was something in the air, some change in the making. Just then, a policeman walked up to the bench and stood over him. UG probably looked like a hippie or a vagabond come to the park to spend the night. The policeman asked UG to 'scoot', and threatened to lock him up if he didn't. UG stood up and heard a voice within him command: 'Go to the Ramakrishna Mission.'

After travelling by the tube as far as five pence could take him, he walked the rest of the distance and reached the campus of the Ramakrishna Mission. It was past ten at night, quite late by ashram standards, so the staff member on duty refused to let UG go in and meet the swamiji. But luckily for UG, the head of the Mission, Swami Ghanananda himself happened to come out. UG introduced himself and requested the swamiji to permit him to stay in the meditation room for the night. It was not possible, said the swamiji. He would not break the rules of the Mission. But he gave UG enough money to stay in a hotel for the night and come back the next day.

The next day, the swamiji was kind enough to invite UG for lunch. 'For the first time in a long time', UG had a real meal. Upon hearing about UG's Theosophical background and his career as a lecturer, the swamiji straightaway asked UG if he would work as an editor for the Vivekananda Centenary Issue that the Mission planned to bring out. UG was in a quandary because he did not know whether the work would suit him. Nevertheless, he accepted the offer because of the swamiji's repeated requests, and, of course, five pounds a week was too attractive an offer to decline.

UG now stayed at the Mission and worked on the Centenary Issue in the mornings. After lunch, he would take the tube to the city, watch a film and return to his room in the evening. This routine lasted for about three months; quite unmindful of his future, he spent almost all his earnings in travelling and seeing films.

UG has a strange relationship with the film world. It actually goes back to his school days when he used to be very fond of films, and even met film actors who would occasionally drop in at the big house in Gudivada. In Madras, while he was studying at Madras University and even while he was working at Adyar for the Theosophical Society, he would regularly go and see Tamil films. That's how, he says, he picked up his Tamil. Later, in the 1970s and 1980s, some of the film people who had been one-time followers of either J. Krishnamurti or Rajneesh (teasingly called 'widows of JK' and 'divorcees of Rajneesh'), were to gravitate towards UG and become his admirers and friends. Mahesh Bhatt and Vijay Anand, both directors, and film star Parveen Babi, the *Time* magazine cover girl, are among the most notable of the long list of his admirers from the world of cinema.

UG continues to watch films, although he gleefully dismisses them as sentimental nonsense. Twenty years ago, when I was writing an article on him, I remember him saying that romantic films bored him, religious ones repulsed him, and he found musicals noisy and irritating. But action films held his attention, for there was nothing there to understand, nothing to feel, but only *see*. Advertisements take the cake, he would say, for they show brilliantly that the advertising world has taken over the strategies of religious language and teachings!

But to return to his days in London, it was during this time that certain changes began to manifest themselves in UG's body. In 1953, he had brushed aside the mystical experiences he had undergone in the caves of Rishikesh and his 'near-death experience' at Adyar as of no great consequence. But now, it seems that all these experiences were to converge and build up as it were, and steadily begin to alter his being. From the Hindu traditional perspective, this may be interpreted as the awakening of Kundalini energy, the 'serpent power'. One day, while sitting in the meditation room of the Ramakrishna Mission, he came upon the following experience. It was only the beginning. In his own words:

> I was sitting doing nothing, looking at all those people, pitying them. These people are meditating. Why do they want to go in for samadhi? They are not going to get anything— have been through all that—they are kidding themselves. What can I do to save them from wasting all their lives, doing all that kind of thing? It is not going to lead them anywhere. I was sitting there and in my mind there was nothing—there was only blankness—when I felt something very strange: there was some kind of movement inside of my body. Some energy was coming up from the penis and out through the head, as if there was a hole. It was moving in circles in a clockwise direction and then in a counter-clockwise direction. It was like the Wills cigarette advertisement at the airport. It was such a funny thing for me. But I didn't relate it to anything at all. I was a finished man. Somebody was feeding me, somebody was taking care of me, there was no thought of the morrow. Yet inside of me something was happening . . ..[37]

Three months passed. It was time to quit the Mission. Whether it was a conscious decision on UG's part or it just happened, one does not know, but the fact is that he has not stayed in one place for more than three months. Before leaving the Mission, however, UG wrote to the swamiji who was in hospital for an eye operation. The letter, dated 7 September 1963, is most revealing.

> . . . I wish to God I knew what hidden hand led me to the Centre. When you suggested helping you out with some kind of editing work, I did not for a moment hesitate to fall in with your kind suggestion. What I did not know was that I would be having the most Blessed Moments of my life here at the Centre. It is needless to add that it has been a great privilege to have associated myself with you, and I feel greatly

refreshed both in mind and body. That, however, apart, my continued stay here at the Centre and the necessary atmosphere for alert and strenuous discernment in meditation has helped me tremendously. The hidden agony of my life which no human being could understand has dissolved itself into thin air, as it were, and this has awakened me to what may loosely be called a kind of spiritual sleepwalking. I have pulled myself out from what looked like the edge of an abyss.

You know that there are very rare occasions in the lives of most of us when we have brief experiences of existing beyond time. I too have had several such moments. But this has been more than fleeting and has indeed become an abiding certainty. Nevertheless the strains and stresses of adjusting myself to a whole new way of life resulted in a peculiar state of mind hedged with some kind of indolence, maybe a form of conceit, which only meant greater and greater sorrow but left with a kind of empty expectancy. I may have achieved a certain calmness, but that calmness was of death-producing languor. But I have always felt and still feel that one has to haul oneself out of one's own swamps by one's own bootstraps. However, all my strenuous and directed attention hasn't helped me much to break the vicious circle. Well, now, through the touch of the inscrutable Divine power of Sri Ramakrishna, I have been blessed beyond words with the clarity of perception. And this calmness is a calmness without a trace of languor or contentment or watchful expectancy but one of completeness and wholeness. Need I say that when I burst forth into the world—the joy which overflows the heart is indeed bursting forth—I will be a new man?[38]

Indeed, the 'new man' was in the making; it was as if he was programmed for it from birth, or some mysterious force was slowly but surely leading him to it. However, it was not going to be what he had imagined it would be like, and that is the most mind-boggling, most enigmatic, part of his story.

In any case, his stay in London was over. He moved on to Paris, turned in his return air ticket to India and made a handy 350 dollars. For another three months he let his hair down and stayed at a hotel in Paris. And as he had done before in London, he wandered the streets of Paris and devoured varieties of French cheese, a habit that continues to this day, though in very small quantities now.

Again, as had happened in London, at the end of three months he ran out of money. There were no immigrants from India here for him to give cooking lessons to and make some money on the side and no friends to approach for help either. Out of the blue, an old friend did meet him and even offered to help him. The friend happened to be the woman from Texas, a divorcee and a millionaire, with whom he had spent a night during his lecture tours in America. She was on holiday in Paris. It was an unexpected meeting. UG spent some time chatting with her in a restaurant. When she understood his pathetic situation, she took UG to the office of the American ambassador in Paris and made out a cheque for a million dollars. The transfer of the large sum of money required the endorsement of the ambassador, who was intrigued. He had no idea who UG was. The lady wanted UG to take the money and spend it in any way he wished. She expected nothing in return from him except his friendship, she said. UG took the cheque, tore it into pieces and said quietly that she could not buy him for any amount of money. It was like an emotionally charged scene from a film. The ambassador felt awkward. The lady was obviously disappointed, to say the least. UG bade her goodbye and left.

Having rejected the money that could have made him a rich man, UG scraped up whatever little money he could and went to Geneva. Again, like an amnesiac, he took a room in a hotel and started wandering about. Two weeks passed and yet again he found himself without money even to buy his meals, let alone pay the hotel bills. He had reached the end of his tether and there seemed no way out except going to the Indian consulate and requesting the authorities to send him back to India.

Fortunately, he still had his scrapbook with him, which saved him from being thrown out of the consulate. Reading through the praises heaped on UG by the American press, which included the high opinions of the notable Norman Cousins, and of Dr S. Radhakrishnan, the Indian ambassador to Russia, the vice-consul was quite impressed.

But he was helpless, since UG could not be flown back to India at the expense of the government. The only alternative was for UG to write to his people in India and get some money. At that time, the head of the Ramakrishna Mission in Geneva, Swami Nityabodhananda, happened to be in the vice-consul's chamber. The swamiji straightaway offered UG 400 francs to clear all his bills, and then turning to the vice-consul, he is believed to have advised him not to treat UG as an ordinary person and to see what he could do to help him. It seems the 'inscrutable power of Sri Ramakrishna' had yet again come to the rescue of UG.

There is nothing like a 'coincidence', believers are wont to say. And now, even scientists would agree, though a little reluctantly, that coincidence is but a set of possibilities which cannot be conceived of logically. At least in UG's life, it seems that the apparent coincidences, if not exactly predetermined, are a sort of prearranged set of possibilities. Whatever the case may be, UG's pathetic yet candid submission had attracted the attention of the staff of the consulate, too. Among them was a rather unusual woman, Valentine de Kerven. Something about UG touched a deep chord in her. Talking to him a little later, her impulse or sudden resolve to help this strange man from India only grew stronger; she told UG that she could arrange for his stay in Switzerland, and if he really didn't want to go back to India, he shouldn't. For UG it was like a new lease of life and he accepted the offer without a second thought. In point of fact, there was no choice and UG let himself flow with the tide.

A few months later, Valentine gave up her job and the two lived like friends who had been separated for ages but were now reunited on the cusp of a new age. The pension Valentine received was not large but was sufficient to take care of their household expenses and travel. At UG's suggestion, she sold almost all her jewellery, and antique art pieces she had collected over the years and had inherited from her father, and put the money in the bank. Later, Valentine also set up a separate fund for UG's travels.

What was the nature of their relationship? Why should a woman who was fiercely independent dedicate the rest of her life to caring for UG? What was her fascination with UG? Was there something physical too? There have been many such questions about their

UG with Valentine

relationship over the years. She was sixty-three when she met UG, who was seventeen years younger than her. Valentine, of course, never cared to answer these questions. In fact, people who knew her well say that she hardly talked about her relationship with UG, and that she never cared to explain why she took the extreme step of quitting her job to take care of UG. Between the two there was certainly something that cannot be put into words, something mysterious.

Valentine was not religious and she did not look upon UG as a spiritual man. The best thing she has said about UG, plain and simple, is found in her diary, written in French: 'Where can I find a man like him. I have at last met a man, a man the like of whom can be met very rarely.'[39]

In some ways, their relationship reminds one of the strange relationship between Aurobindo and Mirra Alfassa, who later came to be known as the Mother. Mirra first saw Sri Aurobindo 'in a dream'; and ten years later, in 1920, she met him at Pondicherry and stayed with him thereafter as his disciple and co-worker. Aurobindo was nearing fifty when Mirra, six years younger than him, joined him in his spiritual adventure. But UG was no guru to Valentine, and Valentine was no follower or interpreter of UG's 'teaching', as the Mother had been of Aurobindo's philosophy. She only took care of UG and physically followed him everywhere, until she was struck down by Alzheimer's disease.

It was an extraordinary life; in UG's own modest words: 'In fact, Valentine's life-story is more interesting than mine.'

Valentine de Kerven was born on 1 August 1901, in the village of La Chaux de Fond in the Zura mountain region of Switzerland. Her father, Alfred de Kerven, was a well-known brain surgeon. Valentine was the second of three daughters and even as a girl was fiercely independent. She developed artistic tastes at an early age and at the age of eighteen left home to move to Paris, in spite of great opposition from the family. Her father knew that if he tried to stop her she wouldn't hesitate to run away, so he allowed her to go and even arranged for her to have a yearly income of two thousand francs. Valentine loved him deeply which partly explains why, contrary to the custom, she insisted on keeping her maiden name after her marriage. She moved freely in the artistic circles of Paris, knew the noted poet–philosopher Antonin Artaud and got involved in the production of some important plays of the time.

Photography was another of her passions, which eventually led her into films. She founded de Kerven Films and produced a number of documentaries, notably one on the life of the gypsies, which was shown all over Europe, and earned her a reputation as a prominent director. She also produced documentaries about her father's medical research. During this period, she met a theatre personality, Walmar Schwab, and fell in love with him. Since the idea of marriage was anathema to her independent spirit, the couple lived together as lovers for twenty years. In 1939, just before the Second World War broke out, Valentine and Schwab decided to cross the Sahara Desert on Valentine's motorbike. It was an extraordinary feat, fraught with danger. With Schwab behind her, Valentine herself rode through hundreds of miles through scorching heat and stormy winds.

The Second World War forced the couple to leave Paris and move to Switzerland. At that time, according to Swiss law, it was a crime to live together without marrying. In order to avoid police harassment and possible imprisonment, the couple decided to get married, but not before Valentine drew up a contract of her own which said that although they were husband and wife legally, neither of them could exercise any rights over, or impose restrictions on each other, and both could feel free to lead their own lives without interference from the other. It was an extraordinary document considering the conservative nature of the law and the institution of marriage at that time. The story goes that during this time Valentine got involved with the revolutionary movement, against the dictatorship of General Franco.

In 1954, when UG had just returned from Europe with his wife, and when he was still contemplating a trip to the USA for his son's medical treatment, Valentine and Schwab came to India in her Volkswagen, via Iraq, Iran and Afghanistan, and drove from Kashmir to Kanyakumari. So India and the people of India were not unknown to her before she met UG.

Back in Switzerland after the long journey through South Asia, the forty-year relationship between Valentine and Schwab began to break up. They had no children; it had been Valentine's wish not to have any. When Schwab fell in love with an eighteen-year-old, Valentine decided to annul the marriage, although according to the contract which she herself had drawn up, Schwab was free to have relationships outside marriage. It was then that she took up a job at the Indian consulate in Geneva as a translator. Years later, to K. Chandrashekar and Suguna who took care of her during her last days in Bangalore, she was to say: 'As long as there is a tendency among men and women to own each other, no matter how sweet the relationship is, it will have to turn bitter. No matter how many ideals you cite, and no matter what you do, that tendency will not go away. If the lives of married couples are horrible, the lives of unmarried couples are even more horrible.'[40]

When UG landed in Geneva, Valentine had still not come out of her shock and depression. It seemed to her then that her whole life had been in vain. For someone who had never cared about her future and had led a Bohemian life, the present now seemed terrible. That night, feeling low and depressed and unable to sleep, Valentine sat on the banks of Lake Geneva, wondering about her future.

The next day, UG had walked into her life. Valentine was never to think of her future again, nor of her past. UG says, 'Ever since she met me, Valentine has had no life of her own as such. She has pretty much led my life.' But actually, one could as well say that her life with UG was yet another (but climactic) adventure, though of a different order, and it had to happen to her.

After leaving her job, Valentine took care of UG, but with no idea of what was to come. The next four years were relatively calm. With all the time in the world and no pressing tasks to attend to, UG and Valentine went travelling outside Geneva. For UG, the search had nearly come to an end. He ate, slept, read *Time* magazine, occasionally travelled, and went for long walks either alone or with Valentine. It was what may be called the period of 'incubation'. The body was preparing itself for the 'metamorphoses' that would challenge the very foundation of human thought built over centuries.

In the summer of 1964, UG and Valentine rented a 300-year-old chalet, Chalet Pfynegg (meaning 'windy') in the village of Saanen. UG recalls that in 1939, when he had visited Switzerland as a twenty-one-year old, something in him wanted to 'get down' and make a home at Saanen. Then again in 1953-54, on a world tour with his wife, UG had visited the beautiful valley of Saanen and had felt yet again that if he had to choose to live in any one part of the world, it would be here, among the seven snow-capped hills of Saanen, but his wife had turned down the idea. And here he was now, in the Saanenland of his dreams. He moved into the chalet, surrounded by the breathtaking beauty of the Alps.

In the 1960s, JK usually held a series of public talks and dialogues in Saanen in July, when people from all over the world converged in the sun-bathed valley to listen to JK and pursue their spiritual quest. Though UG kept a respectful distance from JK and his admirers, almost every evening inquisitive seekers would drop in at the chalet to chat with UG. The chat would invariably turn into a fierce conversation on spiritual matters and UG would debunk the many spiritual concepts thrown at him and generally tear apart JK's teachings.

Altogether JK gave ten public talks and held seven dialogues at Saanen that year. As the days passed, gradually more and more Krishnamurtiites started to drop in on UG, some out of sheer

curiosity to see who the 'other Krishnamurti' was, others to clarify
their doubts or challenge UG with ideas gleaned from the talks.
This was to become a pattern every summer. Even JK's close
associates would sometimes amble in to the chalet, if only to quench
their curiosity, among them Madame Scaravelli and David Bohm.
Some, after extended conversations with UG, were to turn their
backs on JK and become UG's close friends.

JK obviously knew of UG's presence in Saanen but made no
attempt to meet him. It was impossible, however, to walk through
the small town of Gstaad (adjacent to Saanen) without running into
each other. One afternoon, while UG was returning to his chalet,
he was caught in a sudden downpour. JK, who was coming that
way in his Mercedes, stopped, flung the door open and shouted,
'Hop in, old chap!'

UG was soaking wet. He turned, saw that Krishnaji was at the
wheel, and said, 'Thanks. I would rather walk singing in the rain.
Thanks anyway.'

'Suit yourself,' shouted back JK and drove away.

Years later, on yet another summer day in Gstaad, both UG and
JK happened to be walking on the same sidewalk in opposite
directions. Valentine said softly to UG, 'Look who is coming!' UG
looked up and saw that it was J. Krishnamurti. There was no way
he could have avoided him. As they neared each other, like two
cars bound for a head-on collision, neither uttered a word; both
folded their hands in the respectful gesture of greeting, and then
passed on silently.

Round about this time (1964), UG had started writing his
autobiography, but with his 'will' breaking, he had difficulty
recalling past events, particularly his various encounters with JK,
which formed a vital part of his life. In order to get the 'hang' of
what JK was saying, and for the added reason that Valentine had
never heard JK before, UG attended a few talks by JK. One would
like to believe that there was something more to it than that. Be
that as it may, UG's autobiography never saw the light of day. Three
years later, after his 'calamity', once he was 'cleansed of the entire
past of mankind', he was to make a 'bonfire' of the manuscript.

More importantly, it was during this time that things started
building up in his body, and started to prepare itself for the eventual

'mutation'. He started suffering from constant headaches, from what he called 'terrible pain in the brain'. He would swallow dozens of aspirins and cup after cup of coffee, but nothing would give him relief. One day, Valentine remarked, 'You are drinking fifteen to twenty cups of coffee every day. Do you know what it means in terms of money? It's almost 400 francs per month. What is this? What is happening?'

But UG did not discuss what was happening to him. In fact, he never talked about his mystical experiences or even his religious background with Valentine. He couldn't have, for, in point of fact, all his search for truth, for reality, for moksha was at an end. Yet, though he was not seeking anything spiritual or mystical, strange, 'funny' things had started happening to him. If he rubbed his palms or part of his body, there used to be a sparkle, like a phosphorous glow, and when he rolled on his bed with unbearable headaches, again there would be sparks. It was electricity! His body had become an electromagnetic field!

One night, Valentine came running out of her room to see what was happening. When she saw UG lying quietly in bed, she went back feeling relieved, thinking the flash of lights came from the car passing on the nearby road. UG says that he not only avoided talking about these strange experiences to Valentine, he did not even relate these happenings to 'liberation or freedom or moksha'. By that time, he had reached a point where he said to himself: 'Buddha deluded himself and deluded others. All those teachers and saviours of mankind were damned fools . . . They fooled themselves!'

This strange yet bewildering physiological process—which may not sound all that strange to those who are familiar with Kundalini Yoga—went on for three years, but it was only a sort of groundwork for the eventual 'calamity', which was to be something so utterly new and radical, something that went beyond any of the texts on Kundalini Yoga or reports of the Kundalini experiences hitherto known.[41]

All these years, JK came to Saanen every summer to hold his talks and discussions. It seems that he was destined to come there, if not to preside over UG's bewildering transformation, at least as a sort of distant witness to the birth of a phenomenon that would challenge not only his teachings, but the teachings of all religions whether of the East or of the West.

With all these physical changes and in spite of the bouts of severe headaches, UG began to appear much younger than his age. In photographs of him taken at the time, he truly looks like a young man of eighteen or twenty. But this was to change and he was to start ageing after the completion of his forty-ninth birthday, although he still looks much younger than his age.

Gradually, the headaches diminished and disappeared altogether, but now he began to feel as if 'the head was missing'. And he came upon certain occult powers. This was not something entirely new, for he had experienced these powers on several occasions and dismissed them as of no great importance. By merely looking at someone, he could see his entire past and predict his future. UG refers to such occult powers as natural attributes, or powers and instincts of the human body. Reports of Kundalini experiences reveal similar development of 'siddhis', but the similarity ends there.

UG never mentioned these developments to either Valentine or his friends. Outwardly he looked the same, carrying on as if nothing had happened, letting the body do its work. As he neared his forty-ninth year, when he went for a walk one day, up the Oberland hills, he experienced what he was to later refer to as 'panoramic vision'. It was as if his eyes opened unbelievably wide and took in a 360-degree vision of the entire landscape, as if there were eyes all round his head; the observer disappeared and the objects seemed to pass right through his head and body.

It was only a beginning. There was more to come. Two months before the completion of his forty-ninth year, UG and Valentine happened to be in Paris. JK was there, too, giving public talks. One evening, friends suggested that they go and listen to JK's talk. Since the majority, including Valentine, was in favour of the idea, UG relented and joined them. But when they got there, they realized that they had to pay two francs each to get in. UG thought it was ridiculous to pay money to listen to a talk however profound or spiritual. Instead, he suggested, 'Let's do something foolish. Let's go to Casino de Paris.'

And to Casino de Paris they went. What happened to UG at the casino may sound stranger than fiction. Sitting with his friends watching the cabaret, UG says: 'I didn't know whether the dancer was dancing on the stage or I was doing the dancing. There was a peculiar kind of movement inside of me. There was no division there.' This experience, after his thymus gland was fully activated, was eventually to become his everyday 'normal' experience; for instance, while travelling in a car, he would feel as if oncoming cars were passing through his body.

A week after this experience, one night in a hotel room in Geneva, he had a dream in which he saw himself bitten by a cobra and die instantly. He saw his body being carried on a bamboo stretcher and placed on a funeral pyre at some nameless cremation ground. As the pyre and his own body went up in flames, he was awakened.

It was a prelude to his final, 'clinical' death and awakening into the Natural State. And in his Natural State, a time would come when real cobras would take a walk with him!

Although Valentine was not religious in the orthodox sense of the term, and did not attribute any religious meaning to what was happening to UG, she was now convinced that willy-nilly she was a witness to something extraordinary happening in the history of humankind and that she ought to tell the story to the world. She worked hard and wrote nearly 350 pages of a biography of UG. But the work met the same fate as the autobiography UG had penned before the 'calamity'. One evening, when Valentine returned home after a long walk, she saw to her utter horror, UG feeding the manuscript to the flames in the living room fireplace.

10

The Mystique of Nirvana

The story goes that 2500 years ago, on the first day of the Buddha's awakening, in Bodh Gaya, now a town in the state of Bihar in India, the land was suffused with an enchanting yellow light. And through the land flowed gently the great Ganges, like a witness to the many plays or lilas of Brahman over several kalpas or ages. Now, having overcome the forces of Mara, the future Buddha sat under the Bodhi tree in deep meditation. For seven days seven times he was to penetrate the secret of secrets, break the veil of ignorance, of Maya, and reach Nirvana.

With the breaking of the veil of Maya came about the rejection of all traditions, of the old ways of seeing and experiencing life and the world. It involved too the rejection of the traditional dualism between *jiva* and *ajiva*, between *prakriti* and *purusha*, turning on its head the Upanishadic negative way, neti-neti, and also its great positive assertion *tat tvam asi*, thus wiping out the self.

In the first watch of the night, the future Buddha is believed to have looked deep into the past and present and discovered that he is this, that, and everything, he is the star-studded sky and the earth that rumbles, he is everything that breathed, every stone and every blade of grass.

In the second watch of the night, it became clear to the Buddha that there is no security, no joy or happiness in samsaric existence, that the fear of death is ever present, that desire is the cause of all sorrow.

As the third watch of the night drew on, he surveyed the twelve-linked chain of causation, all of which is linked and dependent upon ignorance, the cessation of which alone can lead to liberation.

Thus, for seven nights the Buddha broke through the different layers of ignorance and came to see without a shadow of doubt that there is no self, and since all creatures are without self, nobody has to attain extinction, for everybody is always already extinct and has always been so. Without this realization, human beings struggle with their non-existent selves, and the world suffers; therefore, what is required is not disdain or loathing, but compassion towards humanity.

Thus Awakened, the Buddha stood up.

Something utterly new and unique had occurred on earth. A new life, a unique yet radical expression of life had come into being, and the earth rejoiced at this new birth. A pleasant breeze blew softly, a gentle rain fell from the heavens, and the earth itself shuddered with great joy.

But the Buddha looked around and sighed. And then he asked himself and the elements of the universe as it were: 'But how shall I teach a wisdom so difficult to grasp?'

★

It was summer in Saanen and the sun was on the rugged peaks of the Oberland in full glory, when it happened to UG—or rather a prelude to the most incredible changes that were to happen over the next few days. His body was now like rice chaff burning inside. The fire was not visible, but it was there, smouldering inside, slowly and steadily moving in circles towards the outer surface. The previous day, on 13 August 1967 to be exact, he had been dragged to listen to JK's last talk. UG had sat there, under the huge tent, listening and not listening. At some point JK started saying: '. . . in that silence there is no mind; there is action . . .'

Stunned, UG listened, and suddenly it all seemed funny. JK was actually describing *his* state of being! How could that be? But it was true. So, 'I am in that state!' UG thought to himself. If that was so, then what the hell had he been doing all these thirty-odd years, listening to all these people, struggling, wanting to attain the state of Jesus, of Buddha, when in fact he had already been there! 'So I am in that state,' the self-assertion, along with a sense of huge wonder, continued for a while. And then it suddenly seemed ridiculous to sit there listening to JK's description of *his* state of being. He got up and walked out of the tent. But he was not finished. He was in that state, certainly—state of the Buddha and all the enlightened masters. But what exactly is that state? The next moment the question transformed itself into yet another question: 'How do I know that I am in that state?' The question burned through him like a maddening fury. 'How do I know I am in that state of the Buddha, the state I very much wanted and demanded from everybody? How do I know?'

The next day, still consumed by the question burning through his whole body, he sat on a little wooden bench under a wild chestnut tree overlooking Saanenland with its seven hills and seven valleys bathed in blue light. The question persisted, the whole of his being was possessed by that single question: 'How do I know?' In other words, he had become the question! And it went on thus: 'How do I know that I am in that state? There is some kind of peculiar division inside of me: there is somebody who knows that he is in that state. The knowledge of that state—what I have read, what I have experienced, what they have talked about—it is this knowledge that is looking at that state, so it is only this knowledge that has projected that state. I said to myself: "Look here, old chap, after forty years you have not moved one step; you are there in square number one. It is the same knowledge that projected that state there when you asked this question. You are in the same situation asking the same question, *how do I know*? Because it is this knowledge, the description of the state by those people, that has created this state for you. You are kidding yourself. You are a damned fool." So, there was nothing in it. But still there was some kind of a peculiar feeling that this was the state. And yet again the question "How do I know that this is the state?"—I didn't have any answer for that question—it was like a question in a whirlpool—it went on and on and on...'

Then suddenly the question disappeared. He was finished truly and wholly. It was not emptiness, it was not blankness, it was not the void of Buddhism, it was not the state that all the enlightened persons are supposed to be in. The question just disappeared.

The disappearance of the question marked the extinction of thought, thought crystallized and strengthened over centuries by cultures, and religions. The 'I' linking the thoughts, 'the psychic coordinator collating, comparing and matching all the sensory input so that it could use the body and its relation for its own separative continuity', was suddenly gone. Now, the link broken, the continuity of thought snapped and exploded, releasing tremendous energy: repairing, cleansing, invigorating, cathartic . . .

UG was to describe the process thus:

Everything in the head tightened—there was no room for anything there inside of my brain. For the first time I became conscious of my head with everything 'tight' inside of it. So, these vasanas (past impressions) or whatever you call them— they do try to show their heads sometimes, but then the brain cells are so 'tight' that it has no opportunity to fool around there any more. The division cannot stay there—it's a physical impossibility; you don't have to do a thing about it, you see. That is why I say that when this 'explosion' takes place (I use the word 'explosion' because it's like a nuclear explosion) it leaves behind chain-reactions. Every cell in your body, the cells in the very marrow of your bones, have to undergo this 'change'—I don't want to use that word—it's an *irreversible* change. There's no question of your going back. There's no question of a 'fall' for this man at all. *Irreversible*: an alchemy of some sort. It is like a nuclear explosion, you see—it shatters the whole body. It is not an easy thing; it is the end of the man—such a shattering thing that it blasts every cell, every nerve in your body. I went through terrible physical torture at that moment. Not that you experience the 'explosion'; you can't experience the 'explosion'—but its after-effects, the 'fall-out', is the thing that changes the whole chemistry of your body.[42]

UG deliberately calls it a *calamity* for he doesn't want people, particularly religious people, to interpret it as something blissful, full of beatitude, love, ecstasy, or even as 'Enlightenment'. No. It is physical, physiological; a torture! It is a calamity from that point of view.

For the next seven days seven bewildering changes took place that catapulted him into what he calls the Natural State.

On the first day, he noticed that his skin had become as soft as silk and had a peculiar golden glow. When he tried to shave, the razor slipped. He changed blades, but it was of no use. He touched his face to see if something was wrong. His sense of touch was different and also the way he held the razor. The whole thing seemed 'funny'.

On the second day, he was thrown into a sort of 'declutched state'. He was upstairs in the kitchen looking at the tomato soup which Valentine had made. He could not figure out what it was. Surprised at the sight of UG staring at the bowl, Valentine told him it was tomato soup. UG tasted it and thought to himself: 'This is how tomato soup tastes.' He drank some soup, and then returned to this odd frame of mind, rather a frame of 'no mind'. He asked again, 'What is that?' Again she said it was tomato soup. Again he tasted it and again he forgot. This went on for some time like some funny game, which, of course, exasperated Valentine who had no clue as to what was happening to UG.

This 'declutched state' has now become normal, says UG. He says he no longer spends time in reverie, worry or conceptualization. His memory has come back; it is there in the background and only comes into play when it's needed, for instance, when we ask questions, or when he has to fix a meal or a tape-recorder or something like that. The rest of the time the mind is in the 'declutched state'. It is a state of no mind, no thought; there is only life.

On the third day, some friends happened to come over for dinner, and UG, who at one time used to give cooking lessons, agreed to 'prepare something'. But somehow he couldn't smell or taste the ingredients he had to use. He became aware that his sense of smell and taste had been transformed. Whenever an odour entered his nostrils it only irritated his olfactory nerve. He couldn't recognize the smell. All smells, he was to discover later, whether from the most expensive scent or from cow dung, caused the same irritation. Whenever he tasted something, he tasted the dominant ingredient only, the taste of the other ingredients seeped in slowly afterwards. From that moment, perfume made no sense to him, and spicy food had no appeal either, for he could taste only the dominant spice, the chilli or whatever it was.

On the fourth day, UG happened to be sitting in the Rialto restaurant with some friends, and he became aware of a tremendous sort of 'vista vision', like a concave mirror. Things rushed towards him, moved into him, as it were. It was as if his eyes were like a gigantic camera, changing focus without his doing anything. Now he is used to the puzzle, he says. That is how he sees everything. For instance, while travelling in a car, he is like a cameraman dollying along; he feels the cars coming in the opposite direction go through him, and the cars that pass by go out of him. When his eyes fix on something they fix on it with total attention, like a camera. The same day, after returning home from the restaurant, he looked in the mirror to see what was odd about his eyes. He looked and looked in the mirror for a long time, and then observed that his eyelids were not blinking. Just to make sure, he looked in the mirror for nearly forty-five minutes; still there was no blinking. Instinctive blinking was over for him, and that's how his eyes function today.

On the fifth day, he noticed a change in his hearing. When he heard the barking of a dog, the barking originated inside him, and he felt the same with the mooing of a cow, the whistle of the train, the ringing of a phone or any sound coming from the kitchen. Suddenly all sounds originated inside him, as it were. The sensation has remained to this day: All sounds, whatever they may be, seem to originate from within him.

Thus, over five days, his five senses were transformed.

On the sixth day, his body disappeared. That day, he was lying down on a sofa; Valentine was in the kitchen. There was this sudden feeling that his body was missing. He looked at his hand and wondered: 'Is this my hand?' There was actually no questioning there, just the feeling that the body was not there. Being a total sceptic he touched his body, and felt that there was nothing, except the touch, the point of contact. Then he called Valentine and asked: 'Do you see my body?' Being used to his quirky ways, Valentine touched his body and said: 'This is your body.' Yet that assurance didn't give him any satisfaction. 'What is this funny business? My body is missing,' he thought to himself. Truly, his body had gone away, and it has never come back, says UG. Further, he declares: 'The points of contact are all that is there for the body—nothing else is there for me—because the seeing is altogether independent of the sense of touch here. So it is *not* possible for me to create a complete image of my body even, because where there's no sense of touch there are *missing* points here in the consciousness.'

On the seventh day, he 'died'—this was not metaphorically dying to all 'yesterdays' as religious people believe. It was actually a 'clinical death', says UG. That day he was again lying on the same sofa, relaxing, enjoying the peculiar state of 'no mind', the 'declutched state'. He would see Valentine coming in and recognize her as Valentine, but when she went out of the room, there would be nothing, no memory, no Valentine and he would have reverted to his blank state of 'no mind'. He also discovered that all his senses were functioning independently without any coordination. The 'link' was missing, the coordinator was gone, never to come back again.

Then there was a tremendous burst of energy and all these energies seemed to draw themselves to a focal point from different parts of the body. It was frightening. UG thought he was going to die. He called Valentine and said, 'I am going to die, Valentine, and you will have to do something with this body. Hand it over to the doctors—maybe they will use it. I don't believe in burning or burial or any of those things. In your own interest you have to dispose of this body—one day it will stink—so, why not give it away?'

She was shocked, but being a woman capable of extraordinary humour even in a crisis, and used to his eccentricities, she quipped, 'You are a foreigner. The Swiss government won't take your body. Forget about it. But what is this? Every day you say something has changed. What is this whole business?' Uninterested in religion, she did not attribute any religious meaning to what UG was saying. She said again, 'Look, you say you are going to die, but I know you are not. Forget it. You are all right, hale and healthy.' And she went back to whatever she was doing.

The frightening movement of the life force continued and it seemed to be converging at some point in his body. He did not know what was going to happen. He lay down, as if to die. Then a point arrived where the whole thing looked as if the aperture of a camera was trying to close itself. UG says: 'It is the only simile that I can think of. The way I am describing this is quite different from the way things happened at that time, because there was nobody there thinking in such terms. All this was part of my experience, otherwise I wouldn't be able to talk about it.'

So, the aperture was trying to close itself, but something was there trying to keep it open, perhaps the 'I', the residue of 'thought' refusing to die. Then, after a while, there was no 'will' to do anything, not even to prevent the aperture closing itself. And then suddenly, it closed.

UG does not know and cannot say what happened after that. This process 'lasted for about forty-eight minutes', this process of dying. It was like a physical death. His hands and feet turned cold, the body became stiff, the heartbeat slowed down, the breathing slowed down, and he started gasping for breath. UG cannot say what exactly happened. It was a clinical death. But, unbelievable as it may sound, when the landlady came up and said that there was a telephone call for him, he came out of it, as he was destined to. He went downstairs to answer it. He was in a daze. He didn't know what had happened. What brought him back to life? Was it the phone call? UG cannot answer. It was a miracle!

Douglas Rosenstein, the man who had made the phone call that momentous day which had brought UG back to life, was also a witness to a part of UG's 'calamity'. Here is his account.

Twenty-four summers ago I was a witness to that rarest of all transformations, arguably the only real one—the death and rebirth of an ordinary human being. This was an ordinary man rather than a 'god man', a chosen one or a world teacher. It all began in the summer of 1966 when I went to Saanen to listen to the talks of J. Krishnamurti . . .

On the last day of the talks I saw UG again. He didn't appear to be very involved in what Krishnamurti was saying. The next day I was having lunch with UG and Valentine. UG began telling the story of how on the previous day he was lying on a couch and he asked Valentine where his body was. And she had answered that his body was there on the couch. Valentine admitted that this crazy conversation had indeed taken place. We were talking about all this between bites of

our lunch. The conversation took place in the past tense. UG
went on repeating how his body had disappeared. I asked him,
'What about now? Is your body there for you now?' And with
the certainty that I have ever seen in UG, he said, 'No, it's
gone for good. It can't come back.' I asked, 'How can you
be sure?' And he switched emphatically into the present tense,
and for the next twenty-five years I have never again heard
him use the past tense in reference to how he is functioning.

That day I was at my apartment in Gstaad. It was evening
time. The moon was just coming up on the horizon.
Something told me that I should call UG at his chalet. I did.
The landlady answered the phone. I could hear her yelling,
'U.G. Krishnamurti, phone for you.' Valentine came on the
phone. She sounded upset, 'Something is going on with UG.
His body is not moving. He may be dying.' I said, 'Go and
get UG, I'll talk to him.' Valentine said, 'I don't think he will
come.' I insisted. And then UG came to the phone. His voice
sounded very far away, and he said, 'Douglas, you better
come over and see this.' It was an invitation to see a 'dead'
man. So I ran. At that time the trains weren't running. The
distance between Gstaad and Saanen is about three kilometres.
I entered the chalet and went up to UG's room. I remember
the scene very vividly: Valentine was looking white with
terror, and UG was lying on the couch—gone. His body was
in an arched position. In yoga you would call this posture
Dhanurasana (the posture of the bow). The full moon was just
coming over the mountain. I asked UG to come to the window
and look at the moon. He got up. I will never forget the
manner in which he looked at the moon. There was something
strange going on in that room. I asked him, 'What was all
that?' He said, 'It's the final death.'[43]

An utterly new human being was born, not the 'new man' UG
had imagined he would be when he wrote to Swami Ghanananda
in the Sri Ramakrishna Ashram in England in 1963. There was no
reference point here, nothing to compare and contrast this Natural
State with.

UG after the 'calamity'

★

But the body was not finished; the total transformation was not yet over. From the next day, UG started experiencing an outburst of tremendous energy; it was as if along with the body, the sofa, the chalet and the whole universe was shaking, vibrating. Cascades of energy invaded his body like huge waves, lashing into a tiny house with shattering effect. It was terrific; it was also painful because the body has limitations, has a form, a shape of its own and cannot withstand the flow of this tremendous energy. UG would say, 'It is not your energy or my energy or God's, and it does not feel the limitations of the body; it has its own momentum.' And the experience is not what is generally assumed to be a state of ecstasy or bliss, asserts UG.

It moved clockwise and anti-clockwise, this way and that way, the impact was such that the body went into some sort of epileptic fit. Where was this energy coming from? From outside or inside, from below or above, UG couldn't locate the spot. It was all over. The body had virtually become like a sea in spate. For three days, as UG lay on his bed, his body contorted with pain. He was to experience similar outbursts of energy intermittently throughout the next six months, particularly whenever he lay down or relaxed. Sometimes the energy flow would slow down and move like 'ants'. For three days he went through terrific pain, over the next six months it diminished, and it took another six months for the whole process to disappear altogether.

It was a cellular revolution, a full-scale biological mutation.

Every cell started changing and his body was covered with 'ash', owing to what UG calls the ionization of cells, ionization of thoughts. The sex hormones too started changing. He didn't know whether he was a man or woman; there was a breast on the left-hand side. Then the movement of his hands changed, they turned backwards.

Up and down his torso, neck and head, at exactly the spots called *nadi chakras* in the Kundalini Yoga, large swellings of various shapes and colours appeared and disappeared. 'On his lower abdomen the swellings were horizontal, cigar-shaped bands. Above the navel was a hard, almond-shaped swelling. A hard, blue swelling, like a large medallion, in the middle of his chest was surmounted by another smaller, brownish-red, medallion-shaped swelling at the base of his throat. These two "medallions" were as though suspended from a varicoloured, swollen ring—blue, brownish and light yellow—around his neck . . .'[44] At one point, his throat was swollen to a shape that made his chin seem to rest on the head of a cobra, as in the traditional images of Shiva. Just above the bridge of the nose appeared a white lotus-shaped swelling. All over the head the small blood vessels expanded, forming patterns like the stylized lumps on the heads of the Buddha statues. These swellings came and went over a period of six months.

Only later, UG was to ascertain that these swellings were due to the reactivation of the ductless glands: the thymus, pituitary and pineal. In UG's own words: 'These glands are what the Hindus call chakras. These ductless glands are located in exactly the same spots where the Hindus speculated the chakras are. There is one gland here (slightly to the right of the midpoint of the chest) which is called the thymus gland. That is very active when you are a child; they have feelings, extraordinary feelings. When you reach the age of puberty it becomes dormant—that's what they say. When again this kind of a thing happens, when you are reborn again, that gland is automatically activated, so all the feelings are there. Feelings are not thoughts, not emotions; you *feel* for somebody. If somebody *hurts* himself *there,* that hurt is felt *here*—not as a pain, but there is a feeling,—you automatically say "Ah!".'

Then the pituitary gland, called the 'third eye' or ajña chakra was reactivated. UG says that once the interference of thought is finished, it is taken over by this gland. It is this gland that then gives instructions or orders to the body, not thought; thought cannot interfere. That is why perhaps it is called *ajña* meaning 'command'. Since there is nobody who uses this thought as a self-protective mechanism, it burns itself up. In his words, 'Thought undergoes combustion, ionization. Thought is, after all, vibration. So, when this kind of ionization of thought takes place, it throws out, sometimes it covers the whole body with an ash-like substance. Your body is covered with that when there is no need for thought at all. When you don't *use* it, what happens to that thought? It burns itself out—that is the energy—it's combustion. The body gets heated. There is tremendous heat in the body as a result of this, and so the skin is covered—your face, your feet, everything—with this ash-like substance.'

Once these glands were reactivated and the 'interference of thought' ceased, UG was thrown into what he calls the *Natural State*, which is also considered to be the state of 'Undivided Consciousness'. In this state, even the so-called good thoughts, holy thoughts, mystical experiences including visions of God or gods are only 'contaminations' and, therefore, have to be flushed out.

In UG's own words:

There are no purificatory methods necessary, there is no sadhana necessary for this kind of a thing to happen—no preparation of any kind. The consciousness is so pure that whatever you are doing in the direction of purifying that consciousness is adding impurity to it. Consciousness has to flush itself out: it has to purge itself of *every* trace of holiness, *every* trace of unholiness, *everything*. When once the frontiers are broken—not through any effort of yours, not through any volition of yours—then the floodgates are open and everything goes out. In that process of flushing out, you have all these visions. It's not a vision outside there or inside of you; suddenly you yourself, the whole consciousness, takes the shape of Buddha, Jesus, Mahavira, Mohammed, Socrates— only those people who have come into this state; not great men, not the leaders of mankind—it is very strange—but only those people to whom this kind of a thing happened. One of them was a coloured man (not exactly a coloured man), and during that time I could tell people how he looked. Then some woman with breasts, flowing hair—naked. I was told that there were two saints here in India—Akkamahadevi and Lalleswari—they were women, naked women. Suddenly you have these two breasts, the flowing hair—even the organs change into female organs. But still there is a division there— you, and the form the consciousness has assumed, the form of Buddha, say, or Jesus Christ or God knows what—the same situation: 'How do I know I am in that state?' But that division cannot stay long; it disappears and something else comes. Hundreds of people—probably something happened to so many hundreds of people. This is part of history—so many rishis, some Westerners, monks, so many women, and sometimes very strange things. All that people have experienced before you is part of your consciousness. I use the expression 'the saints go marching out'; in Christianity they have a hymn 'When the Saints Go Marching In'. They run out of your consciousness because they cannot stay there any more, because all that is impurity, a contamination there. You can say (I can't make any definite statement) probably it is because of the impact on the human consciousness of the 'explosions' of all those saints, sages and saviours of mankind that there is this dissatisfaction in you, that whatever is there is all the time trying to burst out, as it were. Maybe that is so—I can't say anything about it. You can say that they are there because they are pushing you to this point, and once the purpose is achieved they have finished their job and they go away—that is only speculation on my part. But this flushing out of everything good and bad, holy and unholy, sacred and profane has got to happen, otherwise your consciousness is *still* contaminated, *still* impure. During that time it goes on and on and on—there are hundreds and thousands of them—then, you are put back into that primeval, primordial state of consciousness. Once it has become pure, *of and by itself*, then nothing can touch it, *nothing* can contaminate that any more. All the past up to that point is there, but it cannot influence your actions any more. All these visions and everything were happening for three years after the 'calamity'. Now the whole thing is finished. The divided state of consciousness cannot function at all any more; it is always in the undivided state of consciousness—nothing can touch that. Anything can happen—the thought can be a good thought, a bad thought, the telephone number of a London prostitute. It doesn't matter what comes there—good, bad, holy, unholy. Who is there to say 'This is good; that is bad?'— the whole thing is finished. That is why I have to use the phrase 'religious experience' (not in the sense in which you use the word 'religion'): it puts you back to the source. You are back in that primeval, primordial, pure state of consciousness—call it 'awareness' or whatever you like. In that state things are happening, and there is nobody who is interested, nobody who is looking at them. They come and go in their own way, like the Ganges water flowing: the sewerage water comes in, half-burnt corpses, both good things and bad things—everything—but that water is always pure.'[45]

Now the body is affected by everything that happens in nature, for the Natural State is affected by everything; UG calls it simply 'affection'. It is what is otherwise called 'compassion': compassion not in the sense of showing kindness or being affectionate, but meaning 'to suffer with'.

During the phases of the moon, swellings appear around his neck. I was a witness to one such phenomenon when I met him on the last day of his stay in Bangalore, on 2 September 2002. It was the night of the quarter moon. I was sitting beside UG on a sofa. There was a sudden pause in the conversation, and exactly when the phenomenon occurred, UG sensed the swellings in his neck and showed them to us. I looked at my watch, it was 6.45 p.m. The swellings, on both sides of his neck, felt like the soft flesh of a baby. On full moon night, several friends have observed the swellings in UG's neck become more prominent and take the shape of a cobra.

Mahesh Bhatt saw another strange phenomenon during the solar eclipse in Bombay, on 16 February 1980. As the eclipse occurred and the day turned dark, UG noticed that the sex glands in his body had become active. UG, Valentine and Mahesh Bhatt, were standing in the balcony in Mahesh's house when UG commented on the bodily change.[46] The next day, a newspaper reported that at the time of the total eclipse all the animals in the zoo had started to copulate.

On the day of another total solar eclipse, 24 October 1995, UG happened to be staying with K. Chandrasekhar. For nearly a week, newspapers, and TV channels, had been talking about the eclipse and about thirty-two teams of scientists from different countries had come to India to study the phenomenon. UG felt his sexual instinct activated. There was nothing more to it. 'All this hoopla is a waste. What do they know? They are fools . . . Man, who supposedly has achieved so much progress in the scientific field, cannot even predict precisely when an earthquake is going to occur. How can he know of the astronomical secrets occurring millions of miles away?' he said. 'There is not the slightest difference between their theories and the superstitious beliefs of my grandmother. The contemporary astronomer's theories are just as ridiculous as the belief that Rahu (a mythical dragon) swallowed the Sun, and the Sun emerged out of the throat of Rahu . . . Science supplies the technological know-how to the world. Our lives become easier and more comfortable because of it. Because of our faith in that technology, we believe implicitly whatever gains currency in the name of science. In fact, none of those theories are true; they are mere speculations.' He told Chandrasekhar not to stupidly believe in all the warnings and advice of the scientists published in the newspapers and, much against the practice, he ate his breakfast of idlis before the eclipse.[47]

inkink.........

Once, while talking about the thymus gland and how 'feelings', not emotions, are felt there, he narrated an incident to illustrate the point. It happened in 1967, while he was staying at Chikkamangalur, in a coffee plantation. One evening, he heard a child wailing and was drawn to the spot. He saw a mother beating her child. She was mad, hopping mad, and she hit the child so hard, that it almost turned blue. UG did not, or rather could not intervene, for he felt both the anger of the mother and the pain and fear of the child. He simply could not move. Later, when one of his associates asked him why did he not stop the mother from beating the child, he said, 'I was standing there—I was so puzzled, you see. "Who should I take pity on, the mother or the child?"—that was my answer—"Who is responsible?" Both were in a ridiculous situation: the mother could not control her anger, and the child was so helpless and innocent. This went on—it was moving from one to the other—and then I found all those things (marks) on my back. So I was also part of that. (I am not saying this just to claim something.) That is possible because consciousness cannot be divided. Anything that is happening there is affecting you—this is affection, you understand? There is no question of your sitting in judgement on anybody; the situation happens to be that, so you are affected by that. You are affected by everything that is happening there.'

Another instance of this strange 'affection' occurred when UG, Valentine and a few friends were staying in a hill station in north Goa in the mid-seventies. One morning, UG and friends climbed down the hill and sat chatting and basking in the sun. Valentine, who found the path down the hill too steep and slippery, decided against joining the group. The men now got talking as to what each one would have done if Valentine had decided to come with them, slipped and fallen. UG said nothing. After a while, Valentine came out of the cottage, ventured down the treacherous path, and indeed she slipped and fell. Even the man just behind her couldn't manage to help her, let alone the ones sitting with UG. A stunned silence fell over the group as Valentine got up and limped down. With a bemused smile, UG pointed out to the men that they had done nothing even though each of them had said they would help her. One of them asked UG, 'How come you yourself did nothing to help, then?' UG said quietly, 'I never said that I would give her a helping hand. If, however, you want to see for yourself how I myself was involved in that event...' and he rolled up one leg of his trousers. They found scratches on his knee similar to those found on Valentine's knee.[48]

★

Towards the end of 1967, UG happened to be in Sringeri. Upon hearing of the bewildering physical changes in UG, the Sankaracharya of Sringeri was keen to meet him. At that time, UG was not interested in talking to people about his state nor did he believe he had any teaching to impart to the world. Nevertheless, upon the insistence of a friend, he did meet the Sankaracharya. Given his religious background, the Sankaracharya had no doubt that UG was a jivanmukta. He is believed to have said, 'When I heard of the extraordinary things that happened to you, I am reminded of my guru Sri Chandrasekhara Bharati. I don't know of these things from my own personal experience, but my teacher used to describe his experiences just the way they have occurred in your case. We were afraid that perhaps his mind was deranged. It is very rare that the body survives the shock of such a thought-less state. According to the scriptures, within three days or seventy-two hours after such an event the body dies. If the body could sustain its vital force and not die, it must surely be for the sake of saving humanity.'

UG did not think he was a saviour, nor did he believe the world needed to be saved from anything. What had happened to him was not something he had sought, and it had happened despite all his search and sadhana. He just wished to stay put in some quiet spot and let things be. The peaceful environs of Sringeri, on the banks of the river Tunga, seemed an appropriate place for him to retire. He listened silently to the swamiji for some time and then quietly broached the subject of his retirement. The Sankaracharya, Sri Abhinava Vidya Tirtha Swami, is reported to have said, 'I will arrange to get you any place around here, if you so wish, but your idea of living alone will never work. Whether you stay in a jungle or in a mountain cave, people won't stop coming to see you.'

It was truly said. One could not hide a sun, nor could the sun choose to go incognito. UG abandoned his resolve to stay away from people.

But the question remained: 'What is there to say after a thing like this?'

Days passed, and then suddenly it occurred to him:

'I will say it exactly the way it is.'

★

UG gave his first public talk at the Indian Institute of World Culture in Bangalore, in May 1972. It was his first and last public talk.

> . . . I was trapped into this kind of a thing. I don't like to give talks at all. You all seem to be very fond of listening to speeches, talks, lectures, discussions, discourses, conversations, and so on. I do not know if at any time you realize for yourself and by yourself that you never listen to anybody or anything in this world. You always listen to yourself. I really don't know what to say. I don't know what you want to listen to and what I am expected to do. This is supposed to be a discourse and a dialogue. I very often point out to those who come to see me and talk things over that no dialogue is possible and no dialogue is necessary. It may sound very strange to you, but, nevertheless, the fact does remain that no dialogue is possible and yet no dialogue is necessary.
>
> If you will permit me, I will say a few words, to set the ball rolling, as it were. I am going to say a few words about the state of not knowing. How can anybody say anything about the 'state of not knowing'? I have necessarily to use words. Can we use words without indulging in abstract concepts? I say we can. But I do not, at the same time, mean that it is a non-verbal conceptualization. That is a funny thing—there is no such thing as non-verbal conceptualization at all. But, perhaps, a few words like this will enable you to understand (that) the methods of thought prevent you from understanding the limitations of thought as a means to directly experience life and its movements.

This 'state of not knowing' is not (just) my particular state. This is as much your natural state as it is mine. It is not the state of a God-realized man; it is not the state of a Self-realized man. It is not the state of a holy man. It is the natural state of every one of you here. But since you are looking to somebody else and you are reaching out for some kind of a state of liberation, freedom, or moksha—I don't know what words you want to use—you are lost. But, how can one understand the limitations of thought? Naturally, the only instrument we have is the instrument of thought. But what is thought? I can give you a lot of definitions, and you know a lot of definitions about thought. I can say that thought is just matter; thought is vibration; and we are all functioning in this sphere of thought. And we pick up these thoughts because this human organism is an electromagnetic field. And this electromagnetic field is the product of culture. It may sound very inappropriate on this occasion to say that in order to be in your natural state, all that man has thought and felt before you must be swept aside and must be brushed aside. And that means the culture in which you are brought up must go down the drain or out of the window. Is it possible? It is possible. But, at the same time, it is so difficult, because you are the product of that culture and you are that. You are not different from that. You cannot separate yourself from that culture. And yet, this culture is the stumbling block for us to be in our natural state. Can this 'Natural State' be captured, contained and expressed through words? It cannot. It is not a conscious state of your existence. It can never become part of your conscious thinking. And then why do I talk of this state of not knowing? For all practical purposes it does not exist at all. It can never become part of your conscious thinking.

Here, I have to explain what I mean by the word 'consciousness'. I don't know. When do you become conscious of a thing? Only when the thought comes between what is there in front of you and what is supposed to be there inside of you. That is consciousness. So, you have to necessarily use thought to become conscious of the things around you, or the persons around you. Otherwise, you are not conscious of the things at all. And, at the same time, you are not unconscious. But there is an area where you are neither conscious nor unconscious. But that 'consciousness'—if I may use that word—expresses itself in its own way; and what prevents that consciousness to express itself in its own way is the movement of thought. What can anyone do about this thought? It has a tremendous momentum of millions and millions of years. Can I do anything about that thought? Can I stop it? Can I mould it? Can I shape it? Can I do anything about it? But yet, our culture, our civilization, our education—all these have forced us to use that instrument to get something for us. So, can that instrument be used to understand its own nature? It is not possible. And yet, when you see the tremendous nature of this movement of thought, and that there isn't anything that you can do about it, it naturally slows down and falls in its natural pattern. When I say that, I do not, of course, mean what these people in India talk about—that thought must be used in order to get into a thought-less state or into a meditative state. But there is no such thing as a thought-less state at all. Thoughts are there; they will be there all the time. Thoughts will disappear only when you become a dead corpse—let me use these two words—'dead corpse'. Otherwise, thoughts are there and they are going to be there. If all the religious teachers tell us that you are going into a 'thought-less state,' they are taking us all for a ride. They can promise you that in that thought-less state—in that state of silence, in that state of quietness, or in that state of a 'Quiet Mind', or whatever phrase you want to use—there will be this real 'bliss', 'beatitude', 'love', 'religious joy', and 'ecstatic state of being'. All that is balderdash. Because, that state—if there is any state like the state of bliss—it can never become part of your consciousness. It can never become part of your conscious existence. So, you might as well throw the whole thing—the whole crap of these ideas, concepts and abstractions about the blissful states—into a cocked hat.

So, what is one to do? Can anybody help you? No outside agency can help you. That means a complete and total rejection, as I said in the beginning, of all that man has thought and felt before you. As long as there is any trace of knowledge, in any shape, in any form, in your consciousness, you are living in a divided state of consciousness. He (Mr Kothari) referred to my coming into a state of 'not knowing' or 'the calamity', as I myself refer to that. What happened? I don't know. Suddenly thought has fallen into its natural state. The continuity has come to an end. So, what I am saying is not the product of thinking. It is not manufactured by my thought structure inside. Nor is it a logically ascertained premise. But what is happening here is only the expression of that state of being where you do not know what is happening. You do not know how this organism is functioning. This is a pure and simple physical and physiological state of being. It has no religious undertones or overtones. It has no mystical content whatsoever. And, at the same time, this extraordinary thing, the extraordinary intelligence that is there, which is a product of centuries of human evolution, is able to express itself and deal with any problem and any situation without creating problems for us.

Q: May I interrupt you? I was told by people who are around you that when this calamity befell you, you couldn't recognize even ordinary things. You were asking like a newborn child, 'What is this?' Even if there was a flower in front of you, you did not know if that was a flower. Then you would ask, 'What is this?' And the Swiss lady who was keeping house for you, who was looking after you, Valentine (she is here with us), said 'This is a flower.' Then you would ask again, 'What is this?' You mean to say that at the time when the calamity took place, all recognition was gone?

UG: Not only then, but even now, as I said, this is a state of 'not knowing'. Since the memory is there in the background, it begins to operate when there is a demand for it. That demand is created by an outside agency, because there is no entity here. There is no centre here. There is no self here. There is no Atman here. There is no soul here at all. You may not agree. You may not accept it, but that unfortunately happens to be a fact. The totality of thoughts and feelings is not there. But (in you) there is an illusion that there is a totality of your feelings and thoughts. This human organism is responding to the challenges from outside. You are functioning in the sphere—so, thousands and thousands, perhaps millions and millions of sensations are bombarding this body. Since there is no centre here, since there is no mind here, since there is nothing here, what is it that is happening? What is happening here (is that) this human organism is responding to the challenges, or to the stimuli, if I may put it that way. So, there is nobody here who is translating these sensations in terms of past experiences. But there is a living contact with the things around. That is all that is there. One sensation after another is hitting this organism. And at the same time there is no coordinator here. This state of not knowing is not in relationship to your Brahman, or your Nirguna Brahman or Saguna Brahman or any such thing. This state of not knowing is in its relationship to the things that are there around you. You may be looking at a flower. You may think that it is a crazy state. Perhaps it is—I don't know. You do not know what you are looking at. But when there is a demand for that—and that demand always comes from outside, (asking) what is that, and then the knowledge, the information that is there, locked up in this organism comes and says that it is a rose, that this is a microphone, that's a man, that's a woman, and so on and so forth. This is not because there is a drive from inside, but the outside challenge brings out this answer. So, I say that this action is always taking place outside of this organism, not inside. How do I know that these sensations are bombarding or hitting this organism all the time? It is only because there is a consciousness which is conscious of itself and there is nobody who is conscious of the things that are happening. This is a living organism and that living state is functioning in its own way, in its natural way.

Mr Kothari: UG, it appears to me this Nirguna Brahman, Atman, whatever it is—when somebody uses the word *Bhuma*, another uses the word 'unknown', the third man says *'akal'* (the timeless), the fourth one says something else—all of them say that this cannot be described, *'Neti, Neti.'* Probably they meant the same thing; I don't know. I think they meant probably what you are saying as 'totality'. As I understand it, Brahman means 'totality'. If I would translate this state into terms of those times, probably it is the same thing as being in the state of Brahman and (it is) thought which is limiting the 'alpa', which is limiting the 'bhuma', which is limiting the limitless, since it does not function like that, creating an individuality within you. Maybe I am wrong, maybe I am translating, but I say that it is possible that the person who listens to you doesn't know the old terms. You are not going to use the old terms, because the new terms are your terms. And every teacher, every person who has come into some state like this has generally used a different term, a different word, according to his background. But personally I think you mean the same thing. This is a commentary on what you are saying.

UG: What do you want me to say? (Laughter) If they have understood what there is, they wouldn't be here. They wouldn't go to anybody. They wouldn't ask these questions at all. If they translate what I am saying, in terms of their particular fancy or their particular background, that's their tragedy; it would be their misery. It hasn't helped them. This is my question: Has it helped you? Why are you hung up on these phrases? They are after all phrases. When once you realize, when once this is understood—how this mechanism is operating, how automatic it is, how mechanical it is, you will realize that all these phrases have no meaning at all. You may very well ask me why I am using these phrases: (it is) because you and I have created this unfortunate situation where you have put me here on the dais and asked me to talk, and naturally, as I said in the beginning, I have to use words. So, the moment I stop talking, the whole thing has come to a stop inside. Is that so? It is so here (in my case), because there is no continuity of thought.

. . . There is nothing to achieve, there is nothing to accomplish, nothing to attain, and no destination to arrive at. And what prevents what is there, this living state, from expressing itself in its own way is the movement of thought which is there only for the purposes of functioning in this world. When the movement of thought is not there—I have to use the clauses in terms of time—but time is thought. When thought is there, time is there. When thought is there, sex is there, when thought is there, God is there. When thought is not there, there is no God, there is no sex, nothing is there. But the drug of virtues you practise, the practice of virtues is not a foundation for it at all. And the practice of abstinence, continence, and celibacy is not the path to it. But if you want to indulge in them and feel greatly superior, it's your own business. I am not here to reform you. I am not here to lead you anywhere. But this is a fact. You have to understand a fact as a fact. It is not a logically ascertained thing, it is not a rational thing (so as) to understand it rationally. A fact is a movement. Truth is movement. Reality is movement. But I don't want to use these words, because they are all loaded words. You know all about them. The unfortunate thing about the whole business is that you know a lot about these things, and that is the misery of you all. This is a thing which you do not know at all. I am not claiming that I know it. I myself don't know. That is why I say I don't know. It's a state of not knowing. Let alone God, let alone reality, ultimate or otherwise, I don't know what I am looking at—the very person who has been with me all the time, day and night. That is my situation. If I tell this to a psychiatrist, he will probably put me on a couch and say something is radically wrong with me. Probably I am functioning like any other human being. He doesn't understand that. That's his problem, it is not my problem any more. So, all your search—for truth, God, Reality—you use any phrase you like, is a false thing. You are all on a merry-go-round, and you want to go round and round and round.

. . . You want to imitate the life of Jesus, you want to imitate the life of the Buddha, you want to imitate the life of Sankara. You can't do it, because you don't know what is there behind. You will end up changing your robes, from rose to saffron, saffron to yellow, or from yellow to rose, depending upon your particular fancy. How can you ask for a thing which you do not know? How can you search for a thing which you do not know? That is my question. So, search has no meaning at all. Only when the search comes to an end, what there is will express itself, in its own way. You cannot tamper with that. You cannot manipulate that. You cannot manipulate the action of the thing which is there, which has an extraordinary intelligence.

. . . I am making assertions, statements and conclusions— you will object to them. Take it or leave it. I don't expect you to accept anything that I am saying. You are not in a position to accept or reject it. You can reject it because it does not fit into the particular framework of your philosophy— Sankara, Gaudapada, Ramanuja, Madhvacharya, God knows what—we have too many of them here. So how can you understand this? The only thing to do is to throw in the towel. Turn your back on the whole business. That is why, it takes extraordinary courage, not the courage or the bravado of these people who climb Mount Everest or try to swim across the English Channel, or cross the Pacific or Atlantic— whatever their fancy—on a raft. That is not what I mean. What I mean is the courage. You quote your Bhagavad Gita, or your Brahma Sutras, 'kaschid dhirah'. All these phrases. What do they mean? 'Abhayam Brahma'. (Fearless is Brahman.) Why do you all repeat these phrases? It has no meaning. It's a mechanical thing. 'How are you?' 'I am all right, I am fine. Just fine. I couldn't be better.' In America, you know, (they say) 'How are you this morning,' 'I am just fine. I couldn't be better.' In exactly the same way, you throw these phrases at everybody. If you understand the way this mechanical structure is functioning inside of you, you see the absurdity of the whole business of discussing these matters everlastingly. Can you throw the whole business out of the window and walk out?

Mr Kothari: Not now . . .

UG: Yes, throw stones at me and walk out.

Mr Kothari: They don't have any.

UG: My interest is to send you packing, as the expression has it. If you can do that, you will never go to listen to anybody.

That's enough, I suppose. I haven't said anything. What all you think I have said is a 'bag'. You think it makes sense. How can it make sense? If you think that it makes sense, you haven't understood a thing. If you think that it doesn't make any sense, you haven't understood it either. It's just words, words, words . . . I am not trying to be clever with all these phrases. I don't know a thing about it. Am I talking, am I saying anything? This is like the howling of a jackal, barking of a dog or braying of an ass. If you can put this on that level and just listen to this vibration, you are out, you will walk out, and you will never listen to anybody in your lifetime. Finish. It doesn't have to be the talk of a self-realized man. You will realize that there is no self to realize. That's all.[49]

UG never again gave another public talk, nor would he accept invitations to talk at universities or institutions. But he could not stop people from meeting and talking to him. He responded to their queries and answered their questions in the way only he could. For the last thirty-six years now, UG has travelled to practically every country in the world. And this man with 'no message', 'no teaching' has probably met and talked to more people than any person alive today.

The first book, *The Mystique of Enlightenment—The Unrational Ideas of a Man Called UG*, appeared in 1982. In 1986, JK passed away, bringing to an end what was probably the most intense 'spiritual phase' of the twentieth century. Now, it was as if the task of breaking away from the tradition, from the old ways of seeing and being, and teaching new ways of questioning and looking at life was passed on to UG. Two years after JK's death, UG went public and gave his first TV interview, which was soon to be followed by several TV and radio interviews the world over.

Now wherever he goes, people meet him in increasing numbers. There is absolutely no restriction. People can walk in and out as in a shopping mall. But there are no wares sold in this shop. People are, of course, welcome to ask him questions, even questions they dare not ask their parents, their spouses, their intimate friends, let alone their gurus. 'Why do you speak? Where do you get money to travel so much? What do you mean you are neither man nor woman? What is there in your pyjamas? What is love? Do you have sexual urges? Do you get dreams? Why do you criticize and condemn spiritual gurus? What is moksha? Aren't you an enlightened man? What is your teaching? Do you have a message?' and so on and on. He answers them all in his own inimitable style.

The 'shop' is kept open from early morning to late evening for people to feel free to come without an appointment, and to leave whenever they want. 'This is how it should be. There should be no special duration, prior appointment, and such,' UG would say, and his hosts everywhere have maintained the rule without fail.

Some years ago, one evening at K. Chandrasekhar's house, UG remarked: 'This has turned into a barber shop.'

Everyone present thought it was a good joke and broke into hearty laughter.

'They have been coming since morning without a break,' UG added. 'They come and get their hair cut.'

Not enlightenment, not wisdom, not anything profound or spiritual. But *haircut*! There couldn't have been a more apt, a more unspiritual or blasphemous description of what UG gives or does to people!

But that's the way it is with UG.

BOOK TWO

INTERPRETING U.G. KRISHNAMURTI

11

God(s), Fear and Ultimate Pleasure

The world has always been full of gods. They don't go away even when they appear to disappear. They cannot be killed or burnt like you burn down a tree. They come back, reincarnate themselves in new forms and take on new names. Gods have a way of surviving and perpetuating themselves. Once created, they can never be destroyed. They live in a totem as much as in a science-fiction movie or a politician's head. They exist in the minds of scientists in the form of some notion as easily as in the mind of a priest. They are made of the stuff of thought, of the non-existent 'I' that refuses to go away. This is not a mere paradox. It is the source of great mischief and wisdom, of great fantasy and terror.

In her fascinating book, *The History of God*, Karen Armstrong says that the idea(s) of God probably emerged in the Middle East (Joseph Campbell would call it the Near East) about 14,000 years ago. How the scholars have arrived at this figure is hard to understand. However, it is enough for us to know that it is the most ancient of human ideas, rooted in a sense of wonder, mystery and fear of the unknown. Add to it the deep-rooted innate urge to transcend the individual separative consciousness which constitutes the heart of the great human drama on earth.

Be that as it may, the ideas of God(s), the worship of gods and rituals have undergone remarkable changes over the centuries. According to Karen Armstrong, like all other great ideas, the idea of God too has an indisputable history. The study of the evolution or development of the idea of God would reveal that it 'has always meant something slightly different to each group of people who have used it at various points of time'. There is no objective meaning or view of 'God'; rather, the word 'God' contains a whole spectrum of meanings and these meanings could sometimes be contradictory to each other, or even mutually exclusive. To put it differently, history reveals that when one conception of God has ceased to have meaning or relevance, it has been rejected and replaced by new ones or new and different understandings of God. If not for this flexibility, or openness of mind, the notion of God wouldn't have survived to become one of the greatest ideas. A fundamentalist fails to see this cleansing fact and remains ignorant and intolerant of new understandings. In the words of Karen Armstrong, '. . .fundamentalism is anti-historical: it believes that Abraham, Moses and the later prophets all experienced their God in exactly the same way as people do today. Yet if we look at our three religions (Judaism, Christianity, and Islam), it becomes clear that there is no objective view of "God": each generation has to create the image of God that works for them.'[50]

The study of ancient paintings and carvings, myths and legends and stories shows that throughout history mankind has worshipped not just one God but a number of gods and deities, literally a 'government of gods', although the worship of the great Sky God and the cult of the Mother Goddess appear to have been in vogue for a considerable period in certain ancient cultures. It is interesting to learn that both Joseph Campbell, through his lifelong study of the mythologies of the world, and Karen Armstrong, through a rigorous historical inquiry, register the radical difference in the historic emergence and development of the idea of gods in the East and the West. It is a fascinating story which is too complex to go into here. Suffice it to say that in the West, God has been predominantly seen and experienced as 'transcendental' and in the East as 'immanent'. This could perhaps be best explained with reference to the two major creation myths, the myth of Adam and Eve, and the myth of Prajapathi.

The myth of Adam and Eve is the story of man's fall, his exile, of temptation and knowledge, of alienation from 'innocence'or 'unity', of God as the Creator separate from His creation, separate from Nature. Tied up with such a transcendent God in the Occidental consciousness are the ideas of sin, retribution, Satan, surrender and mercy, logos (the wisdom of God, the Divine Plan), and salvation.

The story of Adam and Eve also marked the emergence and establishment of monotheism, of One (male) God (as opposed to the Mother Goddess). It was the beginning of an era marked by wars and violence. The God of mercy and justice had to be a jealous God and a God of vengeance as well. Mercy and vengeance, justice and punishment always went together.

Adam's fall and exile was seen not as symbolic, as the beginning of self-consciousness and separation from Nature (as Joseph Campbell interprets it), but interpreted quite literally to mean alienation from God's law, His Divine Plan, from the garden of 'innocence', and as an event in history.

In other words, the birth or emergence of 'I', of self-consciousness, was interpreted as violation of God's law, a sin to be atoned for. The only way out was to accept God's decree, surrender and seek His mercy for salvation from 'evil'.

The story of monotheism is also the story of organized wars against other gods and goddesses, other ways of being and experiencing life. It is the story of eternal conflict: man vs woman, man vs nature, man vs God, good vs evil, God vs Satan and so on.

Feminists quite rightly find monotheism, rooted as it is in binary thinking, not merely problematic but as the source of the oppression of women. One Truth or One God not only becomes a source of violence and irreconcilable division, it also, as Rosemary Radford Ruether says, 'strengthens patriarchalism to the extent that the one God is presumed to be male and represented by males, thus setting up the hierarchy of God over human as analogous to male over female.' To put it differently, in the words of Mary Daly: 'The image of God as exclusively a father and not a mother, for example, was spawned by the human imagination under the condition of patriarchal society and sustained as plausible by patriarchy. Then, in turn, the image has served to perpetuate this kind of society by making its mechanisms for the oppression of women appear right and fitting.'[51]

This dichotomy, or dualism, between the spirit and matter, soul and body, is characteristic of monotheism. Religious institutions and authority have been built upon this dualism, which has created an eternal dichotomy between man and woman, body and soul.

As some feminists have tried to show, this has led to fear of
sexuality, and a sense of alienation from the earth, and the
movement from a cyclical, organic, religious world-view to a
historical, dualistic world-view, has been the primary cause of
oppression by race, class, and sex, of militarism and the domination
over, and mindless exploitation of, nature.[52]

It is almost impossible to overcome or kill this God of destructive
dualism. Nietzsche thought this vengeful God was dead, or that he
found Him dead in the European consciousness. Rather he wished
Him dead! But Nietzsche should have known better, for gods too
transmigrate—they are deeply entrenched in man's will to power!

In the East, however, the myth of God as immanent in all
creation has had a dominant influence on the development of
Eastern religions and shaped its psychology and philosophy. The
myth of Prajapathi as recounted in the *Brihadaranyaka Upanishad*
(around 700 BC) goes thus:

> In the beginning, this universe was nothing but It, the Self in
> the form of a person. It looked around and saw that there was
> nothing but itself, whereupon its first shout was, 'It is I!';
> whence the concept 'I' arose. (And that is why, even now,
> when addressed, one answers first, 'It is I!' only then giving
> the other name that one bears.)
>
> Then he was afraid. (That is why anyone alone is afraid.)
> But he considered: 'Since there is no one here but myself, what
> is there to fear?' whereupon the fear departed. (For what
> should have been feared? It is only to a second that fear refers.)
>
> However, he still lacked delight (therefore, we lack delight
> when alone) and desired a second. The person was exactly
> as large as a man and woman embracing. This Self then
> divided itself in two parts; and from that man and woman
> came into being. (Therefore this body, by itself, as the sage
> Yajnavalkya declares, is like half of a split pea. And that is
> why, indeed, this space is filled by a woman.)
>
> The male embraced the female, and from that the human
> race arose. She, however, reflected: 'How can he unite with
> me, who am produced from himself? Well then, let me hide!'
> She became a cow, he a bull and united with her; and from

that cattle arose. She became a mare, he a stallion; she an ass, he a donkey and united with her; and from that solid-hoofed animals arose. She became a goat, he a buck; she a sheep, he a ram and united with her; and from that goats and sheep arose. Thus he poured forth all pairing things, down to the ants. Then he realized: 'I, actually, am creation; for I have poured forth all this.' Hence he became known as creation.

Anyone who understanding this becomes, truly, himself a creator in this creation . . .[53]

Variations of this primary myth of God splitting itself into male and female and becoming all creation can be found in almost all ancient cultures. How this myth was transmogrified into monotheism, into a transcendent male God, is indeed the story of Western civilization.

However, in the context of the East, what the Prajapathi myth says is that what had been one became two, hence man and woman, life and death. In other words, the split in consciousness was the beginning of a separate ego-self ('I'), of a sense of separation which in turn led to a tremendous dissatisfaction and yearning to return to the state of primordial or unitary consciousness. The Hindus, therefore, interpret human life as a play, a lila, played out by Brahman on the stage of fear and desire (samsara).

So, if a human being, yearns to be free from this deep dissatisfaction or lack, to go beyond this drama of life and death, beyond this play of dualism, these pairs of opposites, of good and evil, of I and thou, of samsara, he or she has to return to the source and ground of all creation.

However, if God is transcendent, as in the Western view, if man and God are distinct from the beginning, if the Self is not that of God nor is it one with the universe, then there is no freedom in such a scheme of life but only surrender to God. 'The goal of knowledge cannot be to *see* God here and now in all things; for God is not in things. God is transcendent. God is beheld only by the dead. The goal of knowledge has to be, rather, to know the *relationship* of God to his creation, or, more specifically, to man, and through such knowledge, by God's grace, to link one's own will back to that of the Creator.'[54]

Joseph Campbell captures the essence of these two different modes of knowing and being beautifully: 'The fall of Adam and Eve was an event within the already created frame of time and space, an accident that should not have taken place. The myth of the Self in the form of a man (person), on the other hand, who looked around and saw nothing but himself, said "I", felt fear, and then desired to be two, tells an intrinsic, not errant, factor in the manifold of being, the correction or undoing of which would not improve, but dissolve, creation. The Indian point of view is metaphysical, poetical; the Biblical, ethical and historical.'

To put it differently, if man has been removed from the divine through a historical event, it will be a historical event that leads him back. But if it has been by some sort of psychological displacement then psychology will be his vehicle of return.[55]

To probe this point further and understand the basic difference between the dominant Oriental and Occidental approaches to life and freedom, again in the words of Joseph Campbell, '. . . in the Indian myth the principle of ego, "I" (aham), is identified completely with the pleasure principle, whereas in the psychologies of both Freud and Jung its proper function is to know and relate to external reality (Freud's 'reality principle'): not the reality of the metaphysical but that of the physical, empirical sphere of time and space. In other words, spiritual maturity, as understood in the modern Occident, requires a differentiation of *ego* from *id*, whereas in the Orient, throughout the history at least of every teaching that has stemmed from India, ego (*aham-kara*: 'the making of the sound "I") is impugned as the principle of libidinous delusion, to be dissolved.'

Two thousand five hundred years ago, the Buddha tackled this subject differently. He knew the mischief that is God. He did not deny God, for this was quite unnecessary. It is the ego, the self that is the creator of God. So what the Buddha did was to simply reject God and wipe out the self. What UG does is not very different. 'God is irrelevant,' he says. And then, as one who has seen it all, he asserts, 'There is no power outside of a human being.'

But the battles in the name of God(s) have not ceased; more people have been killed in the name of God than in all the wars put together. Arthur Koestler writes: 'No historian would deny that the part played by crimes committed for personal motives is very small compared to the vast populations slaughtered in unselfish loyalty to a jealous god, king, country, or political system', or what Koestler calls 'transpersonal ideals'.[56]

Notwithstanding this terrible fact of history, it seems man cannot help but cling to his God(s) with a desperate hope of finding answers to his nagging (metaphysical) questions and solutions to all his existential problems. The sceptical thought that perhaps there are no answers to all our metaphysical questions, and that the idea of God far from being a solution is probably part of our problem, hardly ever strikes us. We find it almost impossible to understand and accept that these various gods (whether one or many) are nothing but our converted fears, desires, ideals, and ecstasies, too. And the notion of One God, the Universal, Supreme, Absolute, is the totality of these different gods, the totality of these fears, desires and ecstasies.

UG, of course, speaks about God variously as Greed, Fear,

Ultimate Pleasure, or as search for Permanent Happiness. In effect, God is the totality of our fears, desires, ideals, and our yearning to be in a state of uninterrupted happiness. According to him, God is the most destructive of man's inventions; if man has to be saved from destroying himself, he has to be first saved from God. What he means is that we have to be saved from the beliefs associated with the concept of God, such as the concepts of truth, the beyond, timelessness, bliss, permanent happiness, rebirth, and life after death, as well as political ideals born out of religious thinking such as progress, order, reason, or the belief in utopias.

We cannot get rid of these concepts through any sort of political or social revolution, whether communist or otherwise. It doesn't work that way. Never. Nor does it help to become anti-God or an atheist. UG warns:

> To me, the theist (the believer in God), the non-believer in God, and the one that comes in between and calls himself an 'agnostic'—all of them are in the same boat. I personally feel that there is no power outside of man—whatever power is out there in the universe is inside man. So, if that is the case— and that is a fact to me—there is no point in externalizing that power and creating some symbol and worshipping it. That's why I say that God, the question of God, is irrelevant to man today. It's not that you should burn all the religious books and tear down all the temples. That is too silly, too ridiculous, because what temples and religious books stand for is in the man, uh? It is not outside. So there's no point in burning all those libraries and making a bonfire of all the religious books—that is too silly; that is not the way to do it. What 'God' stands for is already there in man—there is no power outside of man—and that has to express itself in its own way, express itself in a new form, otherwise there is not much hope . . .

When UG asserts 'there is no power outside of man' he sounds like an 'avatar' in whom all fears have come to an end, truly an embodiment of 'undivided consciousness'. One is tempted to ask if in effect he is in agreement with Joseph Campbell's interpretation of the myth of Prajapathi as against that of Adam and Eve, and that actually he is giving expression to the Upanishadic saying: *Aham Brahmasmi*, 'I am that infinite', or *tat tvamasi*, 'Thou art That'. UG would probably disagree, saying that these phrases, far from expressing the 'undivided state', only express the yearning to be in that state because countless sages have expressed the view that it is the highest state a human being can aspire to. But actually, says UG, there is nothing to these expressions, they are all empty words. Even supposing there is such a state, he would argue, it cannot be known, for it would be a state of not knowing. It is not the state of a God-realized man or a Self-realized man. He calls it, simply, the Natural State. And there is no power outside of that state.

The following incident demonstrates UG's stance on gods forcefully.

Sometime in the 1990s, UG happened to visit the temple of the goddess Chamundi in Mysore. Sri Chamundi is the tutelary goddess of the (eighteenth century) Mysore Wodeyar dynasty, and is a variant of Durga and Kali, the two most powerful manifestations of the Mother Goddess. She is seen as the Shakti or energy of the universe, which envelops the three *lokas* (worlds). She embodies paradox—she is gentle and fierce and destructive, beautiful and ugly, erotic and chaste, and she is worshipped and feared not only by human beings, but also by the (male) gods.

Inside the *sanctum sanctorum* of the Lakshmi Narayan temple, behind the Chamundi temple, the priest of the temple, Anandji, had placed a photograph of UG by the side of the deity. UG visited the temple in order to tell the priest to remove his photograph.

Anandji had met UG in Mysore some years ago. Once, in UG's presence he is supposed to have felt an intense movement of energy within him. From then on, reportedly, he began to look upon UG as a divine power, perhaps as the god Shiva himself in the flesh. He placed a picture of UG on the altar and worshipped it every day. Now, at UG's admonition, he removed the photograph from the temple and put it in the puja room of his house.

That day, however, he took UG and his friends into the *sanctum sanctorum* of the Chamundi temple. In his report of the visit, K. Chandrashekhar writes:

'The priest led Valentine, Parveen Babi and Mahesh, along with UG, directly into the inner sanctum. The honour that was done to them that day was not normally accorded even to the Maharajah. It was inconceivable that people like Valentine, Parveen and Mahesh would be allowed into the inner sanctum where even orthodox Brahmins would not normally be allowed. A special puja was performed for them. It was another wonder that the sacred conch shell (called *Panchajanya*) belonging to the Goddess, and the Sri Chakra (a design for meditation with sacred syllables carved on a metal plate worshipped in the temple) that was installed there were also brought to them, and UG was allowed to touch them. That honour too is not normally accorded even to the Maharajah. From the moment he stepped into the inner sanctum, UG was feeling the effect of the energy that was there and appeared to be in a semi-conscious state. The Sri Chakra and Panchajanya stirred the energies in him. Mahesh later said that he had seen on UG's forehead a swelling of the skin in the form of the vertical marks worn by Vaishnavaites (*namas*). The swelling had remained for a length of time, and there was also another mark evident around UG's neck in the form of a serpent.

'When asked about the nature of these swellings, UG's explanations, as always, were of a scientific nature. He says that the worship that was done with great devotion and devoutness, and the *Yantras* (mystical diagrams on metal plates) that were installed there all fill the area with powerful vibrations. These swellings are an end-result of his body mechanisms reacting to these energy vibrations. They show up for a little while and then subside. UG says there is no need to attribute any more spiritual significance to such manifestations. "Such things happen to me even when I am on the toilet," says UG.'[57]

In one of my meetings with UG in January 2002, when I asked him about the incident, he talked of it in a rather clinical way as if it were a visit not to a temple but to a barber shop, and pooh-poohed Chandrashekhar's mystical interpretation of it.

'But, sir,' I persisted, 'temples, churches and mosques are spaces invested with tremendous energy . . .'

He didn't let me complete the sentence. 'Thought-induced energy, sir,' he said.

Then, to my utter shock, he hissed, '*Chamundi* . . . *chi-mundi* . . . *chi munda.*'

The manner in which he dismissed the Goddess, calling her *chi munda*, meaning a widow with a shaven head, seemed not only blasphemous but arrogance of the highest order. If the terrible one happened to be there, she would surely have fled.

It seems for UG this is all fairly simple and natural. In the state of 'undivided consciousness' even God is a contamination!

12

Mysticism Demystified

All experiences belong to the past. A new experience is a contradiction in terms, for experience involves recognition, recognition entails memory, and memory is of the past. The so-called 'ever present', or living in the present, is but a fiction. You can never know or experience the present, says UG; it is always in terms of the past.

However, for a long time now, believers and theologians, as well as philosophers and scholars of mysticism, have interpreted mystical experience as something beyond memory, beyond the mundane, even beyond the 'natural'. In particular, classical scholars (such as Underhill, Otto, and Zaehner) have interpreted mystical experience as 'pure', 'unmediated', 'numinous' union with God, with the Absolute, bearing no relation whatsoever to the culture and social conditions in which a mystic lives; in short, no connection with the past. There is a strong belief that a mystic with God-experience, comes into possession of truth and wisdom and becomes an embodiment of compassion. Further, writers on religion and mysticism are of the opinion that despite different backgrounds, there is something common among the mystics, in the sense that they all experience a higher truth that is not accessible to non-mystics, that they all seek and experience God or Truth but express the experience differently because of the difference in their social background and language.

These assumptions need to be examined. Is a mystic's experience truly 'unmediated', 'pure'? What does experience of God, or communion or union with God mean? And which God, one may ask? Is any experience possible at all wherein recognition, memory and knowledge are not involved?

Atheists and sceptics in all ages have, from certain rational perspectives, questioned religious teachings. But in modern times, from within the religious framework, it was JK who was probably the first to question most vehemently yet creatively all religious or spiritual authorities, the authority of the scriptures, as also the tremendous value and significance attached to mystical experiences. He said:

> 'All experiences must be questioned, whether your own or of another. Experience is the continuation of a bundle of memories, which translates the response to a challenge according to its conditioning. That is, experience is, is it not, to respond to a challenge, and that experience can only respond according to its background. If you are a Hindu, or a Muslim, or a Christian, you are conditioned by your culture, by your religion, and that background projects every form of experience. So we must question, doubt . . . especially the so-called religious, spiritual experiences . . .'[58]

A critical consideration of reports of mystical experiences (often given by mystics themselves) should, in the light of what JK and UG have said, reveal that these experiences are basically projections of one's own mind, that they are all invariably culturally conditioned or 'thought induced'. Such experiences are not necessarily 'liberating', as is generally made out; on the contrary, they could be imprisoning in the sense that the interpretations of these experiences often reinforce religious authority and thereby block a genuine search for truth and freedom. Interestingly, recent studies on mysticism [59] show in clear and unambiguous terms that all mystical experiences are conditioned responses, although these studies, unlike JK or UG, do not reject the spiritual value attached to such experiences.

Generally, mystics are seen as great religious rebels on the one hand, and on the other as embodiments of true and genuine spiritual search and experience as prescribed by the scriptures. They are seen as rebels when they appear to undermine the spiritual authority of orthodoxy and place their own experience above the doctrines of religious institutions. Over the centuries, particularly in Christianity and Islam, when the experiences and teachings of mystics were seen as too radical a challenge to the established spiritual authority, they were excommunicated or even put to death. However, a critical examination of the lives of mystics reveals that they were most often rather conservative than radical.

All experiences, whether ordinary and mundane or artistic and mystical, are dependent upon or informed by the history, culture and tradition in which a person functions. In other words, it is romanticism to think that a mystic is independent of the culture and religious traditions within which he lives. His or her experiences are no more unmediated than the experiences of a person who goes to a temple or watches a game of soccer. This might seem like an extreme position, a trivialization of mystical experience; it is not.

In deconstructing the character of mysticism, Steven T. Katz writes: '. . . there are *no* pure (i.e. unmediated) experiences. Neither mystical experience nor a more ordinary form of experience gives any indication, or any grounds for believing, that they are unmediated. That is to say, all experience is processed through, organized by, and makes itself available to us in extremely complex epistemological ways. The notion of unmediated experience seems, if not self-contradictory, empty at best. This seems to me to be true even with regard to the experiences of those ultimate objects of concern with which mystics have intercourse, e.g., God, Being, Nirvana, etc., and this "mediated" aspect of all our experience seems an inescapable feature of any epistemological inquiry, including the inquiry into mysticism. Yet this constitutive epistemic element has been overlooked or underplayed by every investigator of our subject. Thus, contrary to the prevailing scholarly view— that of James, Stace, Underhill, Otto, and even Zaehner and Smart—we must recognize that a right understanding of mysticism is not just a question of studying reports of the mystic after the experiential event but also of acknowledging that the experience itself, as well as the form in which it is reported, is shaped by concepts which the mystic brings to, and which shape, his experience.'[60]

To be more specific, orthodox Jews, Christians and Muslims do not seek union with God, because losing one's identity and becoming one with the 'cosmic ground' is a deadly heresy in these teachings.[61] Hence, a Christian mystic does not experience neutral something or nothingness, or Brahman; he or she experiences Jesus, the Trinity, Christ, or the Godhead. Similarly, a Hindu experiences the Higher Self, atman, Brahman, unlike a Buddhist who experiences sunyata. Since in Islam it is blasphemous to visualize God in human form, a Sufi would experience God as Light, as the Mystery of mysteries, as the Spirit of spirits, in contradistinction to, say, a Christian mystic who would see Jesus as the Christ. A Muslim would respect Jesus as a prophet, but never see Jesus as the Christ.

It is not as if mystical experiences are predetermined, but they are conditioned by one's past. For that is the character of religious experience, it is Koranized, Christianized or Hinduized, depending upon one's allegiance and training. A person exposed to, say, both Christianity and Hinduism might see or experience Christ in Krishna and Krishna in Christ, but that would only indicate another kind of affiliation. The same may be said about Zen, considered so mind-boggling, and subversive. For Zen too is a tradition, dependent and constructed upon the paradox of the koan. The paradox of the 'sound of one hand clapping' is seen as essential to satori, illumination. It is a sophisticated method which uses a different language and technique compared to other conventional discourses, in order to shape and produce 'the ultimately translinguistic character of Zen mystical experience'.[62]

The stories of mystics, their mystical experiences and their languages, therefore, only express different mystical worlds, different cosmologies, which are influenced and shaped by the scriptures and the experiences of the 'founders' of religions, which are internalized, taken as ultimate models to be followed and imitated. To put it differently, all religious experiences are only recreations and re-enactments of experiences that are already there, which is the past. And these mystical experiences, which are shaped by the past, in turn, further strengthen that very past.

Steven T. Katz expresses this fact cogently: 'Though Christian mystics will adopt St Paul's language and speak of being "born again in Christ", of "suffering with Christ", of "dying with Christ", of "rising with Christ", transforming these incidents into existential experiences, this interiorizing, this contemporizing, this mystical mimetic re-enactment is possible only because of the dominant belief that there was a historic Jesus who was born of a Virgin by God, that this Jesus did suffer the torments of Good Friday described by the synoptic authors, that Jesus did die only to be resurrected in the body on Easter Sunday, and that this Jesus ascended to Heaven to co-rule the world with the other Persons of the Trinity.'

There should be no doubt whatsoever of the significant role these great religious *models* play in all religious as well as mystical experiences. Just as Christ becomes a supreme model for Christian mystics, so do the religious-mystical models of the Buddha, Krishna and Mohammad for other mystics. Therefore, 'in sum,' Katz argues, 'our deconstruction and re-conceptualization suggests that *models* play an important role in providing our map of reality and of what is real and, thus, contribute heavily to the creation of experience—I repeat, to the *creation* of experience. This is a fact to be pondered, and pondered again.'[63]

Indeed, when we ponder deeply, we realize that there is something truly extraordinary about thought, and the power of thought is such that it can create almost anything, even solid objects, and touch it, feel it, experience it as something very real. To use UG's words, these experiences are all 'thought-induced', God, bliss, and beatitude being the most profound of its inventions. And these experiences, created by thought, further strengthen thought, which is knowledge. It is a vicious circle, like a dog chasing its own tail, going round and round and round! 'Whatever you experience,' asserts UG, 'peace, bliss, silence, beatitude, ecstasy, joy, God knows what—will be old, second-hand. You already have knowledge about all of these things. The fact that you are in a blissful state or in a state of tremendous silence means that you know about it. You must know a thing in order to experience it. That knowledge is nothing marvellous or metaphysical; 'bench', 'bag', 'red bag', is the knowledge. Knowledge is something which is put into you by somebody else, and he got that from somebody else; it is not yours. Can you experience a simple thing like that bench that is sitting across from you? No, you only experience the knowledge you have about it. And the knowledge has come from some outside agency, always. You think the thoughts of your society, feel the feelings of your society and experience the experiences of your society; there is no new experience.'

Surely it would be difficult for religious scholars or mystics, to accept what Katz says and UG asserts. Still, one might ask: Is there really nothing to mystical experiences? How does one then understand the lives of mystics whose lives have been transformed after whatever they have experienced? And how do we account for the tremendous influence mystics have had on the religious consciousness of people?

These are tricky questions. Nevertheless, to say that mystical experiences are culturally conditioned or thought-induced does not necessarily mean there is no significance whatsoever to these experiences. However, we need to point out that these experiences are still in the field of duality. A mystic might experience something beyond his or her ordinary sense of time and space, and bring home a sense of wonder and mystery, but it is actually not outside of time and space, or his or her cultural background.

While mystical experiences can be liberating to the extent that they help one to break out of the tyranny of religious or scriptural authority, most often this is not the case. More often than not, a mystic falls under the illusion that he or she has come upon the ultimate truth and becomes yet another authority, another 'model' to be imposed on others.

UG responds to this tricky issue thus: 'The saint or mystic is a second-hand man who experiences what the sages have talked about, so he is still in the field of duality, whereas the sages or seers are functioning in the undivided state of consciousness. The mystic experience is an extraordinary one because it is not an intellectual experience; it helps them to look at things differently, to feel differently, to experience things differently and to interpret the statements of the sages and seers for others.

'The world should be grateful to the saints rather than to the sages. Had it not been for the saints, the sages would have been clean forgotten long ago. The sages don't depend upon any authority; what they say *is* the authority. This the sages talked about, and the saints—some of them—had experiences, and this became a part of their experience. They tried to share that (experience) through music and all kinds of things. But this is not an experience which can be shared with somebody else; this is not an experience at all.'

We are grateful to the saints and mystics who share their experiences and kick us into questioning all our assumptions and keep alive that great yearning for freedom. But, like UG, we cannot also help but be critical of those saints, mystics, and religious leaders who exercise great spiritual authority, who not only interpret the sages and the scriptures in exclusive and dogmatic ways, but also give people the impression that they have arrived at a final understanding of everything and become autocratic gurus. A wise saint or mystic, however, would see through this mischief of the mind, this power politics of the mind, and would move on. For he or she would know that mystical experience, contrary to the popular understanding that it is something transcendental, holy and liberating, could well-nigh be imprisoning. And so, he or she would refuse to privilege his or her experience, and refuse to convert that into a teaching.

13

Gurus and Holy Business

According to the Upanishads, a guru is a dispeller of darkness, of ignorance. But one wonders if such a being exists anywhere on this earth. Perhaps it only means that a genuine guru is one who leads a student up the hill and lets him see for himself, or leads him to the water and lets him drink and quench his thirst. Maybe even that is not true. Maybe a genuine guru would only point and say, 'Look, there is the hill, and there is the lake. Now you are on your own; whatever happens, learn from it, and don't ever come back to me again.'

Such teachers do not teach or preach, not because they have made a conscious choice, but simply because they cannot. For they know what it means to live, to be honest with oneself, and to respect others. They know that wisdom and virtue cannot be taught. So they try and live what they believe in, live by what they have discovered for and by themselves; the way they lead their lives itself radiates and affects the lives of others and the world in positive and creative ways.

In other words, the genuine ones regard religion as something deeply personal and sacred. They know God and compassion are not something to be talked about, much less something to be taught. For they know that they do not know. It is a deep search, a lifelong search. And such people, who are truly embodiments of wisdom and love, never climb on to a platform to teach. For they know it is not something to be taught, something to be capitalized upon to become gurus, although they may be ready to share their many insights and experiences, and doubts too, as fellow travellers.

These are the genuine teachers who teach without teaching. They are, of course, small in number. But phoney ones who pose as gurus are aplenty, who insist on teaching you and want to change you, who are proud to wear the mantle of guru and strut around the world, giving talks and conducting workshops on meditation and spirituality. Such gurus exist because there is a demand for them, because of the widespread implicit belief that *they* know the way, that they have solutions to all our problems. But in actuality, gurus are part of our problem, and they succeed only in complicating our problems further. Still, we go to them, because the need to follow someone, follow the 'head sheep', seems to be deeply ingrained in our psyche.

Therefore, the problem is not in the guru, but in us. 'You want to smoke cigarettes, and there are always peddlers selling their own brands of cigarettes,' says UG. 'Each one says that his is the one and only one, the best cigarette; and someone comes around and says that his is nicotine-free. So the problem is not the *gurus*, but you. If you don't want to smoke, all these brands will disappear. These *gurus* are the worst egotists the world has ever seen. All *gurus* are welfare organizations providing petty experiences to their followers. The guru *game* is a profitable industry: try and make two million dollars a year any other way.'

And then UG goes on to add: 'I don't want to be called a guru, a god-man, or a religious teacher. It bothers me just as you would be bothered if I called you a thief or a crook.'

Does this mean gurus are only crooks and frauds? Isn't there anything positive about them at all? Thousands of gurus and their followers would surely be up in arms against such criticism, which would, of course, only prove the chauvinistic and reactionary nature of all teachings.

One needs only to pause for a while and ask oneself seriously: Can one really teach love and wisdom? One can understand the idea of teaching, say, carpentry, swimming, dancing, mathematics or astronomy and other such subjects and skills. But can anyone teach goodness, kindness, let alone compassion? More importantly, why does one want to teach any virtue for that matter? Could it be that gurus, too, are not outside of conflict and greed, and by accepting followers, are seeking some symbolic security, or are in search of power?

Virtue cannot be taught, declared Arthur Schopenhauer. Nietzsche, who concurred, and understood the underlying danger too well, warned against all gurus, all teachers who teach perfect happiness, order, paradise, by way of imposing their grand ideas, their visions on people, which eventually lead to what he called caustically but rightly, 'the hangman and the gallows'.

They are the great systemizers, the codifiers, the impostors, and they are driven by what both Schopenhauer and Nietzsche would call the will to power.

Looked at that way, all teachers are dictators, and all teaching is geared towards social engineering.

The worst among the lot are the religious or spiritual teachers. The other ones, the managerial, the political and the intellectual, are but an extension of the spiritual guru.

The division of life into spiritual and material has been the handiwork of the spiritual teachers, into which trap the others too have willy-nilly fallen. But the spiritual man is the first culprit. 'The so-called spiritual authority is an evil thing,' raged JK. 'And that is one of the major causes of disorder, because that is what has divided the world into various forms of religions, into various forms of ideologies.'

UG, of course, turns the heat on JKites and rejects JK too, yet he does concur with JK on this artificial division of life into spiritual and material. UG never tires of saying, '. . . unfortunately we have divided life into material and spiritual—that is the greatest and biggest escape that we have created. It's all one; you can't divide life into material and spiritual. That is where we have gone wrong.' Putting it differently, he declares: 'Religion has placed before us the ideal of perfect man and that has put the whole thing on the wrong path.'

Religious gurus thrive on this artificial division. They bewilder and torture people with their 'transcendental' ideas and charming smiles; they beat them into feeling inadequate, worthless, selfish, sinful and guilty. They first sow the seed of conflict in the minds of people, and then dedicate themselves to serving their sinful, ignorant, unfortunate brethren. They are the 'vessel and vehicle' of religious thinking, which is in its very origin and nature divisive. If religion is a neurological problem, as UG would say, the religious teacher is the one who is pathologically sick.

In his book, *The Light at the Centre, Context and Pretext of Modern Mysticism*, written almost thirty years ago, Agehananda Bharati, a swami of rare honesty, lays bare the many lies and frauds that religious gurus indulge in. His rigorous yet trenchant analysis of mystical experiences, wherein he discusses his own 'zero experience', as also drug-induced mystical states, offers a rational, well-balanced yet no-nonsense view of mysticism. Mystical experience, Agehananda Bharati says, is value-free and non-ontological. This assertion is made in response to the views of scholars and apologists for religion, and sometimes mystics themselves, who erroneously attribute ontological status or a priori meaning to mystical experience. To give teeth to his argument, Agehananda Bharati quotes Nagarjuna, the great Buddhist sage, who denied ontological status to mystical experience. Further, he also refers to the authority of Patanjali, who discusses the nature of mystical experiences, even saying, '*Isvara*, i.e., the divine person or object contemplated upon, is a crutch, a construct.'

There is no experience that is not related to the senses. All experiences involve the senses, and so, as UG would assert, and Agehananda Bharati, who is no stranger to mystical experience, would argue, all experiences are sensuous—even the so-called purely transcendental experiences. The gurus, mystics, and scholars would not agree, because of the emotional and intellectual investment they have made in it. Or, as Agehananda Bharati would say, it could be because 'a practitioner of the art (of mysticism), whose use of the pleasure principle is so rarefied or so highly submerged in exegetical or homiletic language, that the hedonistic ground remains all but invisible'.[64]

If we have to look at this issue from a slightly different perspective, the problem with spirituality or spiritual pedagogy is that it is born out of the classical dichotomy between matter and spirit, body and soul, God and the world, good and evil, and all such binary or dualistic thinking.

Gurus who play God or prophet, perpetuate this dangerous dichotomy, and make a mess of people's lives. They interpret mystical experiences and religious texts for use in non-religious contexts. They project religious practice or spirituality as the panacea for all the ills of society, and project the mystic or the spiritual person as a perfect human being, as a model to be followed by others. They do this either because it has become their second nature to lie, or the self-deception is so deep that they do not realize it. Commenting upon this fraud, Agehananda Bharati writes: 'There have been mystics who were good carpenters, but there have been much better carpenters who were not mystics; there have been mystics who have been poets, but there have been a great many poets who were not mystics . . .' Agehananda Bharati's argument here is that mystical practice does not confer any special skills on a mystic or a guru. It does not necessarily make him or her more intelligent, or a better historian, psychologist, philosopher, or even a better human being, much less a model for others to follow. Therefore, it should not come as a shock to come across gurus, even mystic–gurus, who are misogynists or rapists, gluttons and dullards, chauvinists and communalists, idiots and megalomaniacs.

But the con game goes on, and we are only too willing, out of our own anxiety, confusion and insecurity, to be taken in by spiritual frauds. Compared with modern gurus, the old, traditional gurus may appear simple and vulnerable. The modern ones are quite sophisticated, articulate and charismatic, and have even taken over the role of scholars and religious apologists. A close look at their discourses leaves us in no doubt that they teach a hotchpotch of mysticism, science, occultism, pure common sense and management philosophy. They are the CEOs of modern spirituality, the likes of Sri Sri Ravishankar and Deepak Chopra. They are good salesmen, who do some good to some people, while, of course, making sure they themselves live in great comfort and style.

Practices like meditation, asanas and pranayama do not make one spiritual any more than the practice of science makes one a better human being. Such practices may have a therapeutic value and effect (just as jogging and physical exercises do); they can help one relax, become more effective and productive, alert and intelligent. Similarly, Vedanta, Yoga, Zen, Hare Krishna and Transcendental Meditation are all cultural practices that could serve some social purpose. But these pose no danger to the status quo, no danger to the dominant ideologies that divide humanity and become a source of great violence. In fact, they only domesticate the energies of people, never encouraging one to question, reflect and experiment on one's own, and become a light unto oneself. Rather, they only abort whatever potential there may be for an individual to become an Individual.

To quote Agehananda Bharati again: 'If what the swamis teach people helps them in any manner—by relieving anxiety, diminishing mental agony, overcoming fright, fatigue, nausea, or mitigating despair—then there is merit in these teachings. I have no doubt that some such therapeutic action does indeed take place where the swamis roam. But when the swamis claim that their teachings can give people omniscience, "realization", i.e., zero experience, and that acceptance of their teachings will usher in world peace, then the swamis are frauds or self-deceivers.'[65]

UG would trace this self-deception and fraud to the traditional dichotomy between the spiritual and the material, and more importantly, to the (non-existent) ideal of a perfect man created by religious thinking, which is modelled after the founders of religions and religious masters. In his own words:

Perfection and absolutes are false. You are trying to imitate and relate your behaviour according to these absolutes, and it is falsifying you.

The spiritual people are the most dishonest people. I am emphasizing that the foundation upon which the whole of spirituality has been built is false. I am emphasizing that. If *there is no spirit*, then the whole talk of spirituality is bosh and nonsense. You can't come into your own being until you are free from the whole thing surrounding the concept of 'self'. To be really on your own, the whole basis of spiritual life, which is erroneous, has to be destroyed. It does not mean that you become fanatical or violent, burning down temples, tearing down the idols, destroying the holy books, like a bunch of drunks. It is not that at all. It is a bonfire inside of you. Everything that mankind has thought and experienced must   go.

By using the models of Jesus, Buddha, or Krishna we have destroyed the possibility of nature throwing up unique individuals. The one who recommends that—to be like someone else and forget your own natural uniqueness—no matter how saintly that person may be, is putting you on the wrong track. It is like the blind leading the blind.

14

Avatars as Ultimate Models

All ancient cultures believed that battles could not be won without the help of gods or divine forces.[66] Several of the Vedic hymns are invocations of and prayers to gods—Indra, Agni, Vayu and so on—to come to the aid of people both in their pursuit of livelihood and in their battles against their enemies. Just as in Hindu myths, in Greek myths too, we find gods taking sides with humans and participating in their affairs. These gods were biased and protective gods, whose existence was tied up with the fate of the human beings they sided with. They were not gods of knowledge or wisdom, or even of love. Those came later.

The idea of the Messiah, which is again found in all ancient cultures, was basically an extension of the communal or tribal God, who protected his people against their enemies, against the so-called forces of 'evil' or oppression.

To put it differently, a Messiah represents God's technology of intervention in the lives of his subjects, in order to establish good over evil—evil often being the 'other'. In the Occidental context, the Messiah has always been in the shape of a messenger, while in the Oriental cultures it is in the form of an incarnation (avatar) of an aspect of God or Divinity itself. It is only over a period of time that this idea of Messiah was modified and expanded to mean divine intervention for the welfare and salvation of the whole of humanity. But since historically there has been more than one Messiah, signifying more than one God, one evil, one way, and one teaching or revelation, this has also resulted in a clash of ideas, symbols and visions; a clash between the so-called Truths.

Reflecting upon the causes of conflict and violence among the various religious groups, Joseph Campbell talks about the needless conflict and antagonism among three great religions: Judaism,

Christianity, and Islam. Each group says, 'We are the chosen group, and we have God' and they can't get on together. This is because the three of them have three different names for the same biblical God and are stuck with their metaphor. In Joseph Campbell's own words, 'They haven't allowed the circle that surrounds them to open. It is a closed circle. . . Look at Ireland. A group of Protestants was moved to Ireland in the seventeenth century by Cromwell, and it never has opened up to the Catholic majority there. The Catholics and Protestants represent two totally different social systems, two different ideals . . . Each needs its own myth, all the way. Love thine enemy. Open up. Don't judge. All things are Buddha things. It is there in the myth. It is already there.'[67]

It is, of course, there in the myths, the plural ways of seeing and being in the world, and the great ambivalence that is 'living'. Apologists for religion might argue, it is there in the teachings of the messiahs too. But is this really so? UG is ruthless when he says, 'Messiahs have only messed up the world.' They have not only divided the world, they continue to be the source of great conflict and violence in the world. 'Why do you want to exonerate these messiahs?' asks UG.

What do we do, then? Dump them in the dustbin of history! Is this possible?

Christianity is undoubtedly the greatest messianic religion, followed by Islam. But the beginnings of the idea of the Messiah are to be seen in Judaism, which Christianity took over, after it had gained power over its people.

In Judaic tradition, messiah meant 'any person or thing possessing of great holiness and sacred power'.[68] Later, the term was inflated to mean the Anointed One, the messenger, the one sent by Jehovah or the One True God, who would avenge the suffering of the Jews, protect them, redeem them and make them great and most powerful on earth.

The Bible records a succession of kings and prophets, including David, Solomon, Isaiah, Jeremiah, and Ezekiel, who all adopted 'a military-messianic lifestyle'. Considering the bloody history of the period, one couldn't have expected anything else. The armies of the Egyptians, Assyrians, Babylonians, Persians, Greeks and

Romans often took part in bloody wars, burning temples and cities, looting, plundering, and indulging in terrible massacres.

It was in the midst of this war-infested world, with several messiahs crying themselves hoarse for revenge, for a new political and religious order, that Jesus was born, apparently one of a line of vengeful prophets, soon to be transformed into a messenger of love and peace. It is indeed a paradox that the Prince of Peace should arrive while the military-messianic consciousness was still accelerating, expanding, soaring towards the untarnished ecstasy of Yahweh's grace.[69]

Many biblical scholars find it impossible to reject the fact that, despite our image of Jesus as a peaceful messiah, he was crucified because he was seen as a political revolutionary. There are, of course, disturbing contradictions and nagging ambiguities in the story. For it is quite possible to quote from the Bible to show that Jesus was as much a political radical, as one who taught forgiveness and love. Perhaps, in that war-torn world, it was time for the gospel of love to emerge, from the bleeding wounds and grief-stricken hearts of the people.

However, several readings indicate that it was Paul who laid the foundation for the cult of peaceful messianism. And it was Paul's willingness to baptize even non-Jews, and later the emperor Constantine's adoption of Christianity, that were hugely responsible for the spread of Christianity.

The first gospel was written by St. Mark some forty years after the death of Jesus, and it took nearly 400 years before the then already established church canonized Jesus as Christ, as divine. Karen Armstrong writes: '. . . the doctrine that Jesus had been God in human form was not finalized until the fourth century. The development of Christian belief in the Incarnation was a gradual, complex process. At his baptism he had been called the Son of God by a voice from heaven but this was probably simply a confirmation that he was the beloved messiah. There was nothing particularly unusual about such a proclamation . . .'

Once the proclamation was made, the military-messianic consciousness that had hid itself, as it were, behind the utterly new teachings of love, of the Kingdom of God, or of eternal life beyond the grave, began to surface. This apparently other-worldly religion—

with its almighty yet compassionate God and with its profound, historically significant teaching, 'Love thy neighbour as thyself'—would wage new battles against other gods and other beliefs. A once defeated and oppressed people were determind to destroy all other structures of belief and power, usurping for themselves enormous power over mind and spirit.

The past has a way of working itself into the future; old gods don't die, they transmigrate and take on new forms and names. Whoever said 'history repeats itself' was very clever, but there is indeed an element of truth in it. There is no disjunction in history, for there is no disjunction in human consciousness. On the one hand, George W. Bush of America declares war against Saddam Hussein's Iraq, and against Afghanistan, in the name of 'freedom', and on the other hand Islamic terrorists sacrifice themselves as human bombs against American imperialism and the evil West (for a seat in heaven), but what is in operation is the same consciousness, the same messianic zeal. It is a clash of gods, a battle between two different images of good and evil, but born from the same source.

UG interacting with a group of admirers

Talking about good and evil, about the nature of religious
traditions, UG once remarked that there are only two religions in
the world: Judaism and Hinduism. All the other religions were born
out of 'reactions' to these two major religious concepts. He also
pointed out the difference between the East and the West, the
difference between their cosmologies, their views in relation to the
ideas of God, of sorrow, of good and evil, and freedom.

In his study of the mythologies of the world, Joseph Campbell
points out more or less the same thing, though he replaces Hebrew
tradition with Zoroastrianism to explain the origin of the myth of
good and evil in the West. The idea of life as a conflict between
the forces of darkness and the forces of light, Joseph Campbell
avers, 'is a Zoroastrian idea, which has come over into Judaism
and Christianity'.[70]

The Persian prophet Zoroaster (thought to have lived sometime
between 1200 and 550 BC) was the earliest prophet of the mythology
of cosmic restoration. If Ahura Mazda symbolized Righteous Order
and Light, Angra Mainyu represented the evil principle, also
referred to as 'the Deceiver, principle of the lie, who, when all had
been excellently made, entered into it in every particle'. Consequently,
Joseph Campbell writes, 'the world is a compound wherein good
and evil, light and dark, wisdom and violence, are contending for
a victory. And the privilege and duty of each man—who, himself,
as a part of creation, is a compound of good and evil—is to elect,
voluntarily, to engage in the battle in the interest of the light. It
is supposed that with the birth of Zoroaster, twelve thousand years
following the creation of the world, a decisive turn was given the
conflict in favour of the good, and that when he returns, after
another twelve millennia, in the person of the messiah Saoshyant,
there will take place a final battle and cosmic conflagration,
through which the principle of darkness and the lie will be undone.
Whereafter, all will be light, there will be no further history, and
the kingdom of God (Ahura Mazda) will have been established in
its pristine form forever.'[71]

Further, according to Joseph Campbell, the first historic
manifestation of this mythic order, of this concept of the battle
between light and darkness, and the coming of a Messiah to restore
the pristine order, was in the Achaemenian Empire of Cyrus the

Great (529 BC) and Darius I (521–486 BC), which later spread to India and Greece. The second manifestation of it was to be seen in the Hebrew religion, then in Christianity, and lastly in Islam.[72]

How this mythic order, this Zoroastrian notion of good and evil was later dealt with in the East is the story of Eastern religions. Today we can only have theories as to how this happened and how the two major modes of knowing and experiencing the world, Eastern and Western, emerged on this planet. But that is of little help to our situation today.

However, it must be said that the idea of the 'Messiah' is a peculiarly Western idea, a product of the Western mode of thinking. If, at the beginning, there was pristine order, everything existed as per the divine law, and the human 'fall' due to knowledge wrecked the divine order, then the coming of the Messiah becomes absolutely necessary to repair that damage, defeat 'evil', and restore human life and the world to its pristine order and glory. Hence, Moses, Christ, Mohammad, Marx, Lenin, and interventionist politics. And so the holy wars, and all the wars in the name of God and Freedom.

The idea of the 'avatar' in the East is not the same as the Western idea of the Messiah, although they are regarded as interchangeable today. In Sanskrit, avatar means 'to come down', or the descent of the divine, and it is generally used with reference to the ten incarnations of Vishnu in different animal and human forms. The myth of the avatar reveals that every time Vishnu descends in human form, he does so to avert a crisis, when there is great danger to humanity. The notion of liberation or moksha, and the establishment of dharma or the socio-religious order are not necessarily linked to the idea of the avatar. Whatever truth or dharma an avatar might express or establish are only relative, specific to the historical context of the avatar. He is not a giver of eternal values or truth, for all values and notion of truth are relative, bound by specific time and space.

In the Bhagavad Gita, Krishna says:

Whenever dharma decays and *adharma* is in ascendancy, I manifest myself. For the protection of the good, for the destruction of the wicked, and for establishing dharma firmly, I am born in every age . . .

But what is this dharma that Krishna establishes and what *adharma* does he destroy? What, in fact, does the story of the Mahabharata reveal? Krishna's role in the life and times of the Kuru dynasty hardly fits the image of the popular notion of the avatar. He is not an angry, vengeful God, eager to establish a new order; rather, he comes through as a shrewd, enigmatic yet charming God who suffers and participates in the trials and tribulations, triumphs and defeats of the Pandavas and the Kauravas. He seldom directly involves himself in the bloody war between the cousins. He knows the Kauravas are not an incarnation of 'evil' any more than the Pandavas are the representatives of 'good'. It is a great drama, a great epic about the human condition, and Krishna the avatar, after offering insights (at times delightful, at times disturbing) into the sorrowful human condition, succeeds only in presiding over an age coming to an end. There is destruction all round, yet with a smile that shows supreme understanding of sorrow and death, quietly, he too goes away.

So it seems that an avatar comes to oversee the end of an age, and thus mark the beginning of a new one. However, this 'new' age is not an utterly new beginning, for there is no such thing; it is only a revaluation and modification of the old, as UG would say. The past never dies or goes away completely, for, the past makes up man, the self-conscious human being! This is not how we generally understand the role of avatars or messiahs. The message of an avatar is limited, relative, specific to the age, and his lifestyle is his own, not something to be imitated or used as a model for a social order. The avatars certainly work as a catalyst for the emergence or development of a radical consciousness, which, over a period of time, degenerates into rigid or dogmatic ways. And we discover that the so-called radical is not radical enough, and there is need yet for another big change, yet another radical revaluation of values.

Seen from this perspective, the present-day avatars of the world are like a practical, rather monstrous, joke! India, the so-called spiritual land, boasts of having many avatars, Sri Satya Sai Baba being the grandest of them all. His followers believe that he is not a mere incarnation of an *aspect* of divinity but, like Lord Krishna, the total incarnation of God on earth.

Sai Baba is famous for performing miracles. He produces ash and trinkets out of thin air. He is believed to have cured incurable diseases. There is certainly an element of universality in his teaching, in the sense that he talks of love and brotherhood, of different religions as only different paths leading to the one, essential or universal truth or God.

He has his detractors, too. Christian zealots dub him the 'prince of darkness', while rationalists dismiss him as a mere trickster or magician. The many socio-economic activities initiated in villages and the hospitals built by the organization he heads surely benefit thousands of people, but what is so extraordinary or godly about that? Can Sai Baba stop war, arrest environmental pollution, put an end to terrorism, find the cure for HIV-AIDS, and help the world overcome poverty—can he help humankind overcome all its problems of existence?

'What is he doing, sir? What is he doing?' demands UG. 'What good is that—miracles? Can he perform the miracle of all miracles? Can he transform the whole of life, the whole way of *thinking*? Can he do that? If he is really the avatar who possesses knowledge about any as yet undiscovered laws, isn't it his solemn duty to inform the world, putting mankind on the right track and thus saving it from its inevitable doom, instead of producing trinkets and ash? If he can perform that miracle, I'll be the first one to salute him.'

Having said that, UG firmly asserts that no avatars can really help us, much less can they be used as models of behaviour. In fact, UG would argue that we should give up the idea of the 'perfect individual', our belief in avatars as 'perfect or ultimate models', for no such creatures ever existed in the past or shall exist in the future. By adopting the models of Jesus, Buddha, or Mohammad we have falsified our lives and destroyed the possibility of nature throwing up unique individuals.

In other words, the mistake lies with us, in wanting to follow some teacher, and in thinking of gurus, and avatars as models of perfection. Such perfection doesn't exist. No individual's life, however noble, profound or spiritual, can be a model for others. On the contrary, these models become a stumbling block to our growth and understanding, for a free and open inquiry into the predicament of the human condition.

As UG says, 'It's not the avatars that can help; it's the individual that can help. It is an individual problem, so it is not the avatar who can help. There is a saviour in every individual, and if that saviour is brought out, blossoms, then perhaps there is a hope.'

Looking at the avatars from a different perspective, Bill Moyers, in his conversations with Joseph Campbell, following Campbell's line of thinking on religious heroes or avatars, says: 'The tribal or local heroes perform their deeds for a single folk, and universal heroes like Mohammed, Jesus, and Buddha bring the message from afar. These heroes of religion came back with the wonder of God, not with a blueprint of God.'[73]

15

Religion in a Secular Mode

UG is extremely critical of politics today because, to him, it is hopelessly, relentlessly pushing humanity in the direction of self-destruction. Yet, he accepts the inescapability of politics and even admits that if the trend has to be reversed (which seems almost impossible), the hope lies within politics itself, unless the biological sciences come up with some antidote to man's self-destructive nature, or a large-scale biological mutation occurs that cleanses man of his self-destructive tendency.

He is quick to point out that 'politics is the warty outgrowth of religious thinking', which, in the first place, had put humanity on the wrong path. What he means is that the ideas of good and evil, sin and redemption, reward and punishment, justice and order, are all woven into the fabric of politics. In short, the religious idea of 'becoming' gets transposed to 'social change' in politics, and the psychological engineering of religion is supplemented with social engineering in politics.

Not only politics but even our fundamental social and cultural values are rooted in religious ideas. To illustrate the point, the great European Enlightenment tradition and culture, out of which grew modern politics and 'modernity', was an offshoot of Judeo-Christian cosmology. Interestingly, in his *The End of Modernity*, Gianni Vattimo writes: 'Only modernity, in developing and elaborating in strictly worldly and secular terms the Judeo-Christian heritage— i.e., the idea of history as the history of salvation, articulated in terms of creation, sin, redemption, and waiting for the Last Judgement—gives ontological weight to history and a determining sense to our position within it.'[74]

A deeper analysis of Marxism, the dominant political discourse of the last two centuries, reveals clearly how religious ideas were recycled as utterly new, revolutionary insights; more specifically, how the Judeo-Christian 'themes and threads' were woven into its philosophy. While post-modernist critics and feminists more or less agree that Freudian concepts have their roots in Western metaphysics, they do not say the same, at least not strongly enough, about Marx, though Marxian concepts too are derived from Judeo-Christian metaphysics, perhaps because Marxism continues to be seen as paradigmatic, pro-people politics. It seems to be the need of intellectuals of many shades and persuasions to belong, at least broadly, to the 'left', which only shows the dominance of Marxism as the master narrative, and Marx as the ultimate guru of emancipatory politics.

But this man who characterized religion as the 'opium of the people', as the 'sigh of the oppressed', did not sufficiently take into consideration the wily nature of religion. Perhaps he believed he had killed, or at least initiated, the destruction of the demon called religion with his weapon of historical materialism. This was an illusion, for, as myths tell us, to swallow the demon is to become the demon!

In a sense, Marx can be viewed as Christ come back into the modern world! He embodies the resurrection of basically the same religious spirit and ideology, though under a different garb, a different language. It could not have been otherwise, for not only Marx, but all thinkers cannot help but build their philosophy upon their past. As Jacques Derrida would say, 'To be . . . means . . . to inherit. All questions about being or what one is to be (or not to be) are questions of inheritance . . . We are inheritors . . . like it or not, know it or not.'[75]

In UG's words, 'All thinking is dialectical thinking about thinking', and it is always in terms of the past. There is no such thing as the present, and even if it exists, there is no way of knowing it. And the future! Is there a future? If it is there, it is nothing but a projection of the past yet again, though in a modified form.

UG adds: 'Thought is not yours or mine; it is our common inheritance. There is no such thing as your mind and my mind. There is only *mind*—the totality of all that has been known, felt, and experienced by man, handed down from generation to generation. We are all thinking and functioning in that "thought sphere", just as we all share the same atmosphere for breathing.'

Freud, therefore, had inevitably to draw his concepts 'unconsciously' from the metaphysical tradition he had inherited. Marx too, despite his apparent rejection of the Judeo-Christian tradition, constructed his political philosophy and political manifesto on the foundation of his inherited traditional concepts. When he declared: '. . . all history is the history of class struggle', and 'The philosophers have only interpreted the world in various ways: the point, however, is to change it', he was, knowingly or unknowingly, speaking like a high priest of the church, to whom 'truth' is already given, or pre-given.

This is not to accuse Freud or Marx of borrowing ideas from their traditions without acknowledging it, but to point out the sheer inescapability of the past in our thinking process (dialectical or otherwise), in our scientific projects or philosophical cogitations, in our seemingly original mystical thoughts and experiences, and even in our day-to-day, so-called mundane affairs.

All concepts belong to the history of metaphysics, declare the post-modernists. UG concurs pithily, 'You are the past . . . Man is memory.' He further declares, 'There is no freedom of thought and action.' This sounds like the terrible judgement of an arrogant God, but it is quite obvious for one who is prepared to see. What UG actually means is not something abstract and metaphysical, but a fact, however harsh and unpalatable: There is no freedom of thought and action within the framework of the past. He explains it thus: 'I maintain that man has no freedom of action. I don't mean the fatalism that the Indians have practised and still are practising: when I say that man has no freedom of action it is in relation to changing himself, to freeing himself from the burden of the past. It means that you have no way of acting except through the help of the knowledge that is passed on to you. It is in that sense, I say, no action is possible without thought.'

A closer examination reveals how the inherited past consisting of Judeo-Christian concepts was reworked and secularized in Marxism. All the central concepts of Christianity—the return of the Christ, the apocalypse, the chosen people, alienation, salvation, judgement, Satan, the kingdom of God, even martyrdom—are all there, reincarnated in different forms. Anyone even slightly acquainted with Marxism knows that in the Marxist scheme of life, the workers or the proletariat are the chosen ones, the new heroes, the modern-day messiahs, who would usher in a new world. Just as the missionaries, sacrificing their personal security and happiness, travelled to the four corners of the world with Bible in hand, to spread the message of Christ and convert people to Christianity, the Marxian activist too (preferably with a beard and a copy of the *Communist Manifesto* in his shoulder bag), would risk his life and travel to remote corners of the earth, to build awareness about socialism, organize people against the tyranny of feudalism, capitalism and the tyranny of the state, and prepare the ground for the coming revolution and realization of the kingdom of socialism on earth. And like his religious cousin, he too would, if necessary, embrace martyrdom for the one and only great cause.

In the act of spreading the message of love or the socialist revolution, violence is seen as inevitable, for Marxism cannot allow the way of Satan (the bourgeois forces) to spread and dominate the world. But it is necessary to give the non-believers (the pagans), a chance to change their lifestyle and beliefs, failing which, one should do the inevitable for the common good. For 'tumult and oppression are worse than slaughter' (*Koran* 2: 191); burn them at the stake, throw them into the concentration camps, slaughter them for the greater good, and the greater glory of God and Revolution. With such world-views, crusades and jihads become inevitable, and a Stalin would feel compelled to silence and neutralize millions of dissenters ('heretics'), to enable the Revolution to reach its ordained destination.

A religious faith is as ideological as a political belief in an imagined utopia, demanding sacrifice of people. The assumption is that since the beginning and end of history are known, all that is required is obediently to follow and live according to the ideology. With its so-called covenant with God, the Church presumes to be in possession of the mystery, and its high priests are ordained to implement the Divine Plan on earth. In an apparent reversal of roles, the political revolutionary too knows what is good for humanity, for he too is in possession of the laws of history. To be more specific, the Marxist revolutionary believes, like his Christian brother, that sooner or later, the kingdom of happiness, of justice and equality, will be a reality, and what he can at best do is to 'shorten and lengthen the birth pangs'. In the process, there will be some violence, some 'collateral damage', but that is all for the greater good of humanity, and, therefore, to be tolerated, in the hope that sooner or later, the good shall triumph, the goal shall be achieved.

Despite his hatred, or perhaps because of his hatred of the Jews as 'brokers of money', as 'the universal anti-social element of the present time', Marx remained a Judeo-Christian to his bones.

In 1816, at the age of thirty-five, following a Prussian decree which banned Jews from the higher ranks of law and medicine, Marx's father became a Protestant, choosing Protestantism instead of Catholicism because he equated it with intellectual freedom. In 1824, his six children were baptized. By then Heinrich Marx, the father, had read Voltaire, Rousseau and Kant and believed strongly in the ideas of the Enlightenment, urging his son to cultivate 'the pure belief in God' as found in Locke, Newton and Leibniz. Talking about Marx as a young man, many biographies talk about the essays he wrote and his passion for poetry, but his poems are generally treated as of no great significance in his growth, or referred to as 'youthful follies', of little biographical interest. For instance, the essay 'Consideration of a Young man on Choosing his Career' written by Marx at the age of seventeen, is often quoted to show how the qualities of a great man in the making were already there in his writings. A part of the essay goes thus: 'According to History the greatest men are those that have worked for the general good and ennobled themselves. Experience calls him the happiest who has made most people happy. Religion itself teaches us that the Ideal towards which all strive sacrificed Himself for humanity, and who shall dare to contradict such claims? If we have chosen the position in which we can accomplish the most for humanity, then we can never be crushed by the burden because these are only sacrifices made for the sake of all. Then it is no poor, restricted, egoistic joy that we savour; on the contrary our happiness belongs to millions, our deeds live on calmly with endless effect, and our ashes will be moistened by the ardent tears of noble men.'

Marx wrote poetry during his university days, and even belonged to a poetry circle in Bonn. These poems come through not as

'youthful follies' but as the compositions of a very passionate
Christian, and the apocalyptic nature of his poetry can be discerned
in his political vision as well. In a collection entitled 'Savage
Poems', he wrote:

We are chained, shattered, empty, frightened
Eternally chained to this marble block of being . . .

In yet another he wrote:

Never can I calmly practise
That which strongly grips my soul,
Never can I rest in comfort
And I rage unceasingly.

Elsewhere, like a jilted lover, he howls 'gigantic curses at
mankind', and has no qualms in wishing: 'Everything that exists
deserves to perish . . .'

This essential Judeo-Christian apocalyptic vision remained with
him to his last days. The evidence of this can be found in his
writings and letters. The myth of good and evil, with the eventual
destruction of 'evil', were transposed into his revolutionary discourses.
'History is the judge, its executioner the proletariat', he thundered.
Marx really did believe that the Judgement Day of capitalism was
coming, that it was inevitable, and then this secularized Kingdom
of God would be established on earth.

There is no doubt that Marx thought of himself as a messiah,
if not as God himself. His reading of history offered a radically
different understanding of society. However flawed some of his
theories were, they set in motion a radical political consciousness
and movements all over the world for justice and freedom. He was
no ordinary soul; he was indeed greater than many geniuses and
his concern for the exploited and the marginalized is well known.
But to say Marx was a man of compassion and that his philosophy
was born out of compassion is ridiculous. Undoubtedly he envisioned
a better world, but the method he advocated towards its realization
was only a little less violent than that of Hitler's Nazism. He was
a visionary, hence the problem for all visions are born out of fear,

lack, and a demand for security. The world has already suffered enough with the visions of visionaries, and we should be better off without any new ones.

Indeed, Marx's vision of a new world proved problematic to many of his contemporaries. In the 1940s, Karl Popper undertook a systematic critique of Marxism and found it quite fascist and a danger to the creation of an open society. His contention was that it is perfectly possible to interpret 'history' as the history of class struggle, or as the struggle of races for supremacy, or as the history of religious ideas, or as the struggle between 'open' and 'closed' societies, or even as the history of scientific and industrial progress. All these could offer interesting points of view, and lead to a plurality of interpretations of life and society. But to present a particular point of view as doctrine or as the law of history was to betray intolerance, an unconscious conservatism and a fascist tendency. As a great believer in democratic principles, Popper argued that if pluralistic ways of thinking and living (the 'open society') have to continue, 'if the growth of reason is to continue and human rationality survive, then the diversity of individuals and their opinions, aims, and purposes must never be interfered with (except in extreme cases where political freedom is endangered)'.

Social engineering, however noble, scientific and realistic one may claim it to be, or any attempt to control and regulate human life and society, Popper said, 'must lead to the equalization not of human rights but of human minds, and it would mean the end of progress'.[76]

Interestingly, the greatest criticism of Marxism today has come from the feminist movement and its writings. The insights offered by feminists are indeed revealing; they find Marxism sharing many ideas and values with the bourgeois order it condemns. More specifically, 'it shares with bourgeois thought a universal representation of humanity that is in fact masculine, phallocentric'. It is also oppressive in the way it assumes 'both the power of self-definition and the power of definition over the whole political field', often relegating other forms of knowledge and struggle to secondary or auxiliary position. It is paranoiac in its adherence to materialism and anti-spiritualism, in its assumption that capitalism is the ultimate enemy and source of patriarchy, in its refusal to understand other modes of existence. It is dictatorial when it decrees the conditions and interpretation of all socio-political struggles in its own terms. To put it differently, Marxism interprets 'all radical movements as variations, and inadequate ones at that, of a true (socialist) revolutionary theory and practice'. Truly, it is intolerant of the possibility of developing 'a completely different perspective on problems of truth, reason, reality, knowledge'.[77]

This is so not merely because Marxism shares the ideas and values of the bourgeois order, but because it is yet another, though sophisticated, face of capitalism itself. Rather, they are like the two sides of the same coin, or like the two faces of basically the same politics of thought. Is that the reason why UG is never tired of reiterating that thought is bourgeois, that thought in its very birth, nature and expression is fascist? This, of course, sounds like extreme radicalism, perhaps because it is indeed an extreme fact! 'Thought' used not to build a bridge or treat an injured person, or thought used to find one's way back home; but thought intended to dominate and change the other, to build a religious or social order, to establish the kingdom of God—in short, the whole politics of change, of whatever kind, is born of the same 'bourgeois' consciousness.

UG, of course, uses the term 'bourgeois' and 'fascist' not exactly in the political sense but to mean that thought controls and shapes our life and our actions and that it is always self-protective. In his words: 'It is a very protective mechanism. It has no doubt helped us to be what we are today. It has helped us to create our technology. It has made our life very comfortable. It has also made it possible for us to discover the (so-called) laws of nature. But (basically) thought is a very protective mechanism and is interested in its own survival . . .'

If one has to offer a simple analogy, it is like creating an order, or creating a story, if you like. To create an order or story means to give a specific reading, or meaning, imposing a purpose on this too-complex-to-comprehend movement of life. It also means to control, to regulate, to change, in accordance with rules, laws, visions that thought has manufactured for its own protection and survival. This is the burden, the curse of all religions, philosophies and political ideologies, which are all parts of the same spectrum of thought. This protective mechanism of thought is the same as what is otherwise called the 'will to power'.

The will to power betrays the fear and insecurity in which human consciousness seems to be deeply entrenched. God, permanent happiness and utopias are some of the greatest inventions of thought to overcome this fear and insecurity.

Approaching the subject from a different position, Arthur Koestler says: 'In one of the early chapters of Genesis, there is an episode which has inspired many great paintings. It is the scene where Abraham ties his son to a pile of wood and prepares to cut his throat and burn him, out of sheer love of God. From the beginnings of history we are faced with a striking phenomenon to which anthropologists have paid far too little attention: human sacrifice, the ritual of killing of children, virgins, kings and heroes to placate and flatter gods conceived in nightmare dreams.'[78]

The nightmare dreams continue, for thought is made of the stuff of such dreams. Writing on *Nietszche, Genealogy, History*, Foucault believes that man, in his pursuit of so-called knowledge, is progressively enslaved to this 'instinctive violence'. 'Where religions once demanded the sacrifice of bodies, knowledge now calls for experimentation on ourselves, calls us to the sacrifice of the subject of knowledge'. And this 'desire for knowledge,' Nietzsche warned, 'has been transformed among us into a passion which fears no sacrifice, which fears nothing but its own extinction. It may be that mankind will eventually perish from this passion for knowledge.'[79]

Nothing has helped. Everything and anything born out of this 'self-protective' thought has been destructive. 'What is called human progress is a purely intellectual affair,' says Von Bertalanffy. 'The human cortex contains some ten billion neurons that have made possible the progress from stone axe to airplanes and atomic bombs, from primitive mythology to quantum theory. There is no corresponding development on the instinctive side that would cause man to mend his ways. For this reason, moral exhortation, as proffered through the centuries by the founders of religion and great leaders of humanity, have proved disconcertingly ineffective.'[80]

In the world of Western philosophy, it is interesting to note that almost all philosophers prior to Schopenhauer, more or less conceived of man as a rational being. Schopenhauer, who had a considerable influence on Nietzsche, Freud and Durkheim, saw that civilization, that great pride of man, is the reverse side of barbarism. He was critical of the Enlightenment tradition, and, in particular, Hegel's grand idea of Progress. He saw nothing rational about the human will-to-life, and understood that the 'human animal' is and always will be barbaric, that 'human evil and irrationality would have to be managed within tolerable limits, because they could never be eliminated completely'. The only way out, if there is one, is for individuals to cut themselves off from this madness, and try and live—not teach—a life of compassion, sympathy and affection. Again, not Kant or Hegel, but Schopenhauer was the one who wrote brutally frankly and directly: 'A man can go to work rationally and thus thoughtfully, deliberately, consistently, systematically, and methodically, and yet act upon the most selfish, unjust, and even iniquitous maxims . . . Reasonable and vicious are quite consistent with each other, and in fact, only through their union are great and far-reaching crimes possible . . .'[81]

Durkheim knew only too well what Schopenhauer meant when he said that any actions springing from duty, fear or any sort of compulsion are actions based on egoistic self-interest, which is the basis for barbarism. Spengler concurred with Durkheim: 'In spite of its foreground appearances, ethical socialism is *not* a system of compassion, humanity, peace and kindly care, but one of will-to-power. Any other reading of it is illusory.'[82]

But why is this so? What went wrong with our species? Did anything go wrong?

Over the centuries, there have been countless attempts to answer the questions, to diagnose the possible cause for man's (self) destructive tendency by invoking the Biblical Fall, or Freud's 'death wish', or Marx's 'Class War', or 'Patriarchy' and what have you. But none of these carry much conviction, because, as Arthur Koestler would say, 'none of them started from the hypothesis that *homo sapiens* may be an aberrant biological species, an evolutionary misfit, afflicted by an endemic disorder'. Not only the incontrovertible evidence from man's past record, but also research strongly suggests that at some point during the biological evolution of Homo sapiens something went wrong. 'There is a flaw,' insists Koestler. 'Some potentially fatal engineering error built into the

native equipment—more specifically, into the circuits of our nervous system—which would account for the streak of paranoia running through our history.'[83]

UG would probably agree with Koestler, for in his own way he almost always speaks about the sheer hopelessness of man's endeavours to overcome his destructive streak. In fact, his very endeavours, whether religious, political or technological, are only strengthening the momentum of the self-destructive trait against which he is wrestling. UG suggests, disturbingly, that somewhere along the line, the birth of the thinking Homo sapiens, the self-conscious human being, marked the beginning of this great mischief that put man against nature, man against man, and man against himself. In his own words:

Scientists in the field of evolution now think that the present breed of humans we have on this planet probably evolved out of a degenerated species. The mutation that carried on the self-consciousness must have taken place in a degenerate species. That is why we have messed everything up. It is anybody's guess as to whether anyone can change the whole thing.

Basically, human nature is exactly the same whether in India or in Russia or in America or in Africa. Human problems are exactly the same. All the problems are artificially created by the various structures created by human thinking. And there is some sort of (I can't make a definitive statement) neurological problem in the human body. Human thinking is born out of this neurological defect in the human species. Anything that is born out of human thinking is destructive. Thought is destructive. Thought is a protective mechanism. It draws frontiers around itself, and it wants to protect itself. It is for the same reason that we also draw lines on this planet and extend them as far as we can. Do you think these frontiers are going to disappear? They are not. Those who have entrenched themselves, those who have had the monopoly of all the world's resources so far and for so long, if they are threatened to be dislodged, what they would do is anybody's guess. All the destructive weapons that we have today are here only to protect that monopoly.

The human being modelled after the perfect being has totally failed. The model has not touched anything there. Your value system is the one that is responsible for the human malady, the human tragedy, forcing everybody to fit into that model. So, what do we do? You cannot do anything by destroying the value system, because you replace one value system with another. Even those who rebelled against religion, like those in the Communist countries, have themselves created another kind of value system. So revolution does not mean the end of anything. It is only a revaluation of our value system.

When everything fails, you use the last card, the trump in the pack of cards, and call it love. But it is not going to help us, and it has not helped us at all. Even religion has failed to free man from violence and from ten other different things that it is trying to free us from. You see, it is not a question of trying to find new concepts, new ideas, new thoughts, and new beliefs. But I am sure that the day has come for people to realize that all the weapons that we have built so far are redundant and that they cannot be used any more. We have arrived at a point where you cannot destroy your adversary without destroying yourself. So it is that kind of terror, and not the love and brotherhood that have been preached for centuries, that will help us to live together.

It all looks truly hopeless! If our very desire for happiness without pain or sorrow, our wish to change the world to a state of permanent justice and peace, is a serious neurological problem, what are we to do?

If this is a fact, and if we somehow know that all our attempts to establish a permanent order and happiness in the world, all our religions and political ideologies are bound to fail, what then are we doing?

It is not all that hopeless, many would want to argue. Surely many religious leaders, activists, and intellectuals would say: Yes, we know we are in a messy situation. Our ideas of an ideal society, our utopias, our unquestioning belief in 'reason' and science as the way to genuine growth, freedom, and happiness have created this mess. Still, can we really not theorize about and practise some minimum politics, a more humane politics that would not be utopian, but address itself to what Popper would call 'dangerous evil'? Yes, we know that all ideologies are geared towards social engineering, control and discipline, and are thus in the last analysis more harmful and oppressive than liberating. Still, it should be possible to develop a non-violent, cultural, political system that would not oppress or destroy plural ways of knowing and being and doing things, that would keep dialogues open-ended. And it should be possible to practise—not preach, but practise—what we deeply believe in, and be honest about it, hoping a wise and sane way of living would emerge in the process!

At times, UG seems to agree with the criticism of all our

metaphysical concepts, political ideologies and spiritual ideals as nothing more than our will to power, when he suggests that we should put our thinking on a different track, implying we should give up our search for (non-existent) origins and truths, our metaphysical and spiritual circus (for there is no such thing as a spiritual side to man) and concern ourselves with our basic needs, comfort and security. In short, his critique of our gods and ideals, the dichotomy between the spiritual and the material, does suggest a way out of the present crisis. But sometimes he also takes an extreme position by declaring that there is *no way out*! That it has nothing to do with dialogue, since in fact there are only monologues! That it is not something to do with trying to develop new concepts or beliefs, new thoughts and ways of doing things, whether non-violent or violent; there is just no way out of this mess! So what do we do? 'You stop,' suggests UG. 'When you are lost in the jungle, what do you do? You stop . . . perhaps out of that a way will open . . .'

This seems more hopeless! For, is it really possible to stop, to fall literally dead? Is that what UG means? If so, can it be an act of volition? Or does it mean that with the acceptance of our helplessness and hopelessness, a way would suggest itself?

16

Theory and Practice

'Practise what you preach' is usually the advice one loves to pass on to others.

'Be truthful' is good advice, a good way to chide anyone, for no one could honestly say that he or she does not believe in the importance of truthfulness.

All spiritual teachers say that an iota of practice is better than a ton of theory, though they may seldom practise what they say. Marxists insist that theory and practice should go together, although they must know by now that their practices have never lived up to the expectations raised by their theories, and that they never will be, for as Popper would say: ' . . . utopian plans will never be realized in the way they were conceived, because hardly any social action ever produces precisely the result expected'.

In point of fact, we should know that action or 'practice' is always more complex and confounding than any theory, for it is governed by factors no theory can totally comprehend, much less shape. Yet within every theory is the stubborn hope, an a priori belief, that if only we strictly and seriously adhere to its rules, laws and visions, the world could be changed.

At least, let us be non-violent in our action, suggests Gandhiji, so that dialogue is kept open, and the possibilities of our coming upon the truth are not closed. All his life, he struggled to practise, to live his ideas; even his enemies grant him that. He lived his ideas and constructed his philosophy from the day-to-day existential experience of life. Looked at from this perspective, he might even be called an anti-philosopher, for he was concerned not so much with constructing a new philosophy as in probing, testing, experimenting with given spiritual truths and values in the laboratory of daily experiences.

For Gandhi, truth was always relative. On the level of faith, however, truth is pure consciousness, the power that holds the universe together. It is God, Love, Nature, Cosmic Order. But it cannot be known. What we know is only relative truth. For absolute truth would mean absolute ahimsa or compassion, incarnation of truth in totality. Relative truth is all that is given to us; hence we can but move from truth to truth, and in the light of this, manage and resolve human problems and conflicts.

This indeed leads us to a paradoxical situation. Since all concepts, all ideas and philosophies are relative, they become the source of conflict as well as the way to its resolution. But conflict resolution has to be transacted through non-violence, Gandhi would argue. In other words, in an imperfect and changing world of relative truths, where man is not God or in possession of absolute truth, he is not competent to punish, kill or destroy. This is why non-violence, or ahimsa, should be the means to resolve a conflict, for only it can keep alive the creative possibilities of dialogue and debate, and the plural ways of knowing and being.

All his life, Gandhi did try to practise his ideas and live an open, transparent life. In fact, he belived that it was essential for one committed to the search for truth and goodness (particularly intellectuals, public leaders and activists) to be honest both with oneself and others and to live a transparent life.

But even a man such as Gandhi, whose life was 'an open book', and who confessed to having nocturnal emissions at the age of seventy-six, had his secrets. In the introduction to *The Story of My Experiments with Truth*, he wrote: 'There are some things which are known only to oneself and one's Maker. These are clearly incommunicable.'

Interestingly, one of his greatest admirers, T.K. Mahadevan, who spoke and wrote profusely on Gandhi's philosophy, also wrote *The Year of the Phoenix*,[84] based on Gandhi's life in South Africa, in which he called Gandhi's story of his experiments with truth a romantic tale! He did not exactly accuse Gandhi of deliberate lying, yet he held him responsible for ignoring certain vital, historical facts in the narrative of his life in South Africa, which in point of fact amounted to lying.

One wonders what it would be like if, with absolute honesty, we start examining our own lives and ideas, and the lives of well-known intellectuals and the great philosophers of the world.

From the earliest times, priests, gurus and philosophers have laid claim to advise and guide society. With the decline of religions, secular intellectuals, political theorists, activists, educationists and scientists stepped in to shape the world according to their theories, insights, findings and ideas. In point of fact, they were but an extension of the religious teacher, who is now threatening to come back to reclaim his lost post, since all ideologies, including science, have failed to resolve human conflict and solve the problems of existence.

However, according to UG, actually there are no problems, only answers, only solutions. Since these answers and solutions offered by our messiahs, intellectuals, leaders and scientists have proved to be no answers, no solutions, we continue to ask questions—these answers and solutions have become our problems. Yet, we go on sentimentally defending the authors of these answers, our messiahs old and new, and we live in the hope of better answers, better solutions, and a better future. For we believe that not to have hope is to be pessimistic, nihilistic, unnatural, and even dangerous.

In this scheme of life, the spiritual man is the first culprit, according to UG. 'The spiritual man is the most egocentric man,' he says. 'He feels superior to everyone. He thinks his teaching is going to save mankind and his teaching should be preserved.' With the decline of religious influence and power the world over, the intellectual and secular messiah has stepped in. With great relish he subjects religions and their messiahs and teachings to critical scrutiny. He is a great unmasker! He unmasks lies, repressions, self-deception, and exploitation embedded in the traditions and old philosophies. He unmasks and dethrones the messiahs but only to enthrone himself there. And he sincerely believes that he could himself—rejecting wholesale religions and their ideas, the legacy of tradition—find cures for the ills of society through his intellect, and devise formulae that will transform people and society for the better. He has answers to all questions, solutions to all problems. He is the priest, guru and messiah, all rolled into one. He has almost succeeded in replacing the tyranny of religious ideas and values with his secular teachings, his social sciences and political philosophies.

'Why do you want to exonerate these people and put them on a pedestal?' asks UG. It is not the followers, (failing to follow their messiahs, religious or secular) who are responsible for the mess we are in, but the messiahs themselves, argues UG. In other words, what he seems to be asking is: Why not hold Christ responsible for the Christian crusades? Why glorify Mohammad and only blame the jihadi? Why forgive Marx for what Lenin and Stalin did to their own people? Why exonerate Einstein? Didn't he encourage Roosevelt to produce and use the atom bomb?

To quote UG again: 'The teachers and the teachings are responsible for this mess in this world. All those messiahs have created nothing but a mess in the world. And the politicians are the inheritors of that culture. There is no use blaming them and calling them corrupt. They (the spiritual teachers) were corrupted. The man who taught love was corrupt because he created a division in his consciousness. The man who spoke of "Love thy neighbour as thyself" was responsible for this horror in the world today. Don't exonerate those teachers. Their teachings have created nothing but a mess in this world, progressively moving in the direction of destroying not only man, but every species (of living beings) on this planet today.'

If the religious messiahs or leaders cannot be exonerated for the mess they have put the world in, the secular leaders and intellectuals who wear the mantle of prophets today have played a crucial role in shaping our attitudes and institutions, and should not be exonerated either. It is time to examine the moral credentials of these modern messiahs to tell humankind how to conduct itself. To quote Paul Johnson, author of the controversial and provocative book *Intellectuals*: 'How did they run their own lives? With what degree of rectitude did they behave to family, friends and associates? Were they just in their sexual and financial dealings? Did they tell, and write, the truth? And how have their own systems stood up to the test of time and praxis?'

Brilliant minds, artists, writers, and intellectuals desire admirers and followers just as much as do the people who want to identify with, admire and follow leaders or gurus. But these gurus are in no way different from their followers. In fact, they are as 'unreasonable, illogical and superstitious as anyone else'. They have their self-interest, their careers, their egos at stake in this game. They are not free of ambition or greed although, without any misgiving or hesitation, they attribute all conceivable 'evil' qualities to business people, politicians, sports persons and filmstars. The only difference between these gurus is that some are more ambitious, some less, and some are real megalomaniacs.

★

The much-celebrated writer and thinker Jean Jacques Rousseau was actually one such megalomaniac. A writer of genius who had tremendous influence on his generation, he is held in high esteem by the intellectual community even today. This was a man with a gigantic ego, yet he suffered from persecution mania; an apostle of reason who was at the same time a very efficient 'psychological conman'. His *Confessions*, in which he paints himself as a sort of 'barbarian', as one who gives importance to sentiments rather than convention, who valued the 'impulse of the heart' as opposed to customary 'good manners', is a brilliant rational justification of his lifestyle. He projected himself as one 'with the greatest contempt for money', yet never missed an opportunity to acquire more than enough for himself. There is no denying the fact that his writings, particularly his critique of class, culture and capitalism, had an impact on the European Renaissance and laid the foundation for the coming of Marxism.

But what is not generally known about this great and 'original genius of the mind' is not so much his ill-treatment of women, but what he did to his own children. This genius, whose reputation rests not only on his political ideas but also his theories about the upbringing of children, did not think twice before abandoning all the five children he had with Therese, his wife. Paul Johnson says that Rousseau did not even note the dates of the births of his five children and never took any interest in what happened to them, except once in 1761, when he believed Therese was dying and made a perfunctory attempt to discover the whereabouts of the first child.[85]

While this shocking and horrifying fact about Rousseau's life may not nullify all his ideas, or bring down his stature as one of the most influential writers of the modern world, his integrity is certainly called into question. We cannot help but ask: was he really the champion of the principles of truth and virtue which he claimed to be?

Humanity suffers from a terrible sickness: falling for ideas. The more brilliant the idea, the greater seems the fall. The fact that other 'great minds' such as Kant, who thought Rousseau had 'a sensibility of soul of unequalled perfection', Shelley who saw in him a 'sublime genius', Schiller who thought of him as one with 'a Christ-like soul', and Tolstoy who declared that Rousseau and the Gospel had been 'the two great and healthy influences of my life', only proves the all-too-human fatal weakness for ideas, and confirms the strange truth that great minds can be greatly naive and stupid.

Perhaps the way we consciously or unconsciously ignore the practices and lifestyle of 'great men' betrays our own self-interest in safeguarding our own private lives from public scrutiny. The deliberate indifference of intellectuals to the lifestyle of other intellectuals only means that they do not want others to look too closely into their own personal lives.

★

There is not much evidence of greatness of character in the life of Marx either. Somewhat like Max Mueller, who never set foot in India or had any direct experience of the tremendously plural religious and social practices and beliefs of the people of India, yet wrote voluminously on the Vedas, Marx too, desk-bound at the British Museum, wrote *Das Kapital*, having experienced hardly any direct contact with peasants and landowners. In Paul Johnson's words, 'Marx never set foot in a mill, factory, mine or other industrial workplace in the whole of his life.'

He borrowed ideas and even expressions from his predecessors and contemporaries and reworked them into short, pithy statements with devastating effect. Absolutely nothing wrong with that—there is nothing original about Shakespeare either; he borrowed ideas and characters from history (we all do), but the genius of the man lay in the way he converted them into great drama on the human condition. However, what Marx wrote were not works of art but philosophical and political treatises, supposedly scientific in method and based on research.

We have already discussed, briefly, in the previous chapter, how Marx's vision was basically poetic and Judeo-Christian, though its expression was couched in rational and scientific language. But now the questions that need to be asked are: Were his studies and thesis based on the real politics and economics of the real world? Or did he make use of the available facts and figures (which were almost twenty or thirty years out-of-date, it is said) and did he not falsify certain case histories (by omitting facts and events which would not fit his theory or would falsify his thesis) in order to bolster his theory of proletarian revolution?

Paul Johnson says that Marx's systematic misuse of sources attracted the attention of two Cambridge scholars in the 1880s. Their study of the material that Marx had used in his work led them to the discovery that it was not a case of inaccuracy or oversight, but showed 'signs of a distorting influence', and that he had manipulated facts and figures in favour of the conclusions he was trying to establish. And 'they concluded that their evidence might not be "sufficient to sustain a charge of deliberate falsification" but certainly showed "an almost criminal recklessness in the use of authorities" and warranted treating any "other parts of Marx's work with suspicion"'.[86]

The philosopher Karl Jaspers had no doubt that 'The style of Marx's writings is not that of the investigator . . . he does not quote examples or adduce facts which run counter to his own theory but only those which clearly support or confirm that which he considers the ultimate truth. The whole approach is one of vindication, not investigation, but it is a vindication of something proclaimed as the perfect truth with the conviction not of the scientist but of the believer.'[87]

It seems Marx was quite blind, if not deliberately indifferent, to the happenings around him and in other parts of the world. He also had problems with 'socialist' working-class leaders with large followings who 'preached practical solutions to actual problems of work and wages, rather than doctrinaire revolution'. Paul Johnson writes: 'In his *Manifesto Against Kriege*, Marx, who knew nothing about agriculture, especially in the United States where Kriege had settled, denounced his proposal to give 160 acres of public land to each peasant; he said that peasants should be recruited by promises of land, but once a communist society was set up, land had to be collectively held . . . Proudhon was an anti-dogmatist: "For God's sake," he wrote, "after we have demolished all the (religious) dogmatism *a priori*, let us not of all things attempt to instil another kind of dogma into the people . . . let us not make ourselves the leaders of a new intolerance".'

It seems that this 'intolerance' is characteristic of all radicals or revolutionaries. Over the years, in one's interactions and working relationship with political radicals, one has seen how both theorists and activists manipulate facts and figures to justify their positions, how blind they are all to facts, events, and experiences that could falsify their revolutionary theories and practices. Of course, they all sound completely sure of themselves, and appear quite genuine about their concerns for the disinherited, marginalized and exploited class of people. Anything that goes against their politics, they tend to see as false, as a conspiracy against their great cause, which is assumed to be always pro-people.

So it is not really surprising to learn that their guru, Marx, could be cruel and malicious with his opponents and critics. It is said that he had the terrible habit of saying: 'I will annihilate you.' One wonders what kind of a leader he would have been, if he had been in the position of a Mao or Stalin. Some of the people who interacted with him had no hesitation in calling him a 'democratic dictator' and one whose 'heart did not match his intellect'. Commenting on his editorship of the *Neue Rheinische Zeitung*, Engels himself once observed: 'The organization of the editorial staff was a simple dictatorship by Marx.' And Bakunin wrote: 'Marx does not believe in God but he believes much in himself and makes everyone serve himself. His heart is not full of love but of bitterness and he has very little sympathy for the human race.'

Did he at least care for and love his family? What was he like as a husband and father? The biographical details today reveal that he had an affair on the sly with Helen Demuth, otherwise called 'Lenchen', who came from peasant stock and worked in Marx's household. He had a child by her in 1851. Eventually his wife, Jenny, came to know about it, which only added to her already miserable life with Marx. But Marx never accepted his responsibility, and lived in constant fear of being exposed and of his image as a great revolutionary and seer being permanently damaged.

What is so terribly wrong about all this? Apologists might argue thus: There certainly will be conflicts and contradictions in the lives of philosophers, intellectuals and artists. That is but human and natural, particularly since we live in an imperfect and evolving society. Therefore, the argument would go on, what is important are the insights and ideas they have offered to the world, and leaders have to be judged or criticized in terms of the validity or otherwise of their philosophies or concepts.

Well, suppose we grant that their concepts and methods too are problematic and questionable, again the usual reaction would be: It is an unfinished task, and we have to carry forward their good work.

All this amounts to saying yet again that the thinkers, the leaders, the gurus are right, but the followers are wrong—that we have not worked hard enough towards the realization of their visions. Never do we suspect that perhaps their very ideas could be wrong and, therefore, ought to be rejected.

More importantly, why shouldn't it be demanded that thinkers and leaders should practise what they preach? If an idea is not adopted in life or lived, particularly by its authors, of what worth is it? Shouldn't one be at least truthful about it?

Trust the tale, not the novelist, said D.H. Lawrence. He probably meant the novel is always bigger, more complex and truthful than its author, who may be a philistine or a megalomaniac in real life. But the same cannot be said of thinkers and gurus. For to say that the teaching is more important than the teacher is to make nonsense of his teaching. One cannot speak in favour of monogamy in public and in private have three wives; or preach non-violence and kindness to animals and be a butcher. This is a question that emerges out of the teaching itself. It is not merely a matter of ethics, but one of truthfulness and integrity.

★

In her unusual, penetrating book *Gyn/Ecology*, what Mary Daly says of the famous theologian Paul Tillich may well be true of most theologians, past and present. The difference would only be one of degree. Writing about Christian theologians, she suggests that theologians have always fantasized about a female hanging on the cross. And quoting passages from Hannah Tillich's lucid autobiography, *From Time to Time*, she lays bare the pornographic exploits of Paul Tillich, the theologian. In her autobiography, Hannah describes how she entered her husband's room during his viewing of a porn film for his own private entertainment.

Tillich was not atypical, says Mary Daly. 'He simply had a wife who was determined to publish the truth after his death, despite all the attempts of theologians, psychologists such as Rollo May, and other "friends" at first to stop her and later to discredit her. His private life and fantasies reflected the essential symbolic content of his and other theologians' Christology. Indeed, these sadomasochistic fantasies were the juice/sap of his impressive theologising.' And so, after his death, when Hannah unlocked his drawers, she found the details of his sex-obsessed life:

> All the girls' photos fell out, letters and poems, passionate appeal and disgust. I was tempted to place between the sacred pages of his highly esteemed lifework those obscene signs of the real life that he had transformed into the gold abstraction— King Midas of the spirit.[88]

★

The greatest and the worst among such gurus was our own Acharya, who later on promoted himself to Bhagwan Rajneesh. So long as he remained Acharya Rajneesh, he was a brilliant expounder and interpreter of religious ideas and spiritual traditions. He had the extraordinary talent to connect Zen with Tao, Tao with Vedanta, Vedanta with Science, and construct out of them illuminating narratives. He was certainly unconventional and radical in his methods, scintillating in his interpretations; indeed he was an eccentric and controversial guru and did make people take notice of him. Several thousands became his willing, and at times blind disciples. But the day he appointed himself as the enlightened master, as Bhagwan, he became an insufferable megalomaniac.

From the reports, stories and books written by several former close disciples, we learn that there was a method to his madness, that he suffered from multiple illnesses and phobias, and that he used his spiritual authority to manipulate and exploit his disciples both sexually and financially.

The reckless and arrogant manner in which he tried to establish himself in Oregon finished him; in a way America finished him. But the rot had set in a long time back.

In 1981, Rajneesh bought the 64,000-acre ranch in eastern Oregon for six million dollars and ruled over the desert empire, which he called Rajneeshpuram, like a warlord with his own private army of disciples. The disciples were judged by their ability to surrender to his will and obey his often bizarre commands. The American society was scandalized, not to speak of the spiritual world, about the libertine indulgences at Rajneeshpuram. JK called Rajneesh a 'criminal' and referred to Rajneeshpuram as 'a concentration camp under the dictatorship of enlightenment'. And UG called him 'the world's biggest pimp'.

So it didn't come as a surprise when Rajneesh was arrested and put in jail for breaking US immigration laws and for other major crimes of conspiracy to commit murder, poisoning, first-degree assault, arson and so on and then later deported from the USA. His return to India marked his descent to a spiritual hell. In the 1970s, as Acharya Rajneesh, he was a brilliant interpreter of the spiritual traditions of the world. But in the 1980s, the day he proclaimed himself as Osho, Bhagwan, he turned autocratic and thus began both his spiritual and social downfall. Back in India, where his spectacular rise in the spiritual world had started, now shattered, and Rajneesh did not live long. Suffering from drug and illness induced dementia, the former university professor died 'a mysterious death' in 1990.[89]

There are also, of course, reports of people having felt spiritually uplifted, and even coming upon some mystical states in Rajneesh's presence, as there are reports of Rajneesh's extraordinary charisma, his mesmerizing voice, his apparently cathartic stories, and his tremendous power that energized listeners. In the end, all this doesn't mean anything. It doesn't make the Bhagwan a decent human being, to say the least. In point of fact, Rajneesh is a classic example of spiritual deception and chicanery. For all we know, deception is built into spirituality and megalomania into spiritual authority.

★

For a long time J. Krishnamurti seemed to stand out as the one great example of the incorruptible guru who actually lived his teaching, one bright lonely star which shone as a beacon light, truly above all forms of deception and untruth. Listening to his talks and reading his books was like embarking on a journey 'on an uncharted sea', full of uncertainties, profound confusions, with a touch of desperation and madness rolled into one. However, at the end of this long journey, sometimes tiresome, sometimes ecstatic, one felt disappointed, and even betrayed. The man who dared to walk out of the Theosophical Society and declared 'Truth is a pathless land and it cannot be approached by any path whatsoever', ended up building a huge organization worth millions of dollars. The man who launched a great critique of gurus and religious traditions, who wanted people to break free of all conditioning, himself became a teacher and encouraged books of his teachings to be published and hundreds of video and audio cassettes to be made. Suddenly, it seemed this was no flight of the eagle in untrammelled air, no freedom from the known!

Indeed, it was an utterly new voice, a radical yet humbling truth when he declared 'defence is offence' and 'choice is bondage'. But what a let-down it was when he went to court against his friend and co-worker Rajagopal to claim authority over the Krishnamurti Foundation of which, of course, he was the president. And it was indeed a terrible blow to his 'followers' and his integrity when Radha Rajagopal Sloss published her book *Lives in the Shadow with J Krishnamurti*, in which she wrote candidly about his clandestine sexual relationship with her mother, Rosalind.

There is, of course, nothing wrong with sex unless one is a prude or believes that sex is anti-God. Indeed it can be a profoundly beautiful experience in a relationship. Talking on the subject of *Love, Sex and the Religious Life*, in Kingston, England, on 2 October 1967, JK asked: 'Why is it that you don't know what to do when there is desire? I'll tell you why. Because this rigid decision of yours is still in operation. All religions have told us to deny sex, to suppress it, because they say it is a waste of energy and you must have energy to find God. But this kind of austerity and harsh suppression and conformity to a pattern does brutal violence to all our finer instincts. This kind of harsh austerity is a greater waste of energy than indulgence in sex.'

In the light of JK's statements and reasonable advice, how does one view his passionate relationship with Rosalind?

In her book *Lives in the Shadow with J Krishnamurti*, Radha Sloss has traced the beginnings and the eventual development of JK's romantic and sexual relationship with her mother. Her narrative impresses one as being fair and quite matter of fact in tone.

In early 1935, Rosalind discovered that she was pregnant, and to decided to abort her pregnancy, more for reasons of health rather than discretion. Radha Sloss says that JK was quite compassionate and comforting and even travelled with Rosalind to Los Angeles, but did not accompany her to her osteopath friend's clinic. A year later, Rosalind was pregnant again. This time she did not go to a doctor, but this was, in a manner of speaking, replaced by the hand of fate. One day it so happened that both JK and Rajagopal got into a fierce argument right in front of Rosalind and Sophia. Later, when Rosalind and JK left that evening to drive back to Ojai, Rosalind, who had been deeply shaken and distressed by the quarrel between her lover and husband, lost her second baby on the way to Ojai, in an isolated field.

Three years later, in 1939, for the third time, Rosalind was pregnant. She was now thirty-six, and somewhat recklessly considered having this child. Partly, Radha Sloss suggests, it could have been her emotional need to test Krishnaji's feelings. However, at her age, given her health problems, she could not take the risk, and Krishnaji, without using too many words (let alone pressure tactics), let her understand that it was not a 'good idea for them to have this baby'. Once again, Rosalind went alone to the clinic at Los Angeles and got her pregnancy terminated.

In the late 1940s, their relationship began to sour when Rosalind began to suspect that he was having an affair behind her back. In the spring of 1950, in London, in a fit of remorse, frustration and anger, she poured out the whole story of her relationship with Krishnaji to Rajagopal. Almost twenty years ago, in 1931, after the birth of their first and only child, Radha, Rajagopal is believed to have decided to lead the life of a celibate and told his wife that now that 'they had their baby there was no more reason for them to live as man and wife'. And so, Radha suggests, Rosalind did not feel guilty towards Rajagopal and for almost twenty-odd years, JK provided the physical love and the warm, attentive companionship that she had not found in her marriage.

What then is the problem here?

Radha Sloss was like a daughter to JK. He was, indeed, more than a father, who performed the duties most conventional fathers wouldn't, who was fiercely protective of her and yet encouraged and enabled her to grow up in an atmosphere of freedom. In her book, Radha is quite grateful to JK for all the love and care he showered on her, but cannot forgive him for living, what she calls, a *sub-rosa* life. Given the fact that Krishnaji had, and even encouraged, an unconventional attitude towards marriage in general, his actions are understandable, says Radha Sloss, but not excusable in the context of his relationship with Rajagopal, who had given his life to helping him. Nor were they excusable in the context of the chaste image he continued to project and was careful not to tarnish. In public he spoke most eloquently of love that does not distinguish between human relationships but is boundlessly there for everyone, yet in private, he would frequently and eloquently declare his love to Rosalind and insist that what was between them was the most important thing in their lives.[90]

What can one make of all this? 'The fault lies with you', says UG, 'They are all just like you, why do you put them on a pedestal? Why do you want to exonerate them? Rajagopal put up with JK's affair with his wife, and looked the other way because of the money and real estate that were involved. He was a willing participant in that sordid drama. Don't exonerate these people. They may claim that they are different from us ordinary mortals, but they are exactly the same, perhaps worse . . .'

Extending the argument, UG adds: 'Not only the teachings but the teachers themselves have sown the seeds of this violence that we have in this world. The man who talked of love is responsible, because love and hate go together. So how can you exonerate them?'

More importantly, UG would argue that we should give up the idea of the'perfect individual', for no such creature has ever existed in the past or shall exist in future. 'We are not ready to accept the fact that nature probably is interested in creating only perfect species and not perfect individuals. Nature does not use any model. It creates something; then it destroys it, and creates something else.'

The mistake, therefore, lies with us in wanting to follow a teacher, and in thinking of these gurus, these intellectuals and leaders, be it a Buddha or a Jesus or a Gandhi, as models of perfection. Such perfection, as UG says, doesn't exist. And no individual's life, however noble or profound, can be a model for others.

If you were to meet the Buddha on the way, goes a Zen saying, kill him. This is generally understood to mean that the Buddha as a model is an obstacle to Buddhahood, so get rid of this attachment, this clinging, and this very desire to want to become something which one is not. Perhaps the greater truth is that there is no such thing as Buddhahood. Or, if at all such a thing exists, then perhaps it exists only for the Buddha and can never be someone else's experience. It would be nothing less than self-destructive madness to talk about it as a goal or model for others, just as it would be sheer lunacy to talk about and force others to believe in some imagined 'proletarian revolution', 'stateless state' or 'Kingdom of God' as the final goal of humanity.

17

Superman Debunked

Have you not heard of that madman who lit a lantern in the bright morning hours, ran to the marketplace, and cried incessantly: 'I am looking for God! I am looking for God!' As many of those who did not believe in God were standing together there, he excited considerable laughter. Have you lost him, then? said one. Did he lose his way like a child? said another. Or is he hiding? Is he afraid of us? Has he gone on a voyage? Or emigrated? Thus they shouted and laughed. The madman sprang into their midst and pierced them with his glances.

'Where has God gone?' he cried. 'I shall tell you. *We have killed him—you and I.* We are all his murderers. But how have we done this? How are we able to drink up the sea? Who gave us the sponge to wipe away the entire horizon? What did we do when we unchained this earth from its sun? Whither is it moving now? Whither are we moving now? Away from all suns? Are we not perpetually falling? Backward, sideward, forward, in all directions? Is there any up or down left? Are we not straying as through an infinite nothing? Do we not feel the breath of empty space? Has it not become colder? Is not more and more night coming on all the time? Must not lanterns be lit in the morning? Do we not hear anything yet of the noise of the gravediggers who are burying God? Do we not smell anything yet of God's decomposition? Gods too decompose. God is dead. God remains dead. And we have killed him.'[91]

Nietzsche's proclamation, *God is Dead*, reverberated throughout Europe for more than a century and continues to echo through what today is called postmodernism. Nietzsche believed that a time would come when the past would be divided into *Before Nietzsche* and *After Nietzsche*—it was a Christian habit he could not overcome. While he was a great genius, he was a great egotist too. However, he effected a wholesome critical review of Western philosophies and institutions that for centuries had been taken for granted as truth.

The way Nietzsche questioned and probed philosophical traditions, inverted almost every celebrated idea, ridiculed every virtue, rejected established notions of morality, and almost turned upside down the very foundation of human thought, makes him an extremely interesting and radically important thinker.

Like UG, Nietzsche too was unsparing in his criticism of religions and religious consciousness as being singularly responsible for the mess humanity finds itself in. He saw religion as a disease, the most 'evil' thing about it being that it is anti-Nature. The religious people, on their way to becoming 'angels', have 'seduced us into the belief that man's inclinations and instincts are evil. It is they who have produced our great injustice against nature, and against all nature . . . They despise the body: they eliminate it from their reckoning—even worse, they treat it as an enemy. Their most deluded comedy was to believe that one could embody a "beautiful soul" in abortion of flesh . . .' In particular, Nietzsche pours out his anger against Christianity and declares it to be the most extreme form of corruption that is possible to imagine. 'The Christian Church has left nothing unsoiled by its depravity, it has devalued every value, it has made every truth into a lie, every kind of integrity as an indicator of a base soul. And yet people still dare to speak of its "humanitarian" good nature! To abolish states of misery has not been its function: it has lived on states of misery, it has created states of misery, in order to project itself into the eternal.'[92] Nietzsche literally breathed fire when, in *Anti-Christ*, he declared: 'The words "God", "holy man", "redeemer", "saint", will henceforth be used as obscenities—as marks of the lowest kind of criminal.'

Where there is life, he declared, there is also a will—the will to power! The passion for power is fundamental, everything is but a weapon in its hands: reason, morality, love, even humility. Philosophers seldom understand this. 'The philosophers all pose as though their real opinions had been discovered through the self-evolving of a cold, pure, divinely indifferent dialectic.' It is not, for they are only 'their heart's desire abstracted and refined . . .'

Nietzsche was no respecter of politics either, like UG, who never tires of telling us that political ideas and philosophies are nothing but a 'warty outgrowth of religious thinking'. Nietzsche too, with the eye of a surgeon as it were, detected the religious origin of political ideas. These grand political ideas and values contain within themselves the anti-Nature attitude of religion, and they are but sickly forms of will-to-power. For that matter, socialism too is nothing but envy, and it is, more importantly, anti-biological, and like all ideologies, it 'desires an abundance of executive power, a wealth of authority comparable only with despotism . . .'

In short, God is dead, and so is the mother of all ideas. The days of idealism are over. Nietzsche warns: 'All idealists imagine that the causes they espouse are markedly better than all the other causes of the world. They refuse to believe that if their cause is to flourish at all, it must spring from the same stinking excremental miasma from which all other human undertakings emerge.'

No one could have been more critical, angry and disgusted with idealism (of whatever persuasion). UG should have no problem with most of Nietzsche's criticisms and attacks on religious and

philosophical traditions, including political institutions. In fact, UG himself has often pointed out that man's assumption of superiority over animals and Nature has been the beginning of his downfall. Indeed man is but an ape, and has inherited all the qualities of the animals he seems to have evolved from. He is not yet a full human being! And all his ideas are lies, illusions, 'heart's desire abstracted and refined'.

However, Nietzsche did not stop with his revolutionary yet cleansing criticisms. He moved on to talk about the 'Superman'. The itch to be a prophet was too overpowering, and so this almost pathologically restless anti-philosopher arrived at the very strange notion of the Superman.

Perhaps Nietzsche believed he had successfully managed to break through the 'fetters' of religious ideas and values, that he had truly overcome man with his idea of Overman. 'I teach you the Overman,' he declared. Man is something that ought to be overcome and surpassed. 'Humanity is really more of a means than an end. Humanity is merely experimental material, the monstrous surplus of bad breeding, a pile of rubble.'[93]

But what would he be like, this Overman? Nietzsche said: 'What is an ape to mankind? Either a bad joke or a cause of bitter shame. And this is what Man shall be for the Overman: a bad joke or a cause of bitter shame.' And this Overman would be 'the meaning of the earth'.

One's first reaction is that Nietzsche is writing about the possible coming of a new species, but he was intensely opposed to the religious idea of 'godlyman' and to the religious faith in 'unearthly, supernatural hopes'; in their place he tried to install the Superman, who would rise out of mass mediocrity but who would not be a slave to values and ideas, however noble or profound, but who would be a master of himself and his own destiny. He spoke for a sort of aristocracy of the mind, 'the kingdom of the mind'.

In *Thus Spake Zarathustra*, he wrote:

Dead are all Gods; now we will that superman live . . .
I teach you superman. Man is a something that shall be surpassed. What have ye done to surpass him? . . .
It is time for man to mark his goal. It is time for man to plant the germ of his highest hope . . .

Nietzsche's Zarathustra was the Superman in the making. It was a secular, physiological hope posited against the spiritual hope of religions, Christianity in particular.

Yet, in his *Human, All-Too Human*, Nietzsche had warned: 'Whoever thinks more deeply knows that, whatever his actions and judgements might be, he is always wrong.'

And so it was!

The Supramental Experiments

The only other notable modern thinker to postulate the concept of the 'Superman' was Aurobindo. His idea of the Superman was, of course very different from that of Nietzsche, something the Nazis would have found very difficult to appropriate.

Aurobindo was indeed a great experimenter in spirituality—a sort of spiritual scientist or spiritual empiricist who for twenty-three years or more, probed, tested and experimented with the depths of his own body-mind, with 'planes of consciousness', to bring home what he called the Supramental Being. After his death in 1950, the Mother carried forward the epic trials and experiments within the cells of her own body-lab, as it were, reports of which make mind-boggling reading, undoubtedly a unique chapter in the history of mysticism.

Almost in the style of Marx, Aurobindo too could well have said: The world over mystics have only talked about their ineffable God-experiences but it is time now to go beyond the mystics, transform the very human creature into a Supramental Being and thus create a new world!

In the light of Aurobindo's teachings, Indian spirituality was at best a great spiritual romance, not deep love, not good enough to bring about a 'terrestrial realisation' or evolution. He did not, of course, dismiss the past as so much nonsense, but sat down to correct its errors. As one exposed to Western education, philosophy and science, his hermeneutic studies of Indian religious traditions, and his criticism of modern Western psychology were distinctive and thought-provoking. He found the philosophy and thought of the

Greeks 'most intellectually stimulating', and the aphoristic philosopher Heraclitus closer to Indian mystical thought and traditions. Among English writers, he thought of D.H. Lawrence as an Indian yogi in western clothes, and regarded Nietzsche as one of the most original thinkers in the history of Western philosophy.

We do not know how much of Nietzsche's criticism of religious thinking and his idea of the Superman were influenced by his reading of the Upanishads and Buddhism. Similarly, it is difficult to say if Aurobindo borrowed the notion of the Superman from Nietzsche. However, Aurobindo acknowledged the fact that it was Nietzsche who first talked about the Superman, though he said he had problems with the idea. He wrote:

'Nietzsche first cast it, the mystic of Will-worship, the troubled, profound, half-luminous Hellenizing Slav with his strange clarities, his violent half ideas, his rare gleaming intuitions that came marked with the stamp of an absolute truth and sovereignty of light. But Nietzsche was an apostle who never entirely understood his own message.'[94]

Aurobindo was quite 'original' in some of his ideas and the way he challenged some of the central notions of Indian philosophy. He declared that Nirvana was not the end or self-extinction, but only a new beginning. He kicked the traditional, still-as-stone idea of moksha into motion. He heard Brahman laugh at Sankara's theory of Maya. There is no such thing as maya, he affirmed, nothing false, but only imperfect and incomplete realities. So, what one needed was a 'constant heightening and widening' of our understanding of life and truth.

He had no doubt that Nature was pushing humankind towards a grand terrestrial realization and fulfilment, towards the creation of a new species on earth. It would not be an aristocracy of mind, not overmind, but supermind. The new man would not be a Nietzschean Superman or Zarathustra, but God! And this God, this genuine Superman, would usher in not a better world, but a New World!

So we should go beyond Mind, beyond even Overmind which can at best create mystics and sages, great scientists and leaders. There is certainly more to Nature's design, to this cosmic play. For, reasons Aurobindo, there seems to be no reason why Life should evolve out of material elements, or Mind out of living forms, unless we accept that Life is already involved in Matter and Mind in Life because, in essence, Matter is a form of veiled Life, Life a form of veiled Consciousness. And that mental consciousness, says Aurobindo, may itself be only a form and a veil of higher states which are beyond Mind. If that is so, then the unconquerable impulse of man towards God, Light, Bliss, Freedom, Immortality can be seen simply as the imperative impulse by which Nature is seeking to evolve beyond Mind, beyond even Overmind. Aurobindo's logic is simple and persuasive: 'The animal is a living laboratory in which Nature has, it is said, worked out man. Man himself may well be a thinking and living laboratory in whom and with whose conscious cooperation she wills to work out the superman, the god. Or shall we not say, rather, to manifest God?'[95]

Thus, Aurobindo goes on philosophizing about the Supramental Descent. However, as one wades through his arguments and descriptions of the would-be Superman, it all begins to sound like science fiction! Well, why not, many might say, arguing that in some distant future it may well become a reality. We really do not know. But the more serious question is not about the future. It is about Aurobindo. What happened to Aurobindo? Did the Supramental Energy manifest in him? Did he become a 'Superman'?

UG is not merely suspicious of such grand ideas, whether secular or spiritual, but rejects them all as products of a mind still caught in the realm of opposites, as being still in the realm of time and space, which is thought, which is hope, which is but the strategies of the self to extend and perpetuate itself. 'What arrogance and impudence on the part of these people,' says UG angrily and rudely, 'to think that they are the channels of supramental manifestation.'

Is there, then, nothing at all to Aurobindo's experiments, insights and ideas?

In Raja Rao's celebrated novel, *The Serpent and the Rope*, the central character, Rama, who is a Vedantin and a seeker in his own right, speaks out against Aurobindo's Superman brilliantly thus: 'The Superman is our enemy. Look what happened in India. Sri Aurobindo wanted, if you please, to improve on the Advaita of Sri Sankara—which was just like trying to improve on the numerical status of zero.'[96]

A recent photograph of UG

UG, of course, is no Vedantin and he does not dismiss the idea of 'Superman' from a Vedantic point of view. Rather, referring to his own 'Calamity', or the Natural State, he does agree, though reluctantly, that perhaps Nature is pushing towards the creation of new species. But this new species is not a Superman—rather it becomes a complete human being cleansed of 'animal traits'! This unique individual, who lives in the natural state, is probably the end product of biological evolution, not the science-fiction superman or some kind of spiritual or supernatural being. UG says:

Once an individual is *freed* from the burden of the past, he or she becomes, for the first time, an individual. *You become yourself.* But there is no relationship between these two flowers at all, so there is no point in comparing and contrasting the unique flowers that Nature has thrown up from time to time. They, in their own ways, have had some impact, although the whole thing resulted in some tiny colonies fighting amongst themselves, that's all. It goes on and on and on . . . Each flower has its own fragrance. If it had not been for the heritage of man, which we are so proud of, we would have had so many flowers like this. So it has destroyed what Nature . . . . (It's not that I am interpreting or understanding Nature's ways, the purpose of evolution, or any such thing; there may not be any such thing as evolution at all.) If it had not been for the culture, Nature would have thrown up many more flowers—so this has become a *stumbling block* to man's freeing himself in his own way . . .

What value has that flower to mankind? What value has it? You can look at it, admire it, write a piece of poetry, paint it, or you can crush it and throw it away or feed your cow with it—but still it is *there*. It is of no use to society at all, but it is there.

18

The Two Krishnamurtis

'What is the difference between JK and UG? Don't they speak the same language, and say more or less the same things? Aren't both enlightened Masters? Don't you think JK was a more compassionate teacher, that UG is crude, sometimes even irrational and cruel? Why does he attack JK all the time, isn't he quite obsessed with JK? Is UG really different from JK? How? In what way?'

Such questions are frequently asked about JK and UG by people who know, or have heard both Krishnamurtis.

Frankly, I was at a loss when I first heard UG speak in the late 1970s. I thought JK was the ultimate; his teaching seemed to be a sort of extreme spirituality that one could not go beyond. Then came UG, the 'Other Krishnamurti', who, I found to my utter shock and horror, debunking all that JK had said as romantic hogwash, sheer unadulterated fantasy and nothing more. If JK had made my head burn and the whole of my body feel as if on fire all the time, with UG my head went missing, and I felt like an absolute moron, a zero.

We always build up ideas dialectically and in frames, as UG says. Our knowledge-building process is a movement in measurement and pleasure. So, once the head was back in its place, I could not help but try and get a handle on the two Krishnamurtis.

For some time I thought JK was a genuine teacher, a compassionate man, a truly enlightened being, one who has reached the other shore. And UG, it seemed, was stuck somewhere on the way, or was still on the move, wading through difficult waters.

Indian enlightenment traditions, and texts such as Patanjali's *Yoga Sutra* and *Yogavashista* register the 'marks' of an enlightened being. But how does one know for sure that this is how exactly an enlightened man speaks, moves and behaves? And, pray, what is this enlightenment? All this only added to my confusion. Then I was influenced by Buddhism and for some time I was content with the idea that JK was a bodhisattva, the compassionate one, who out of his compassion for all living creatures returns to the world to take others along in the boat of gnosis to the other shore, to the shore of Nirvana. I thought UG to be a typical *pratyeka buddha*, who, without a guru, reaches nirvana on his own, and later refuses to be a guru to others—a Buddha who walks alone, with no mission in life, for all sense of goal or mission has come to an end. And since there is no birth, no death, no such thing as bondage, there is no liberation either. How, then, can there be any teaching, any teacher, or anyone to be taught?

It was while listening to UG that I realized that it was silly and futile to indulge in such useless comparisons, and that such speculation deflected one's attention away from the facts one has to come to terms with. The need to compare, assess and judge could well be a trick of the mind in search of security. And so I thought one should see if both JK and UG mean what they say, whether what they say reflects in their lives, and also that one should examine the implication of their teachings in the context of one's own experience and examine the realities as one understands them.

However, this narrative demands that the stories be told and contrasts be made if only to arrive, without being judgemental, at some clearer understanding of things, if that is possible. One should let the facts speak for themselves. But then, one might say, we do not know all the facts, and what we call facts could only be our perception of things conditioned by our background. Indeed, it is a fact that there are no facts as such, rather, what we call facts (not to speak of truth) are but our perspectives on, or our interpretation of, things! Be that as it may, let us allow the story to unfold.

Footprints on a Pathless Land

Since we have already briefly covered some aspects of JK's life and teaching, we shall focus here on only certain crucial aspects of his career as a World Teacher.

In 'Why I Am a Destiny' in *Ecce Homo*, Friedrich Nietzsche wrote: 'I know my fate. One day my name will be associated with the memory of something tremendous—a crisis without equal on earth, the most profound collision of conscience, a decision that was conjured up *against* everything that had been believed, demanded, hallowed so far. I am no man, I am dynamite.'

It seems to me that JK too felt the same about his life and teaching, perhaps much more strongly than Nietzsche. He literally questioned and blasted all forms of authority, whether spiritual or secular. He believed he was not merely unique but someone the like of whom the world had not seen for many centuries. In fact, he has even gone on record, saying: '. . .You won't find another body like this, or that supreme intelligence, operating in a body for many hundred years.' I cannot assess the validity of this statement. But, as a matter of fact, what I have found over the years is that it is UG who has literally questioned, rejected and exploded all the ideas 'hallowed so far', who has truly and wholly questioned the very foundation of human thought. In his own words: 'I am an unconverted member of the human race. My viewpoint throughout life has been in tension with those who readily conform to the middle-class standards and conventions of my generation. I am in revolt against the mainsprings of our faith, the religious customs that propel us and form the impelling motives of our actions.'

He is no man, he is a neutron bomb!

Now to get back to the story of the two Krishnamurtis. Way back in 1921, when JK was only twenty-six years of age and still a budding World Teacher within the mould of the Theosophical Society, he warned his followers thus: 'True spirituality is hard and cruel, and the World Teacher . . . is not going to be lenient to our weaknesses and our failings . . . He is not going to preach what we want, nor say what we wish, nor give us the sop to our feelings which we all like, but on the contrary He is going to wake us all up whether we like it or not, for we must be able to receive knocks as men.'

Two years later, he surprised everyone by declaring: 'Nothing could ever be the same. I have drunk at the clear and pure waters at the source of the fountain of life and my thirst was appeased. Never more could I be thirsty, never more could I be in utter darkness; I have seen the Light . . . I have drunk at the fountain of Joy and eternal Beauty. I am god-intoxicated.'

In 1926, two days after the death of his brother, Nityananda, from tuberculosis, though still in great sorrow and feeling let down by the Masters, JK announced at Adyar: 'An old dream is dead and a new one is being born, as a flower that pushes through the solid earth . . . As Krishnamurti, I have now greater zeal, greater faith, greater sympathy and greater love . . . I have drunk at the fountain of human sorrow and suffering, from which I have derived strength.'

It was a slow and hesitant journey, a preparation, a desperate yet firm decision to drop everything, to escape; it was the death of the old dream, and the beginning of a new one, which, sadly and ultimately, would not be very different from the old. The final rupture with the Theosophical Society, the agony and ecstasy of the birth of the new teacher took place when, on the morning of 3 August 1929, in the forest of Ommen in Holland before an array of Theosophical Society leaders, including Annie Besant, JK dissolved the Order of the Star of the East, and declared: 'I maintain that Truth is a pathless land, and you cannot approach it by any path whatsoever, by any religion, by any sect . . .'

Almost until his death, he held that 'the idea of the teacher and the taught is basically wrong'. What he was trying to do was not teaching, but 'sharing', 'merely acting as a mirror' in which others could see themselves clearly and then discard the mirror. Or, at the most, he was only trying to 'awaken' people from their slumber and see for themselves the truth, 'truth not at the top of the ladder; truth is where you are, in what you are doing, thinking, feeling, when you kiss and hug, when you exploit—you must see the truth of all that, not a truth at the end of innumerable cycles of life'.

Doubt and negation as a method of inquiry was the strong point of JK's teaching. Finally, after he broke away from the Theosophical Society, the way he questioned, doubted, probed, tested and negated the established, sacred beliefs of the religious traditions of the East and West, and opened new ways of seeing and experiencing life was something new. It was a voice, deep, profound and cathartic, a voice that had not been heard for a long time.

He was a witness to two horrible world wars and great social and political upheavals. He was also a contemporary of the path-breaking modern artists and thinkers who have had a great impact on modern consciousness (though some of them now may appear like toddlers trying to dream up new ideas, when compared with JK's mature and deep understanding of the human condition). His great contribution lies in the fact that he developed and encouraged doubt as a method of inquiry. When, in both the religious and scientific spheres Nature was still predominantly seen as an enemy, when religious people still indulged in the repudiation of the actual in favour of the other worldly, when matter was seen as a limitation, when the manifestation of life was damned as a burden and escape from manifestation was celebrated as freedom, JK kicked reality into motion and went on to assert that freedom—not as an escape from matter, manifestation or creation, but as a passage into it, and as Pure Creation and Pure Activity. Thus, for almost seventy years, with doubt as his method, he tried to awaken people from their slumber and goad them into questioning everything, especially all the truths that had been accepted as pre-given. With what may be called a *boddhisattvic* zeal, he wanted to create a new order, a new way of living and being in the world. To bring about this new order, this new way of living, he declared repeatedly, doggedly, 'we must understand disorder. It is only through negation that you understand the positive, not by the pursuit of the positive . . . out of negation comes the right discipline, which is order . . . Negation can only take place when the mind sees the false. The very perception of the false is the negation of the false . . .The total negation of that (old) road is the new beginning, the other road. This other road is not on the map, nor can it ever be put on any map. Every map is the map of the wrong road, the old road . . ..[97]

There is no way we can measure the impact of JK's teaching on the world, but he certainly marked a major departure in spiritual thought. His criticism of religious traditions and authority did change the way we look at religious thought and even at the reports of mystical experiences. In some ways, his teaching also anticipated some of the radical insights and perspectives the postmodernists would use to deconstruct the 'hallowed ideas' of Western philosophy in the 1960s and 1970s. And, in a sense, I would say that he also anticipated the coming of UG and his anti-philosophy.

The professional non-dualists in India found it difficult to appropriate or absorb JK's teaching into their Vedantic philosophy, for JK rejected all the central ideas and symbols of Vedanta too. There was no atman, no Brahman, no sadhana, no samadhi, and no moksha. Of the *mahavakyas* (literally great statements, or scriptural utterances) such as *Prajnanam Brahma* '(Consciousness is infinite'), *Aham Brahmasmi* ('I am that infinite'), *tat tvam-asi* ('Thou art That'), he asked: Why do we always attach ourselves to something which we suppose to be the highest? Why not say: I am the river, I am the poor man? Can a conditioned mind,' he questioned, 'can a mind that is small, petty, narrow, living on superficial entertainments, can that know or conceive, or understand, or feel, or observe the unconditioned?'

What does 'Vedanta' mean? The end of the Vedas, the end of knowledge! 'Therefore, leave it,' he said. 'Why proceed from there to describe what is not? . . . If Vedanta means the end of knowledge . . . the ending of Vedas, which is knowledge—then why should I go through the laborious process of acquiring knowledge, and then discarding it? Why should not I, from the very beginning, see what

UG in a pensive mood

knowledge is and discard it? . . . Why did the traditionalists, the professionals, the scriptures, the spiritual leaders not see this? Was it because authority was tremendously important—the authority of the *Gita*, the experience, the scriptures? Why? Why did they not see this?'

Years later, UG would ask the same question of JK. Why talk about immensity, of beauty, of choiceless awareness, of love and compassion? 'Why don't you stop with *what is*, Krishnaji?'

By UG's own admission, JK did have some influence on him. In fact, he has talked openly of his truly paradoxical relationship with JK. However, it is hard to imagine the impact of UG on JK, if there was any at all, for JK has not, either in public or private, talked of his relationship and strange encounters with UG, though records show that in 1953, when JK was in Madras to give his talks, he did meet with UG and have serious conversations with him every day for over forty days.

UG says that during those forty days of intense discussions, JK was using him as a mirror to understand himself. This could have been true, it is a fact that, at some point during one of those conversations (see Chapter 7) UG went through what he calls a 'near-death' experience. It was an experience, says UG, which altered his being and could have made him a teacher in his own right. In his own words: 'I could have been a spiritual teacher on my own, but I put the idea aside as just another illusion I would be adding to mankind's hope of finding the truth. The majority of those who reach this state that I experienced think that they have reached the final goal, and believe that they have attained liberation. But, unfortunately, there is no measuring stick to differentiate between the few who have attained and those who have gotten stuck in the mystical experience.'

There were, of course, a few more encounters between the two in London and then in Gstaad. It is important to note that UG's 'Calamity' was triggered, in a sense, when for the last time UG attended JK's talk on 13 August 1967 at Gstaad.

This is not to suggest that JK was the cause of UG's 'Calamity', or even that JK was in some way responsible for what happened to UG in 1967. Ultimately, we cannot know the cause of a particular effect; in fact, the very division between cause and effect is artificial and problematic. But then thought can operate only within the framework of cause and effect, within a binary mode. We see fire and we see smoke and conclude that fire causes smoke. All our knowledge systems are based on such binary thinking; all our sciences and even political thinking are rooted in this dichotomy. It is indeed effective, it is result-oriented, otherwise we could not send rockets into space, and we would not support democracy! But then we also realize that life slips through this framework, truth eludes us, and we know that we do not know the cause of anything, or whether there is such a thing at all.

However, what one wishes to suggest is that there was something magnetic, some sort of mysterious connection between JK and UG. Perhaps it is not all that mysterious, it is just how things are in life, for everything is an interconnected whole. We affect each other all the time in more and deeper ways than we can understand. We affect the environment we live in just as the environment affects us. It is all one interconnected whole, the incomprehensible 'participation' of the whole universe in every little thing.

The mysterious connection between the two snapped after JK passed away. A year later, UG said what he had to say. It was time

A sketch of UG

to dismantle the old but not erect or construct anything new in its place. It would not be a new interpretation, amplification or clarification of the old teaching, but a total rejection. It would be a negation of all approaches including the negative approach of JK. UG would claim that there is no method implied in either his negation or rejection of things, and that it could not be made into yet another approach. In point of fact, it would be neither a negation nor an assertion of anything. No apocalypse! No Kingdom of God cometh! No atman, no Brahman, no moksha, no Nirvana! No *sunyavada* or sunyata either!

Many people get either upset or misled by UG's criticism and dismissal of JK. Sentiments don't count here. Yet, as a matter of fact, UG has acknowledged the significant role JK has played in his life, saying 'It was J. Krishnamurti who pushed me to stand on my own two feet.'

In the early years of his acquaintance with UG, Mahesh Bhatt once asked him: 'UG, if I ask you to name the most remarkable man you have met in your life, who comes to your mind first?'

'Jiddu Krishnamurti. But . . .'

He didn't complete the sentence. Mahesh asked, 'Are you backing out?'

'Oh, no,' UG is believed to have protested.

Why, then, does he criticize JK all the time? Why, given the slightest opportunity, does he launch a virtual onslaught on JK's teachings? Some people think that UG is obsessed with JK. Religious-minded people, however, view the relationship between these two as in keeping with the great Indian spiritual tradition in which the disciple annihilates the teachings of his guru.

But ask UG, and he would say:

To me, Krishnamurti is playing exactly the same game as all those ugly saints in the market whom we have in the world today. Krishnamurti's teaching is phoney baloney. There is nothing to his teaching at all, and he cannot produce anything at all. A person may listen to him for sixty, seventy or a hundred years, but nothing will ever happen to that man, because the whole thing is phoney. If the number of followers is the criterion of a successful spiritual teacher, JK is a pygmy.

He is a mere wordsmith. He has created a new trap.

Yes, I am using eighty per cent of his words and phrases, the very phrases he has used over the years to condemn gurus, saints, and saviours like himself. He has it coming. One thing I have never said: he is not a man of character. He has great character, but I am not in the least interested in men of character. If he sees the mess he has created in his false role as World Messiah and dissolves the whole thing, I will be the first to salute him. But he is too old and senile to do it. His followers are appalled that I am giving him a dose of his own medicine. Do not compare what I am saying with what he, or other religious authorities, have said. If you give what I am saying any spiritual overtones, any religious flavour at all, you are missing the point.

Many a former JKite, including this writer, cannot help but agree with UG, although one may not call JK a 'fraud' and dub his teachings 'phoney baloney'. JK taught us to question everything, question all authority, including his own. And so, without dismissing JK, in keeping with the spirit of his teachings, we cannot now help but question the guru and his teachings. That's how it should be, for as Nietzsche would say, 'One repays a teacher badly, if one remains only a pupil.'

On the day that JK dissolved the Order of the Star of the East and declared 'Truth is a pathless land', he narrated the following little story.

'You may remember the story of how the devil and a friend of his were walking down the street, when they saw ahead of them a man stoop down and pick up something from the ground, look at it, and put it away in his pocket.

'The friend said to the devil, "What did that man pick up?"

'"He picked up a piece of Truth," said the devil.

'"That is a very bad business for you, then," said the friend.

'"No, not at all," the devil replied, "I am going to let him organize it."'

The message was fairly simple and clear: You cannot organize Truth or teach Truth. You cannot teach compassion. To put it differently, any attempt at the institutionalization of truth or wisdom can only lead to its corruption, and whatever possibility may exist for an individual to come upon truth and wisdom will be messed up.

Why then did JK let an organization be built in his name? His close associates and admirers might defend the decision, saying it was formed for very simple and practical reasons: To arrange JK's trips and talks, to publish his talks in the form of books and bulletins, and to produce audio and video cassettes of the talks and discussions so that those interested in his teachings could benefit from them.

The result is fantastic—close to 10,00,000 pages of printed material. In all, seventy-five books totalling about 40,00,000 copies sold in twenty-two languages, around 2500 audio cassettes, 1200 video cassettes, not to speak of a considerable number of unpublished letters, transcripts, and other writings.

In the late 1960s, the long, deep relationship of trust between JK and Rajagopal began to fall apart. When JK had walked out of the Theosophical Society, Rajagopal had joined him as a good and loyal friend and had been singularly responsible for establishing Krishnamurti Writings Inc (KWINC). For more than three decades, he had almost single-handedly managed the finances, organized JK's trips round the world and edited his books. Though they were not born of the same mother, they had lived like Rama and Lakshmana, Rajagopal like Lakshmana following the *avatara purusha* and dedicating his life, even at the cost of his health and his marital happiness, to protecting JK and propagating his teachings. However, they were no mythical figures and were not free of contradictions, conflicts, and self-interest.

There are different versions of the misunderstandings and quarrels between JK and Rajagopal. According to one version, JK began to ignore, snub and insult Rajagopal and totally disregard his advice regarding the KWINC. Another version has it that Rajagopal began to mismanage the funds and boss over the master. However, the conflicts intensified after Rosalind, in a fit of remorse and anger, confessed to Rajagopal her nearly-twenty-year intimate relationship with JK.

All attempts made by the trustees of KWINC and close associates to bring the two friends together failed, and in 1968 JK filed a lawsuit against Rajagopal. This did shock some of JK's close friends and admirers, for they could not reconcile the fact of the case with the personality and teachings of JK. How could JK—who had been compared with the Buddha and Christ, and who believed 'If you defend yourself, then the defender becomes the attacker'—initiate a 'war' against his own friend? If JK cannot live his own teachings, who can?

In 1974, an out-of-court settlement was reached. JK resumed full powers over KWINC, which was later converted into a different trust under the new name of Krishnamurti Foundation. However, soon yet another case was filed against Rajagopal, who refused to part with the archival material: letters, manuscripts and important documents concerning JK. Radha Sloss says that JK's fear was that if some of these papers were to be published, it would not only be hurtful but permanently damage his image as the World Teacher. The case was settled, after JK's death in 1986, in favour of Rajagopal. His daughter, Radha Rajagopal Sloss, made use of some of these papers to write *Lives in the Shadow with J. Krishnamurti*, published only after JK had died.

Generally, while discussing sex, relationship, love and marriage, JK would ask, 'Why do you make a problem of sex?' and then proceed to show how the problem is actually not sex, but the self—the self that is possessive, jealous and insecure, which corrupts a relationship and destroys the blossoming of love and compassion. It is from JK, in fact, that we learnt: 'Not being able to find out how to live a chaste life, one takes vows of celibacy and goes through tortures. That is not celibacy. Celibacy is something entirely different. It is to have a mind that is free from all images, from all knowledge; which means understanding the whole process of pleasure and fear.' In other words, we learnt that the imposition of celibacy is puerile, that it is foolish to think of sex as anti-spiritual, anti-God or sinful, and that sex could be a beautiful act, an expression of love so long as it does not become possessive, and does not become an escape from sorrow, or an obsessive pleasure to be pursued again and again.

After Radha Sloss's book, which, of course, came as a shock, one also began to wonder if JK was discussing his own dilemmas and conflicts from the public platform. But at that time, the impression one got of him was that he was beyond all conditioning, all doubts and conflicts, that he was truly an enlightened master.

First the starting of KWINC, then the schools and centres all over the world, then the legal battles, and now the sex scandal!

Looking back and feeling betrayed, one may ask: Was it all necessary? Did JK have to break away from the Theosophical Society only to build yet another massive organization in his name? Did he not know that misunderstandings, quarrels, misuse of funds, threats of blackmail, and power politics are inherent in the very nature of organizations, whether secular or spiritual? Did he really believe that the Krishnamurti schools would succeed in producing individuals free of all conditioning, individuals who would be a 'danger' to our 'corrupt society', to our 'corrupt' spiritual and secular authorities? Did he not realize the implications of it all? Was it all really necessary?

Or should we ask if the 'devil' of whom he warned the Theosophists before breaking away from them and declaring 'truth is a pathless land', returned to take his revenge, to claim his pound of flesh from JK?

After Radha Sloss's book, UG took a hard line and called JK the greatest fraud of the twentieth century: 'He denounces systems and opens meditation schools, talks of the crippling effects of conditioning, then runs schools which foster more conditioning, talks of simplicity and builds worldwide real estate organizations; says you must be on your own, then takes measures to preserve his teachings for the future.' And about the book, he said, 'She has dumped a keg of dynamite! The story of the sex, lies and flippancy of Krishnamurti is more absorbing than his teachings. The picture that emerges from that book tells us that Krishnamurti has successfully remained an undetected hoax of the twentieth century . . .'

But UG's criticism of JK and his teachings concern a much deeper and more fundamental flaw, which may be summarised in the following way:

What JK says does not operate in his life. His teaching does not spring from the state of being which it seems to indicate; rather, it is an expression of his own doubts, problems, and aspirations or yearnings, which, of course, has a tremendous appeal because his listeners too operate within the same realm of doubts and aspirations. Further, there is no such thing as choiceless awareness. It simply is not possible. You cannot exist without choice, even for a nanosecond. The thought, 'I', the self, becoming still or choiceless, would mean the death of the self, which would trigger not a psychological transformation but a kind of clinical death, a biological mutation. In UG's own words:

> To me there is no such thing as mind; mind is a myth. Since there is no such thing as mind, the 'mutation of mind' that J. Krishnamurti is talking about has no meaning. There is nothing there to be transformed, radically or otherwise. There is no self to be realized. The whole religious structure that has been built on this foundation collapses because there is nothing there to realize.
>
> Choiceless awareness is poppycock. Who is the one being choicelessly aware? You must test this for yourself. J. Krishnamurti has gathered about him the spiritual dead wood of a twenty-, thirty- and forty-year club. What good is that? I lived with him for years, and I can tell you he is a great actor. "Gentlemen, we are taking a journey together"—but you can never go on that journey with him. Whatever you do, it is always the same. What you experience with him is the clarification of thought. You are that thought. He is a do-gooder who should have given up long ago.
>
> As long as you think that you can see more and more clearly, I say you have seen nothing. J. Krishnamurti says, "Seeing is the end." If you say you have seen, you have not seen, because seeing is the end of the structure that says that. There is no seeing you can know. In other words, there is no seeing. As long as you think you can understand or see the world around you more clearly, I say you will see nothing and understand nothing.
>
> J. Krishnamurti has subtly enticed people into believing in a spiritual goal, a goal which moreover can be reached through specific techniques—"passive awareness", "free inquiry", "direct perception", "scepticism", etc. I reject the idea of transformation altogether. There is nothing to be

transformed, no psyche to revolutionize, and no awareness
you can use to improve or change yourself.

He is a showman par excellence and master of words.
Krishnamurti's teachings may have sounded very revolutionary
a century ago. But with the emergence of new revelations in
the fields of microbiology and genetics, the ideas taken for
granted in the field of psychology will be challenged. The
'mind' (which Krishnamurti's teaching assumes), the exclusive
franchise of psychologists and religious teachers and all the
assumptions connected with it, will also be undermined.

But JK believed otherwise. He believed that his very coming
and his teaching was a major departure from all the religious
teachings of the world, and that his teaching, far from being
outdated, would last for at least 500 years, before another
Maitreya came to finish it. In 1986, after living through two world
wars, through great historical upheavals and unprecedented
changes in the world, and teaching his 'pathless path' for over
sixty years, when he lay in his home at Arya Vihar, dying of
pancreatic cancer, his close associates asked him: 'When Krishnaji
dies what really happens to that extraordinary focus of
understanding and energy that is K?' And Krishnaji, in a voice
that had lost its thunder but was nevertheless clear, recorded the
following answer on tape:

I was telling them this morning—for seventy years that super-
energy—no—that immense energy, immense intelligence, has
been using this body. I don't think people realize what
tremendous energy and intelligence went through this body—
there's a twelve-cylinder engine. And for seventy years—was
a pretty long time—and now the body can't stand any more.
Nobody, unless the body has been prepared, very carefully,
protected and so on—nobody can understand what went
through this body. Nobody. Don't anybody pretend. I repeat
this: nobody amongst us or the public, know what went on.
I know they don't. And now after seventy years it has come
to an end. Not that intelligence and energy—it's somewhat
here, every day, and especially at night. And after seventy

years the body can't stand it—can't stand any more. The
Indians have a lot of damned superstitions about this—that
you will and the body goes—and all that kind of nonsense.
You won't find another body like this, or that supreme
intelligence, operating in a body for many hundred years. You
won't see it again. When he goes, it goes. There is no
consciousness left behind of *that* consciousness, of *that* state.
They'll all pretend or try to imagine they can get into touch
with that. Perhaps they will somewhat if they live the
teachings. But nobody has done it. Nobody. And so that's
that.[98]

The same night, in a house in Marin County, Mill Valley, 400
miles from Ojai, UG felt it and knew that JK was dying. And
something extraordinary happened. Robert Carr (Bob), who was a
witness to this strange yet mysterious incident, writes:

UG called us at home and asked if we could come over right
away. 'Now,' he said. We jumped into our car and arrived
at UG's house. Kim let us in and said, 'UG is in his bedroom,
go in.' UG was seated in the middle of his bed, cross-legged,
and he was dressed in his pajamas. He looked up at us and
said, 'I don't think I am going to survive; the energy is so
strong, the body can't take it.' He added, 'All the papers are
on top of the chest; everything is in order about what to do.'
Then he became silent, and as we were looking at him we
could see ripples from the top of his head moving down his
face, the skin had waves or ripples moving down. His whole
body was undulating. UG again said that the energy was too
strong. It was strange to be with him during this episode. Paul
and I both felt that by being there we were helping him some
way; but how, I didn't know. We told him, 'No doubt it's the
Old Man (JK); he's going, and the two of you are linked,
whether you like it or not.' UG exclaimed, 'Oh, no!' 'Look
UG, you both are two sides of the same coin,' I said. We
stayed there with him, and the energy kept coming in waves
as he sat still with his eyes closed in a yoga posture. What
a strange scene it was! One man in Southern California was

dying, and another man 400 miles away in some way connected with his death. Here was another mystery unfolding about the two Krishnamurtis: their lives were in some way connected. Yet, even to this day you won't get an answer from UG about it.'99

19

Body, Mind and Soul—Do They Exist?

Whenever Sri Ramana was asked any questions relating to God, atman, and the meaning of life, his usual response used to be: 'Who is asking the question? Who or what is this "I"? What is mind? Enquire into it; find out . . .'

How does one find out? There is no asking 'how', JK would say, yet do inquire, be aware, and see 'what is'. On the other hand, UG would assert that the whole business of self-inquiry is a joke. But in the first place, why do we ask these questions? Who am I? What is man? Is there a God? Is the soul different from the body? What is the meaning of all this?

But are these really our questions? Or are we repeating questions already asked by others in the past, sometimes rephrasing them this way or that? Are we asking these questions because our traditions and gurus have told us that they are very important and that it is possible to find answers? Or is it, to use UG's language, because the old answers are really no answers, that the questions have remained and continue to be asked. Could it be that there are actually no questions but only unsatisfying and unconvincing answers, and these answers are our problem. Is the problem that we hope that one day we should be able to find satisfactory and final answers to all our questions?

Obviously, of all the creatures living on this planet, only the self-conscious human being asks questions. The questioning is backed by a sort of a priori belief that it is possible to know, to understand and share or communicate that understanding to others. Otherwise, all our inquiries, all our searching, all our sciences should come to a grinding halt.

However, there has arisen time and again a strong suspicion about this whole business of the search. For, to ask *what* something is or to ask, say, what the body or the mind or a human being is, is to seek out its essence. Does such a thing as essence exist? This is indeed a metaphysical question and metaphysical answers are no real answers at all. 'Man does not exist', declared Foucault. Actually, what he meant was that the body–mind composite, the empirico-transcendental duo is nothing more than a metaphysical construct. Nietzsche too questioned the very basis of this search for, according to him, it is rooted in the value not only of absolutes but also of opposites, by playing off one against the other.[100]

There is nothing outside the text, announced Derrida, meaning that there is only the text and the language in which it is expressed. The implication is that we have first to examine the text, how it works, examine the language and see if it offers any meaning, stable or otherwise, and whether the text achieves anything at all!

So then, for many postmodernists it is not the question, but language itself that is problematic. The self, or even the body, is not something given, but the significant effect of language. The self is not outside of language, and is always in relation to the 'other'. In fact, it is in and through language and in comparison with others that man constructs himself as a subject, and establishes the concept of self or ego.[101]

It all seems to be a terribly futile epistemological exercise. As G.B. Madison would say: 'So long as we remain bound to epistemology, which is to say, to metaphysics, searching for ultimate basis or "models", sources, grounds, or origins, ultimate causal, essentialist, fundamentalist explanations, we are perhaps condemned to go round in endless circles, like a dog chasing its tail in vain.'[102]

But the chase is on. The dog seems to be getting nearer its own tail, particularly in the non-metaphysical domain. A considerable number of psychologists, neuro-physiologists, geneticists and socio-biologists do not bother too much about whether 'mind' exists at all. They simply grant it a vague epiphenomenal status and get down to talking about behavioural patterns and neural activity. And we see a certain interpenetration of disciplines: The psychologists reduce their science to biology, the biologists to chemistry and physics, and physicists to the enigmatic man who happens to be the observer who seems to create or construct a phenomenon rather than discover it. This epistemological circle, avers Madison, has not led us anywhere closer to a unified theory or non-reductionist understanding of the human person.

However, there are tough molecular biologists and geneticists who believe that they have nearly solved the body–mind problem within their discipline. It is interesting to take a quick look at least at two of their important theories.

The Selfish Gene

Richard Dawkins's celebrated yet controversial book, *The Selfish Gene*, narrates a fascinating story of the evolution of man on earth from the genetic point of view. It is the story of the journey of the ruthless gene, starting its passage from the 'primordial soup' through Darwinian 'natural selection', through 'mutation' and 'adaptation' to 'Homo sapiens', the human body, which is but a fantastic machine used by the gene for its perpetuation.

According to Dawkins, it is erroneous to assume some grand design or purpose to evolution, or that it is for 'the good of the species'. No—it is for the good of the individual or the gene. The argument that culture is more important than genes to the understanding of human nature is at best only wishful thinking. 'Much as we wish to believe otherwise,' writes Dawkins, 'universal love and the welfare of the species as a whole are concepts that simply do not make evolutionary sense.'

Anything that has evolved through natural selection is *selfish*, Homo sapiens included. 'Selfish' in the sense that genes act only for themselves, their only interest being their own replication. Come what may, they copy themselves and 'want' to be passed on to the next generation. 'Selfish' or 'want' ought not to be understood as some grand purpose, aim or intention (which are all only mental constructions) but only as 'chemical instructions' that can be copied. In this relentless journey of the gene, altruism too is but another technique of the gene, another facet that is played out to ensure its continuity. 'To put it in a slightly more respectable way, a group, such as a species or a population within a species, whose individual members are prepared to sacrifice themselves for the welfare of the group, may be less likely to become extinct than a rival group whose individual members place their own selfish interests first.' Altruism is selfishness in disguise and 'often altruism within a group goes with selfishness between groups'.[103]

These genes or replicators are basically the same kind of molecules in all living organisms—from bacteria to elephants. The human body, which has evolved over millions of years, is the handiwork of the very same gene, created for its safe perpetuation. 'We are all survival machines,' declares Dawkins, 'for the same kind of replicators—molecules called DNA—but since there are many different ways of making a living in the world, the replicators have built a vast range of machines to exploit them. A monkey is a machine that preserves genes up trees, a fish is a machine that preserves genes in water . . .DNA works in mysterious ways.'

It is genes that are immortal, not some dreamed-up spirit or soul which we imagine and identify ourselves with. There is no such thing as God or spirit either! There are only genes that leap 'from body to body down the generations, manipulating body after body in its own way and for its own ends . . .' We are merely their survival machines and 'when we have served our purpose we are cast aside. But genes are denizens of geological time: genes are forever.'

What then is 'mind' in this scheme of things? Is it just another technique, another 'machine' used by the gene for its own survival? Towards the end of his book, Dawkins proposes a theory of what he calls *meme*, apparently to solve the niggling body–mind problem: If the 'body' is the survival machine of the gene, the 'mind'—that is, memory—is the survival machine of the meme, proclaims Dawkins. Unlike genes, memes are not physically located, yet, he asserts: 'Memes should be regarded as living structures, not just metaphorically but technically.'

If the gene emerged out of the 'primordial soup', human culture is a product of the 'new soup'—memes. But how and when did memes emerge? Dawkins says: 'The old gene-selected evolution, by making brains, provided the "soup" in which the first memes arose. Once the self-copying memes had arisen, their own much faster kind of evolution took off. And they seem to have taken over the genes and started a new, independent kind of evolution of their own.'[104]

There are different kinds of memes—what Dawkins calls 'meme complexes'—such as fashions in dress and diet, ceremonies and customs, art and architecture, engineering and technology, music, ideas and concepts—all of which 'evolve in historical time in a way that looks like highly speeded up genetic evolution, but has really nothing to do with genetic evolution'. In other words, these new replicators, like selfish genes, perpetuate themselves simply because it is advantageous to them. They plant themselves on or parasitize the brain, 'turning it into a vehicle for the meme's propagation in just the way that a virus may parasitize the genetic mechanism of a host cell'. According to Dawkins, God exists 'if only in the form of a meme with high survival value, or infective power, in the environment provided by human cultures'.

The Meme Machine

Surprisingly, it is not Dawkins's theory of the selfish gene (which many people find reductionist and reactionary), but his novel concept of the meme that has caught the imagination of a considerable number of psychologists, biologists and cultural theorists, although they may not all use the term to mean the same thing. For instance, Ken Wilber finds the theory quite problematic[105] though he too uses the term 'green meme' to mean pluralistic relativism embedded in egalitarian, anti-hierarchical values.

Susan Blackmore, a psychologist who is interested in near-death experiences, the effects of meditation, the paranormal and evolutionary psychology, has applied the idea of the meme to develop a theory of memetics in her book, *The Meme Machine*. Since her theory has some bearing on what UG has been saying about the nature of thought, it is worthwhile to consider some of her central ideas.

Blackmore believes that memetic theory not only solves what

is called the 'hard problem of consciousness' and body–mind dualism more effectively than other theories, but can also open up a whole new way of seeing and being in the world.

We copy each other all the time and with great ease. We imitate and learn through imitation, and that *imitation* is what distinguishes us from animals and makes us special. When we imitate an idea, an instruction, a behaviour, even a gesture, something is passed on again and again and from generation to generation, which takes on a life of its own. It becomes independent and autonomous, for instance, Karl Popper's idea of World 3 (the world of ideas, language and stories, works of art and technology, mathematics and science). This is the meme: the second replicator (after the gene). Memes are stored in human brains or in books and computers and passed on endlessly. Memes spread for their own benefit, without regard to whether they are useful, neutral or harmful. As examples, the idea of God, or revolution, or a particular invention, spread irrespective of whether they are useful or not. Some memes are useful and creative, some harmful and even dangerous. But memes don't care, they just 'want' to spread and perpetuate themselves. 'There is no master plan, no end point, and no designer.' What we call new creative or original ideas are only 'variation and combination of old ideas'. Memes have uncanny ways of perpetuating themselves. But not all thoughts are memes; not our immediate perceptions and emotions, which are ours alone and which we may not pass on. However, once we express them or speak about them to others, be it our feelings or our ideas, they are passed on.

Memes have nothing to do with genes. If 'genes are instructions encoded in molecules of DNA—memes are instructions embedded in human brains, or artefacts such as books, pictures, bridges or steam engines'.[106]

Acknowledging Dennett's idea of 'competition between memes to get into our brain' to make us the kinds of creatures we are, Blackmore believes that our minds and selves are created by the interplay of the memes. For that matter, human consciousness itself is a product of memes.

There are only memes, only thoughts. Thinking involves energy. Much of our thinking is sheer frustration or self-pity, which we could do without, to the huge advantage of the body. Yet thinking goes on, draining the energies of the body. It happens because the memes, replicators or thoughts are trying to get themselves copied, and in this process, language plays a crucial role in helping memes copy themselves and ensure their perpetuation.

Blackmore says that for at least 2.5 million years, memes have co-evolved with genes. Now, for the last century or so, they are 'off the leash' and have become independent of genes. For instance, sex is no longer indulged in for reproduction alone, for sex has been taken over by memes. Similarly, the self or the I is the doing of the meme called the 'selfplex', which, strangely, does not exist. It is an illusion, says Blackmore, in the sense that there is no self separate from the brain, no continuous, persistent and autonomous self. It does not exist, though 'we construct many of our miseries out of the idea of a persistent self'. Blackmore quotes the Buddha: '. . . actions do exist, and also their consequences, but the person that acts does not'.

The self is a vast 'memeplex', the most insidious and pervasive of all memes. Blackmore calls it the 'selfplex', put together by self-protecting memeplexes, by the process of memetic evolution. It is this selfplex that 'gives rise to ordinary human consciousness based on the false idea that there is someone inside who is in charge . . .' but actually it is an illusion, 'a memetic construct: a fluid and ever changing group of memes installed in a complicated meme machine'.

Therefore, Blackmore suggests that to live honestly one must be free of this illusion, this false sense of self, and allow decisions to be made by themselves. 'From the memetic point of view the selfplex is not there to make decisions, or for the sake of your happiness, or to make your life easier, it is there for the propagation of the memes that make it up.' In other words, 'by its very nature the selfplex brings about self-recrimination, self-doubt, greed, anger, and all sorts of destructive emotions'.

Blackmore ends her thesis on a brilliant, 'spiritual' note, going beyond her guru Richard Dawkins's idea of rebellion 'against the tyranny of the selfish replicators'. She writes, 'Compassion and empathy come naturally. It is easy to see what another person needs, or how to act in a given situation, if there is no concern about a mythical self to get in the way. Perhaps the greater part of true morality is simply stopping all the harm that we normally do, rather than taking on any great and noble deeds; that is, the harm that comes from having a false sense of self . . . We can live as human beings, body, brain, and memes, living out our lives as a complex interplay of replicators and environment, in the knowledge that that is all there is. Then we are no longer victims of the selfish selfplex. In this sense we can be truly free—not because we can rebel against the tyranny of the selfish replicators but because we know that there is no one to rebel.'[107]

Alternative Theories

Alternative theories based on the ideas of transpersonal and integral psychology, hyperspace, 'deep structure', quantum mechanics, psychokinesis, the implicate order and so on basically work on the idea of the interconnectedness of life and the universe. Their thesis is that we cannot hope to understand the mystery of the body, the enigma of the mind, and our belief in God or the Spirit, in isolation, but only within this intriguing ebb and flow of reality, of the inextricable, interconnectedness of all things.

These theorists, striving to develop a unified or integral theory of life, reject what they consider to be materialist, linear, reductionist theories of body–mind put forward by biologists such as Francis Crick and Richard Dawkins. The dogma that genes determine behaviour, which has become the conceptual basis of genetic engineering and which is vigorously supported by the biotechnology industry, is viewed with suspicion by writers like Fritjof Capra, the well-known author of The Tao of Physics. Capra thinks that the claim made by geneticists that they have found the 'blueprint', the 'language of life', is premature and misleading. But then, within the family of molecular biologists too, there are a few who are critical of the view of genes as causal agents of human behaviour and of all biological phenomena. For instance, the molecular biologist Richard Strohman, who is quoted with approval by Capra in support of his criticism, thinks that the basic fallacy of genetic determinism lies in a confusion of levels: 'the illegitimate extension of a genetic paradigm from a relatively simple level of genetic coding and decoding to a complex level of cellular behaviour represents an epistemological error of the first order'.[108]

The human body is not a mere survival machine for genes, nor is it just a collection of genes. Genes by themselves do not simply act. They have to be activated. For that matter, William Gelbart and Evelyn Fox Keller, both geneticists, find the term 'gene' to be of limited value; it cannot be 'the core explanatory concept of biological structure and function', and might be a hindrance to the understanding of the genome.

Capra says that 'many of the leading researchers in molecular genetics now realize the need to go beyond genes and adopt a wider epigenetic perspective' to explain biological structure and function. There is 'the growing realization that the biological processes involving genes—the fidelity of DNA replication, the rate of mutations, the transcription of coding sequences, the selection of protein functions and pattern of gene expression—are all regulated by the cellular network in which the genome is embedded'.[109]

In some ways, the 'epigenetic network' seems analogous to the 'morphic field', the term Rupert Sheldrake, a cell biologist and plant physiologist, employs for an understanding of human consciousness and the process of evolution. Explaining his hypothesis of morphic resonance and morphic fields, Sheldrake thinks that 'genes are grossly overrated and that a lot of inheritance depends on the memory which is carried within these organizing fields of organisms. This memory is a kind of cumulative memory, a kind of habit memory, which is built up through a pool of species experience, depending on a process I call morphic resonance.'[110] In effect, Sheldrake proposes 'a field theory of the mind' in order to arrive at a more integral understanding of the nature of the mind, which in many ways ties up with other attempts and theories to overcome the traditional frameworks of biology, psychology and epistemology that have largely been shaped by the seventeenth-century Cartesian division between mind and matter that has 'haunted Western science and philosophy for more than 300 years'.

These alternative theories also question the recent research by neuroscientists on the function of different areas of the brain to explain religious and mystical experiences in terms of neural network, neurotransmitters and brain chemistry. For instance, neuroscientists have put forward the idea that normal functioning of the right frontal lobe, specifically the parietal lobe, helps orient a person in three-dimensional space, and controls much of our sense of self, and the decreased activity of the parietal lobe could cause the blurring between the self and the rest of the world and give rise to a transcendental feeling of being one with God or with the world.

Vilayanur S. Ramachandran, an eminent researcher and author of the widely acclaimed book, *Phantoms in the Brain*, believes that questions on the Self, free will and consciousness can now be approached and explained empirically. He says 'even though it is common knowledge these days, it never ceases to amaze me that all the richness of our mental life—all our feelings, our emotions, our thoughts, our ambitions, our love life, our religious sentiments and even what each of us regards as his own intimate private self— is simply the activity of these little specks of jelly in your head, in your brain. There is nothing else . . . Lofty questions about the mind are fascinating to ask, philosophers have been asking them for three millennia both in India where I am from and here in the West—but it is only in the brain that we can eventually hope to find the answers.'[111]

The alternative theorists, of course, are suspicious of this over-enthusiasm of neuroscientists like Ramachandran and reject their 'findings' on the ground that the neuroscientists haven't been able to repeat their experiments to produce identical results as incontrovertible proof, simply because you cannot really reduce human experiences or human consciousness to purely neural mechanisms. These scientists succeed only in explaining away the complex relationship between the nature of the human brain and consciousness.

So, Capra suggests: 'Mind is not a thing but a process of cognition, which is identified with the process of life. The brain is a specific structure through which this process operates. The relationship between mind and brain, therefore, is one between process and structure. Moreover, the brain is not the only structure through which the process of cognition operates. The entire structure of the organism participates in the process of cognition,

254 The Other Side of Belief

whether or not the organism has a brain and a higher nervous system.' For that matter, 'At all levels of life, beginning with the simplest cell, mind and matter, process and structure are inseparably connected.'[112]

Rupert Sheldrake comes close to UG's opinion when he suggests that 'the brain is like a tuning system, and that we tune into our own memories by a process of morphic resonance, which I believe is a general process that happens throughout the whole of nature'.

Extending this idea as it were, Saul-Paul Sirag, a theoretical physicist, suggests that 'in some cosmic sense there really is only one consciousness, and that is really the whole thing—in other words, that hyperspace itself is consciousness acting on itself, and space-time is just a kind of studio space for it to act out various things in'. Karl Pribram, a professor of neuropsychology, who explores the similarities between current findings in neuropsychology and in quantum physics, thinks that our ideas of mind–brain, for that matter our whole understanding of life, are still caught up in terms of classical mechanics, with cause and effect relationships. In actuality, he says, we can never find out what and where the cause of a particular act or event is. 'The whole system does it. There isn't a start and a midst and so on, because time and space are enfolded, and therefore there is no causality.' Every act is 'very much a quantum type, holographic, implicate order kind of idea'. In view of this, there is no such thing as self or mind as such; rather, there are only 'mental processes, mental activities. But there isn't a thing called the mind'.[113]

UG's Response: The Mind is a Myth

Although the various theories discussed above, on the one hand, seem to contradict and cancel each other out, on the other hand they appear to support, extend and explicate each other in quite complex ways. Some of these theories come close to what UG has been saying for more than three decades now. However, our purpose is not so much to note the parallels, but see where and how UG deepens our understanding of the body–mind relationship and the interconnectedness of life and the universe. This is not just an idea or an insight with him, but the way he moves and lives in the world, he asserts. It is amazing how very spontaneously, without batting an eyelid, and with absolute clarity he answers questions that have troubled philosophers and religious thinkers over the centuries. In this context, one may be tempted to compare and contrast UG's utterances with the Enlightenment traditions and teachings of the sages of the world, although this would not necessarily enhance our understanding of things. In fact, it could even mislead us into thinking that what UG has been saying is as old as the hills, so we should tread carefully here. For, in actual fact, there *is* something new, utterly new in what UG is saying, the implication of which is tremendous and critical for a world that seems to have more or less decided what is right for humanity. Unless we break out of our old, established mode of thinking, our situation will continue to be like that of a dog chasing its own tail in vain.

Outwardly, there is nothing new in the language UG uses. He does not coin any new words as philosophers and scientists do, he uses simple, commonplace terms, free of metaphysical overtones and spiritual content, but what comes through is revolutionary, to say the least.

What is there is only the body, asserts UG. There is no mind. But for centuries we have been made to believe that there is an entity—the 'I', the self, the psyche, the mind. There is no such thing. It's only an illusion.

In the light of what UG says, we need to understand the term 'mind' at two levels.

Mind in the sense of intelligence is life itself and is everywhere. It is present in the seed of a plant as much as in a mosquito. It is there in matter, in every particle of the universe, in every cell of the body. This mind or consciousness as intelligence, as awareness, says UG, 'functioning in me, in you, in the garden slug and earthworm outside, is the same. In me it has no frontiers; in you there are frontiers—you are enclosed in that.'

When Arthur M. Young says that photons can think, or that so-called matter has properties of mind, or when Saul-Paul Sirag suggests that 'hyperspace itself is consciousness acting on itself', they are, in point of fact, saying that mind is immanent in matter at all levels of life. The *Mundaka Upanishad* too seems to suggest the same thing poetically: 'As the web comes out of the spider and is withdrawn . . . so springs the universe from the eternal Brahman . . . Brahman . . . brought forth out of himself the material cause of the universe; from this came the primal energy, and from the primal energy mind, from mind the subtle elements, from the subtle elements the many worlds . . .'

But this mind as intelligence, as primal energy, is not our problem, although it would be if we make that into a philosophy or build a religion around it. It simply points to the inseparability of life and the interconnectedness of everything, which by implication means our sense of separation is an error and an illusion.

Our actual problem is the mind in the sense of self. The Buddha did not find this self inside or outside, above or below, and UG says it is non-existent. But it is this non-existent self that has created religions, cultures, politics, technology, and the market forces that have begun to dominate the world today. It is the same self that not only produces great architecture, wonderful artefacts, and enchanting music but also invents nuclear bombs, wages wars, abuses natural resources and endangers the existence of life on earth.

How does this sense of self arise in the first place? And why? Tradition says we do not know, cannot know, it is *ignorance*. The evolutionary biologists say that self-consciousness probably arose to enable the survival of the hominid. In other words, self-consciousness was the emergent property of the brain, or the result of some strange mutation engineered by the body itself in its fight against the forces threatening its survival. A strange adaptation!

The myth of creation found in the *Brihadaranyaka Upanishad* offers layered meanings and implications: In the beginning there was nothing but It, the Self (in the sense of Awareness), in the form of a person (the Body). It looked around and saw that there was nothing but itself, whereupon its first utterance was 'It is I'; hence the birth of 'I'. Then it was afraid, and desired a second. It split itself into two: female and male. The male and female now desired each other and embraced and from them arose all living creatures, including the human race.

Hence, it is said, the sense of aloneness, the sense of lack, fear and desire (libido or *kama*). To put it differently, in the words of Joseph Campbell: 'Life and death became two, which had been one, and the sexes became two, which also had been one.' One could say that God divided itself into two and thus began the terrific play, the maya; what tradition calls the lila of Brahman.

In other words, this primordial creature(s) was thrown out of the Garden of Eden (not in the orthodox Christian sense but in Joseph Campbell's image), breaking the unitary consciousness. It was a grand illusion, forever accompanied by a sense of separation, alienation, lack, and suffering. As long as this illusion of separation, this ego, remains, in the words of Joseph Campbell again, 'the commensurate illusion of a separate deity also will be there; and vice versa, as long as the idea of a separate deity is cherished, an illusion of ego, related to it in love, fear, worship, exile, or atonement, will be there. But precisely that illusion of duality is the trick of maya.'[114]

UG, however, refuses to use this kind of religious or mythical metaphor, or even any words that may carry philosophical or metaphysical connotations. Terms such as soul, universal mind, oversoul, atman or higher self are all only persuasive words that seduce people and put them on the wrong track—a bogus chartered flight! UG believes life has to be described in simple, physical and physiological terms: 'it must be demystified and depsychologized'.

According to UG, somewhere along the line of evolution, the human species experienced self-consciousness, which does not exist in other species on this planet. (UG refuses to say why this happened, probably because it cannot be known; it is not within the realm of knowing, for thought cannot know its own origin.) With the help of this sense of self-consciousness, man accorded himself a superior position over and above the other species on this planet. It is this separation and sense of superiority that has been the source of man's problems and tragedy.

Since the whole of Nature is a single unit, human beings cannot ever really separate themselves from the totality of what we call Nature. Our sense of separation from Nature is an illusion and it is in this illusion that the 'I' is born (the 'I' itself being the illusion) and tries to perpetuate itself, forever seeking permanence. In actuality, there is no permanence, no security, no permanent happiness, and no 'I', no separate, psychological entity. The search for permanence and the 'I' are the same thing. The institutionalization of this search is what all religions are about. There is only the 'I', as a first person singular pronoun which, UG says, he uses only to make the conversation simpler. There is no other 'I'.

Sometimes, for purposes of convenience, and for want of a better or adequate word, UG uses the term 'world mind' to explain the nature of 'I' or the 'self'. The world mind constitutes the totality of thoughts, feelings, experiences and hopes of humankind.

'The world mind is that which has created you and me, for the main purpose of maintaining its status quo, its continuity. That world mind is self-perpetuating, and its only interest is to maintain its continuity, which it can do only through the creation of what we call individual minds—your mind and my mind. So without the help of that knowledge, you have no way of experiencing yourself as an entity. This so-called entity—the I, the self, the soul, the psyche—is created by that. And so we are caught up in this vicious circle, namely, of knowledge giving you the experience, and the experience in turn strengthening and fortifying that knowledge . . . This knowledge is put into us during the course of our life. When you play with a child, you tell him, "Show me your hand, show me your nose, show me your teeth, your face . . . what is your name?" this is how we build up the identity of the individual's relationship with his body and with the world around.'

So, knowledge is all that there is, says UG. The 'me', the 'self' is nothing but the totality of this inherited knowledge that is passed from generation to generation. Susan Blackmore would be delighted to know that what UG says about knowledge and thoughts, reflects her ideas: Memes and memeplex are passed on through imitation, education, and knowledge systems, for ensuring their own continuity. But she would note that according to UG, thoughts are passed on not only through education and books; thoughts are everywhere, and we have no way of finding out the seat of thought or human consciousness. Sometimes, he uses the phrases 'thought sphere' or 'world mind' to explain the all-pervasive nature of thought. But how this knowledge, these thoughts, this memory is passed on is a mystery. The genetic code is only a part of it; it is much more than the genetic code. He says:

There is no such thing as your mind and my mind. Mind is everywhere, sort of like the air we breathe. There is a thought sphere. It is not ours and not mine. It is always there. Your brain acts like an antenna, picking and choosing what signals it wants to use. That is all. You use the signals for purposes of communication. First of all, we have to communicate with ourselves. We begin as children naming everything over and over again. Communicating with others is a little more complex and comes next. The problem, or the pathology if you will, arises when you constantly communicate with yourself, irrespective of any outside demand for thought. You are all the time communicating with yourself: "I am happy . . . . I am not happy . . . . What is the meaning of life? . . ." and so on. If that incessant communication within yourself is not there, *you* are not there as you now know and experience yourself. When that inner monologue is no longer there, the need to communicate with others is absent. So you communicate with others only to maintain that communication you are having with yourself, your inner monologue. This kind of communication is possible only when you rely and draw upon the vast totality of thoughts passed on by man from generation to generation. Man has, through the process of evolution, learned to draw from this storehouse quicker, subtler, and more refined thoughts than the rest of the animals. They have powerful instincts. Through thinking, man has enabled himself to survive more efficiently than the other species. This ability of thought to adapt is the curse of man.

And it seems to be the curse of man never to know the origin of thought. It is too vast, it has the tremendous momentum gathered over thousands of years of evolutionary history, and within it also survive what UG calls the 'plant consciousness' and the 'animal consciousness'. Whatever insights we might claim to have are arbitrary, the invention of thought itself, for they are a result of thought observing thought, thought thinking about itself. It is not in the nature of thought to know either its own origin or the origin of things. In fact, there is no such thing as the origin of things, the

origin of consciousness, or the origin of the universe, asserts UG—
a position that some scientists seem to have come round to accept
today, though reluctantly. In the study of matter, molecules, atoms,
particles and quarks, the scientists finally say that there is really
nothing there. Indeed it is an exercise in futility, avers UG; we shall
never be able to discover the fundamental particle or the building
blocks of the universe, because 'the fundamental particle does not
exist'.

In a conversation with Jeffrey Mishlove, Capra admits that
'quantum physics has brought a dissolution of the notion of hard
and solid objects, and also of the notion that there are fundamental
building blocks of matter'. The search, however, goes on, although
scientists have more or less come to a tacit understanding that in
effect, all our laws of physics, all our observations and findings
are generated by our minds. The physicist Evan Harris Walker
expresses this position most tellingly when he says that essentially
what makes a quantum reaction finally get to some determinate
end point is a human consciousness observing it.[115]

Thus, we see that in effect, thought manufactures all our ideas
and world-views, for in this lies its illusory existence and continuity.
But this thought, the 'I', separated from nature, from the totality
of life, also knows that it cannot exist forever, that it has to come
to an end. Hence, the 'I' also entails the fear of extinction. And
this fear, which is 'me', the 'I', creates an artificial immortality by
way of

- linking up thoughts and giving them an illusion of continuity,
- projecting an entity, a soul, heaven, etc.,
- depending upon and using the body for its own continuity.

Strange and contradictory as it may sound, thought by itself can
do no damage. However, when the 'I', the 'self', uses thought to
achieve what it cannot achieve the problems begin. In UG's words:
'The thoughts themselves cannot do any harm. It is when you
attempt to use, censor, and control those thoughts to *get* something
that your problems begin. You have no recourse but to use thought
to get what you want in this world. But when you seek to get what
does not exist—God, bliss, love, etc., through thought, you only

succeed in pitting one thought against another, creating misery for yourself and the world.'

The nature of thought or the self is to think always in pairs, in terms of opposites—love and hate, birth and death, good and evil, God and Satan, spirituality and materialism—and always to privilege one over the other. But such a separation cannot be made, for love and hate, good and evil, are born of each other, or rather from the same source; in short, the pairs are made of basically the same self-protective movement of thought.

There is no such thing as spirituality, asserts UG. It is yet another movement of thought or the 'self', that creates this artificial division, hoping to overcome the problem that thought has created for itself in the first place. We could perhaps see through this terrible dualism in yet another way. 'Thought is matter,' says UG. So when the 'I' uses thought to achieve either material or spiritual goals, it is basically the same movement of thought, (that is, matter) to free itself from what may be called self-created anxiety, sorrow, conflict, hate, envy, and the fear of coming to an end. Society may have placed spiritual goals on a higher level than material goals, but actually all values, even the so-called spiritual values, are all materialistic.

The Brain is Only a Reactor

The brain has nothing to do with thought. Thoughts are not manufactured by the brain. Concepts such as synapsis, micro-circuits, Broca's area, and so on do not explain the origin, nature and function of thought. As UG says, thought is everywhere. It is there as traces of the past, as memory in every cell of the body, including the brain. And it is there in the 'thought sphere' or 'world mind'. It is the 'I' that uses thought, and the body, strictly speaking, is not involved in its play. Yet, the body carries, in every cell, the traces of not only human memory, but also of plant and animal consciousness.

To emphasize the point again, the brain is not the 'creator' of the 'self' or of thought, it is only a 'reactor'. 'It is, rather, that the

brain is like an antenna,' insists UG, 'picking up thoughts on a common wavelength, a common thought sphere.'

What UG is saying is that the brain has a minimal function in the protection and survival of the body. Rather, it is only the coordinator of bodily functions. It is not the creator of the coordinator, the 'I', which in fact uses the brain. Left to itself, the brain is only concerned with the safety and survival of the body. It is only a reactor, or as Sheldrake would say, it is 'like a tuning system'. The brain does not generate thoughts, it only picks up thoughts.

Now, in UG's words again:

Thoughts are not really spontaneous. They are not self-generated. They always come from outside. Another important thing for us to realize and understand is that the brain is not a creator. It is singularly incapable of creating anything. But we have taken for granted that it is something extraordinary, creating all kinds of things that we are so proud of. It is just a reactor and a container. It plays a very minor role in this living organism.

The brain is only a computer. Through trial and error you create something. But there are no thoughts there. There is no thinker there. Where are the thoughts? Have you ever tried to find out? What there is is only about thought but not thought. You cannot separate yourself from a thought and look at it. What you have there is only a thought about that thought, but you do not see the thought itself. You are using those thoughts to achieve certain results, to attain certain things, to become something, to be somebody other than what you actually are. I always give the example of a word-finder. You want to know the meaning of a word and press a button. The word-finder says, 'Searching.' It is thinking about it. If there is any information put in there, it comes out with it. That is exactly the way you are thinking. You ask questions and if there are any answers there, they come out. If the answers are not there, the brain says 'Sorry.' The brain is no different from a computer.

Is There a Soul?

Etymologically speaking, it is said that *atman* in Sanskrit, *psyche* in Greek, *anima* and *spiritus* in Latin mean 'breath', as do *pneuma* in Greek and *ruah* in Hebrew. If spirit or soul means 'breath', perhaps there isn't much to say about it except that *prana* or 'breath' is the defining characteristic of all life forms. Linked to it, one might suggest, is the ancient idea of 'spirit' believed in by 'primitive' or tribal people the world over for thousands of years. They believed that a mysterious spirit (or spirits) animates the whole world, not only life forms but also the whole of Nature.

However, the notions of spirit or soul as found in the belief systems of the major religions and even mystical reports are complex, complicated and different from each other. The Hindu notion of *atman* or Self is not the same as the Christian or Islamic *soul*. The one common defining characteristic of these different narratives of the soul is that it is conceived of as an independent or separate entity, and that in its complex relationship with God, mind and body, the soul is always privileged over the body. The soul is pure and transcendental; the body is impure, mundane, subject to decay and death. The body is something to be rejected, abandoned, and transcended in order to realize and experience the soul. Despite the hermeneutical attempts to overcome the dualism of body–soul or soul–God, it has to be conceded that this dualism between the body and the soul is the bedrock on which all religions are built and continues to be the core of all their discourses. It is the same with what goes under the name of spirituality, too. After all, what is spirituality? Isn't it understood as something concerned not with the material or the mundane, but with the sacred, the holy, with Soul, God or things divine? Isn't spirituality seen as an engagement with the soul or spirit as opposed to matter, body, and external reality? This dichotomy or dualism between spirit and matter, body and soul, spirituality and materialism is the warp and woof of all religions and all spiritual traditions.

If one were to consign the notion of the soul to the dustbin, religions would collapse like a pack of cards, and gurus would have to find some other job to earn their living. In UG's words, 'We have been fed on this kind of bunk for centuries, and if this diet were to be changed, we would all die of starvation.'

In many ways, this is analogous to our belief in 'love', without which most of our artists, novelists and poets would not survive, and the gargantuan structures of the film and music industry would soon be a heap of ash.

Just as hate is seen as the enemy of love, the body is seen as the enemy of the soul. The major religions might differ in their interpretations of the soul, but they all pit the soul against the poor body! However, some people may argue that of all religions, Hinduism—or rather, India's different religious groups and spiritual traditions—have developed a more rigorous and sophisticated discourse on atman which is radically different from the other notions of the soul. It isn't. The notion of atman, however sophisticated and complex, is not free of this awful dichotomy.

'While our bodily organization undergoes changes, while our thoughts gather like clouds in the sky and disperse again,' writes S.Radhakrishnan, 'the self is never lost. It is present in all, yet distinct from all.' The nature of atman or soul is 'not affected by ordinary happenings. It is the source of the sense of identity through numerous transformations. It remains itself though it *sees* all things. It is the one thing that remains constant and unchanged in the incessant and multiform activity of the universe, in the slow changes of the organism, in the flux of sensations, in the dissipation of ideas, the fading of memories.'[116] These words more or less summarize the position of Vedanta, which is considered to be the highest philosophy of atman or Self.

In short, the body, the mind, and the world are arbitrary restrictions imposed on *atman*, which in itself is pure, unaffected, unchanged, immutable and eternal, a trinity of transcendental reality (*sat*), awareness (*cit*), and bliss (*ananda*).

Radhakrishnan himself being a Vedantin, a non-dualist, his interpretation does come close to the various discussions on the nature of atman to Sankara's notion of body as impure, limiting, and imperfect, to his distinction between what he called, the empirical, individual self and the Supreme Self: unconditioned, transcendent, absolute, pure and immutable, essentially the same as Brahman, the source and ground of all creation and existence. This again is the notion of atman as found in the Bhagavad Gita, which declares atman, not the body, as immutable, immortal, which 'weapons cut not, fire burns not, water wets not, wind dries not'; which casts off worn-out bodies and takes on new ones in its cycles of births and deaths, until it finds release and becomes one with the Supreme.

Say what you will, in these texts, the opposition between the atman and the body is unmistakably evident. Modern gurus and alternative theorists, who are trying to develop an integral and unified theory of spirituality, might argue that atman or Spirit or the Universal Self is not necessarily opposed to the body; that it is a problem of semantics, and the limitation of the vocabulary of the period when these texts were composed. This is sheer word-play that does not really help the situation. The modern theorists succeed only in dodging the real issue, which is the irreconcilable dualism between body and soul, spirit and matter, that runs through all spiritual discourses. The usage of terms such as pure, transcendental, unchanging, unconditioned, and eternal, simultaneously betrays the fear of the self coming to an end and the search for some symbolic security, permanence or immortality. The more important question for us here is: Why talk of soul or atman as immortal, when, in the first place, there is no death for the body?

The Buddha, of course, did not find the atman. As regards JK, he found the whole thing problematic. He asked why, instead of saying the atman is immortal, '*Thou art That*', 'You are That Brahman,' you cannot say 'I am the river,' 'I am the poor man,' 'I am that tree,' 'I am all that.' How can a narrow, conditioned mind observe or even speculate on the unconditioned? How can one start with a conclusion that one is Brahman? Isn't that the end of the search?

UG is categorical and direct in his response and asserts that there is nothing to our search there. He demolishes the questions and the many answers given by declaring: There is no self, no I, no atman, no God.

What is there inside you is nothing but *fear*, states UG. 'Death' is fear, the fear of something coming to an end. The 'I' knows that this body is going to drop dead as others do, it is a frightening situation and it does not want to come to an end. So it creates the belief that there must be something beyond, it projects an afterlife, immortality of soul, God and so on. The problem, therefore, is not whether there is a soul, whether there is a centre, whether there is a God or not; it is fear, operating as belief, that is passed on from generation to generation. It is this knowledge, says UG, that makes us think that there must be something beyond and even experience it. But there is nothing to it. In other words, ideas of the soul and life after death are born out of the demand for permanence. That is the foundation of man's religious thinking. All religious thinking is born out of that demand for permanence.

But thought is a tricky customer. It cannot exist without grounding itself in some belief. It will appear to abandon a belief only to create a new one in its place. It will even employ the so-called negative approach to arrive at some positive idea. Atheism, agnosticism, pragmatism, nihilism, and what have you, are only the various tricks of thought to anchor itself to some belief in order to seek its perpetuation. And so, UG warns: 'You will replace one belief with another. You are nothing but belief, and when it dies, you are dead. What I am trying to tell you is this: don't try to be free from selfishness, greed, anger, envy, desire, and fear. You will only create its opposites, which are, unfortunately, fictitious. If desire dies, you die. The black van comes and carts you away, that's it! Even if you should somehow miraculously survive such a shock, it will be of *no use* to you, or to others.'

And then, according to UG, all our beliefs in the 'thoughtless state', 'state of awareness', 'choiceless awareness' are nothing but bogus chartered flights. There is no such thing as self-awareness, for the *self* and *awareness* cannot coexist. If one has to give a simple analogy, awareness is something like a mirror, images are reflected upon it, but the image is not the mirror. Awareness is only a medium through which images pass in and pass out. There is nothing more that can be said about it, we cannot call it a soul or build a philosophy or religion around it. Any such attempt will be an attempt to anchor ourselves in something which it is not. In other words, it is only our search for power and security, useful only to spiritual gurus. In UG's words:

You cannot be aware; you and awareness cannot coexist. If you could be in a state of awareness for one second by the clock, once in your life, the continuity would be snapped, the illusion of the experiencing structure, the 'you', would collapse, and everything would fall into the natural rhythm. In this state you do not know what you are looking at—that is awareness. If you recognize what you are looking at, you are there, again experiencing the old, what you know. It is not something that can be captured, contained and given expression to through your experiencing structure. It is outside the field of experience. So it cannot be shared with anyone.

Putting it differently, he says:

I am not particularly fond of the word 'awareness'. It is misused. It is a rubbed coin, and everybody uses it to justify some of his actions, instead of admitting that he did something wrong. Sometimes you say, 'I was not aware of what was going on there.' But awareness is an integral part of the activity of this human organism. This activity is not only specifically in the human organism but in all forms of life— the pig and the dog. The cat just looks at you, and is in a state of choiceless awareness. To turn that awareness into an instrument which you can use to bring about a change is to falsify that. Awareness is an integral part of the activity of the living organism.

20

The Enigma of the Natural State

India boasts of a strong, 3000-year-old enlightenment tradition. The *Yogavashista* speaks of seven steps to enlightenment, the seventh and final stage being moksha—the extinction of the individual, which sounds similar to the concept of Nirvana, the final 'extinction of the self'. Moksha also means release from the cycles of births and deaths, or complete and ultimate liberation from all ignorance and duality through realization of the Supreme or Universal Self and its identity with Brahman. There are, of course, various other descriptions of what constitutes moksha, depending upon the spiritual tradition one belongs to. Are they all speaking of the same state of being, in different words? Is there an 'essence' to moksha or liberation? How can realization of the Supreme Self be the same as 'the extinction of self' or Nirvana?

Are there different kinds of enlightenment? Are there levels to it? Does such a thing exist at all?

In 1939, when UG asked more or less the same question of Sri Ramana, the sage of Arunachalam is believed to have answered in the affirmative.

UG: 'Can one be free sometimes and not free sometimes?'
Ramana: 'Either you are free, or you are not free at all.'
UG: 'Are there any levels to it?'
Ramana: 'No, no levels are possible, it is all one thing. Either you are there or not there at all.'

After his 'calamity' in 1967, in the 1970s and the 1980s to be specific, UG used to offer 'soft' and not entirely negative answers to questions on enlightenment and questions concerning 'spiritual' matters. Today he straightaway rejects the idea of enlightenment. He says: 'There is no such thing as enlightenment. You may say that every teacher and all the saints and saviours of mankind have been asserting for centuries upon centuries that there is enlightenment and that they are enlightened. Throw them all in one bunch into the river!'

Yet, paradoxically, he also states: 'But actually an enlightened man or a free man, if there is one, is not interested in freeing or enlightening anybody. This is because he has no way of knowing that he is a free man, that he is an enlightened man. It is not something that can be shared with somebody, because it is not in the area of experience at all.'

Enlightenment Demystified

I believe there is such a thing as enlightenment but not in the sense in which it is talked about by most gurus and spiritual teachers in the world. It is, of course, as UG says, a state of being that cannot be shared with or communicated to others, as it is not in the realm of experience as we understand it. Still, if we have to approach the subject intellectually and suggest a functional definition of it in plain, non-religious terms, we could perhaps say that it is the cessation of all psychological conflicts, the dissolution of the self, and the birth of the individual into the Natural State.

One prefers the term 'Natural State' to 'enlightenment' for two reasons: One, it is a more creative term than the much-abused word 'enlightenment', which should help us understand at least intellectually this state of being, cleansed of the anti-intellectual, sanctimonious dross indulged in by religious gurus and apologists of religion. Two, the word 'enlightenment' is being (ab)used widely in a way that has nothing whatsoever to do with the state of enlightenment. This is not to say that one knows what enlightenment is all about or that there can only be one fixed meaning to it. Far from it. It is only to point out what enlightenment is not, just as, in the context of our current knowledge of life, we realize that it is a gross error to think that God created the earth and man in seven days (although there is no consensus even among experts as to how many billion years it took and how exactly life forms and Homo sapiens emerged on earth).

Enlightenment has nothing to do with world peace or with the kind of political and social changes we want to bring about to prevent our mutual destruction. It has nothing to do with our values of justice, equality, love, and even compassion. Gurus who claim to be enlightened not only deceive themselves but also mislead people by attributing non-existent ontological status and spiritual values to enlightenment.

In other words, enlightenment has nothing to do with being good or pious. The enlightened state is not a blueprint for a world order, much less for world peace. There is no religious or social content there, yet, in its own way it could make a great social and cultural impact by quickening our insights into ourselves and the world. Genuinely enlightened persons, sages (not saints, gurus or even mystics), do not directly recommend any change in the world, or teach a better way of living. They only point out the errors in our perception of things, question our self-righteous ways of being and doing things, our precious ideas and ideologies, in short, our fragmented existence. They simply go on living as if nothing has happened, as if they are not concerned which the way the world goes, for deep in the marrow of their bones, as it were, they know that life goes on and it has its own ways.

An enlightened person is not an avatar or saviour come down on earth to save humanity, or lead humanity to some promised land, or create the kingdom of God on earth. His or her utterances cannot be converted into a body of teaching and institutionalized. His social or political comments (which are made in response to people's queries and demands) do not carry timeless meaning or values. He lives and moves in a state that is outside the framework of our traditional modes of understanding. Enlightenment is what it is. It cannot be willed, or brought about by an act of volition. Perhaps it comes with the cessation of 'will', the stuff the self is made of. It is the natural state nature throws up now and then for reasons not accessible to our reason. Perhaps it is the last stage of evolution and yet, an utterly new expression of life.

Salvation is Physical

The Mind of the Cells—or Willed Mutation of our Species, is a record of reports of the physical changes and experiences of the Mother of Pondicherry, which occurred over eleven years between 1962 and 1973.

It is a remarkable book that makes other books on mysticism sound like the mere prattling of a child. It is unique not because it is far superior to other texts on mysticism, but because it marks the end of mystical experience. It is an incredible journey on an uncharted sea. One could well call it a journey of billions-of-years-old cells, a cellular journey into utterly new waters of life and intelligence, something the molecular biologists should want to discover and understand. But it is not something that can be seen or studied under a microscope in a laboratory, inside the fish bowl of one's mind.

But strangely, it is an incomplete journey, perhaps only to be carried forward by UG, to reach its final and full fruition and expression in his life.

Aurobindo said, 'Man is a transitional being', and that he has to be surpassed. We do not know if Aurobindo experienced this 'transition'. We know his ideas of 'overmind', 'supermind', 'superman', and 'supramental manifestation'. But did it happen to him? Or, was it only his prediction or, merely philosophical speculation?

Going by the Mother's reports, it seems it happened to her. She presided over this transition, this strange transmutation of the body, this bewildering mutation of the cells. It was something that was certainly not entirely in line with Aurobindo's ideas or predictions.

In 1953, the Mother made a statement to the effect that something new was beginning to take shape in her life. She said: '. . . a New World is born. It is not the old world changing, it is a New World which is born . . .' although, 'the old is still all-powerful and entirely controlling the ordinary consciousness'.[117]

But it seems that only in 1962, when she fell 'ill', did she begin to notice strange changes taking place in her body. It actually was not an illness nor symptoms of illness. Something strange was going

on within the cells of her body, '. . . a sort of decentralization .
. . as if the cells were being scattered by centrifugal force . . .'.
She would feel terribly weak at times, faint now and then, yet
something untouched was fully conscious of what was happening.
'. . .Witnessing everything . . .', something like 'matter looking
at itself in a whole new way.' This process went on for almost eleven
years, until the day she passed away in 1973, at the age of ninety-
five.

At first it seemed her consciousness was breaking out of its limits;
it felt like waves, 'not individual waves, rather a movement of
waves'. It was almost infinite and strangely 'undulatory': vast, at
times, very quiet, and there was a harmonious rhythm to it. 'And
this movement,' she felt, 'is life itself . . .' and it moves by
expansion: 'it contracts and concentrates, then expands and spreads
out'.

Something was trying to get established, an utterly new way or
movement of life! It was the preparation of the body, of the cells,
to mutate. It was not an act of volition. 'You can't try to make
it happen,' said the Mother. 'One can't make an effort, one can't
try to know, because that immediately triggers an intellectual
activity (habit) which has nothing to do with "that".'

Then there came a sort of memory block. She did not know how
to climb stairs, how to read and things of that sort. It seemed
necessary to let go everything, all knowledge, all intelligence, all
capacity—everything. The sense of separation was dissolving. Old
habits were dying.

Taste, smell, vision, touch, sound—the sensory perceptions
began to undergo a complete change. Perhaps 'they belong to
another rhythm,' she suggested. It seemed curious and funny. 'There
is no longer "something seeing" but I am numerous things. I Live
numerous things . . . I See clearly with my eyes closed than with
my eyes open, and yet it is the same vision. It's physical vision,
purely physical . . .fuller.'

Now and then she experienced a tremendous burst of energy that
caused pain. At times she would feel that she was dying, that she
was going to explode. It was not what religious people assume to
be joy or bliss, but a sense of alarm, fear, anxiety, pain. '. . . It's
really and truly terrifying . . . it's a hideous labour . . . it's truly

a journey into nothing, with nothing, in a desert strewn with every conceivable trap and obstacle. You are blindfolded, you know nothing.'

The body had become a battleground. A battle within the cells between the old habit and something new that was trying to emerge. In the Mother's words: 'The battle begins to be fought deep down in the cells, in the material consciousness, between what we call "the will to haemorrhage" and the reaction of the cells of the body. And it is absolutely like a regular battle, a real fight. But suddenly, the body is seized with a very strong determination and proclaims an order, and immediately the effect begins to be felt and everything returns gradually to normal.'

It is the struggle of the body to cleanse itself of the habit developed over thousands of years of 'separate existence on account of ego'. Now it has to learn to continue, without the ego, 'according to another, unknown law, a law still incomprehensible for the body. It is not a will, it's . . . I don't know . . . something; a way of being.'

The way human beings have lived with a separative consciousness has been nothing but a habit. A bad habit! All that must be undone, the so-called laws of Nature, all the collective suggestions, all the earthly habits. 'It is nothing but mechanical habits. But it clings, it's really sticky, oh! . . . what appear to us as "the laws of Nature" or "inescapable principles", are so absurd, so ridiculous!'

And then the body falls into a rhythm all its own. It becomes transparent. 'All vibrations pass through it freely. It no longer feels limited: it feels spread out in everything it does, in everything around, in all circumstances, in people, movements, feelings . . . just spread out.' The Mother felt that the body was everywhere. 'I am talking here about the cells of the body, but the same applies to external events, even world events. It's even remarkable in the case of earthquakes, volcanic eruptions, etc. It would seem that the entire earth is like the body.'

Everything is interconnected. Everything is one. The sense of separation is a complete falsehood, cause and effect only a figment of human imagination. 'It isn't something you see or understand or know, it's . . . something you are.' Consciousness or mind, divides everything up, but here, in the body, everything is one. Literally everything: 'The speck of dust you wipe off the table, or ecstatic contemplation, it's all the same.'

The Mother felt it was something beyond what all earlier spiritual leaders had said till then, which is what UG reiterates today with absolute conviction and clarity. It was beyond moksha, beyond Nirvana; it was something very physical. 'Salvation is physical,' declared the Mother. And she demanded to know: Why did the spiritual teachers of the past all seek liberation by abandoning their body? Why did they talk of Nirvana as something outside the body? 'The body is a very, very simple thing, very childlike,' said the Mother. 'It does not need to "seek" anything: it's THERE. And it wonders why men never knew of this from the start: why, but why did they go after all sorts of things—religions, gods, and all those . . . sorts of things? While it is so simple! So simple! It's so obvious for the body!'

When the Mother says 'the body is very simple' and that it does not need to 'seek' anything at all, she sounds very like UG. She confirms what UG has been saying for the last thirty years, when she asserts: 'All the mental constructions that men have tried to live by and realize on earth come to me from all sides: all the great schools of thought, the great ideas, the great realizations . . . and then, lower on the scale, the religions; oh, how infantile all that seems! . . . Oh, what noise, how vainly you have tried!'

It is fairly clear that the 'process' took the Mother beyond even Aurobindo's philosophy of the supramental manifestation, as well as her own previous ideas about spiritual evolution before the actual physical changes began to take place. Still, her past kept popping up now and then, and she did refer, though reluctantly and hesitantly, to the idea of 'supermind' and 'supramental'. It is surprising to note that even serious followers of Aurobindo have either completely ignored the Mother's report of these great physical and physiological changes, or interpreted them purely in terms of Aurobindo's philosophy.

One might quote from Aurobindo's writings and argue that he was the first to speak about the need, or rather the inevitability, of a physical transformation. Indeed, he was the first to say that if any radical change has to take place, it has to take place in the body, and he did prepare the ground for the Mother's transformation.

Even otherwise, his interpretation of the Upanishads and his criticism of Sankara's Vedanta makes him one of our most radical mystic–philosophers. But all this should in no way distract us from the cleansing fact that the Mother, quite unwittingly as it were, went beyond Aurobindo's philosophy and beyond all known frames of spiritual reference. This would have certainly brought a smile to Aurobindo's face, for he would have intuitively known that something like this would happen; after all, didn't he repeatedly warn that what is to come in future will be something hitherto unknown and unexplored!

What happened to the Mother was something she had least expected, just as UG had not expected his 'Calamity' even in his wildest dreams! A careful consideration of the Mother's report reveals that all through these changes, she felt a sort of total helplessness, 'choicelessness', and had absolutely no precedence or frame of reference to which she could relate. 'I don't know . . . can't say . . . have no idea . . . no words to express . . . blindfolded . . . you see, I feel I am right in the middle of a world I know nothing about, struggling with laws I know nothing about . . . it is something like a condition: the unreality of the goal—not its unreality, its uselessness. Not even uselessness: the non-existence of the goal . . . it happened in my bathroom upstairs, surely to show that it is in the most trivial things, in everything, continuously . . . You see, it's even fairly easy to pose as a superman! But it remains ethereal, it isn't the real thing, not the next stage of terrestrial evolution . . . So simple! It's so obvious for the body!' Her admissions more than reveal her incredible journey into unknown waters of life and intelligence, and she did go beyond Aurobindo and her own ideas and beliefs before the process began.

We do not know. Perhaps the Mother did not live long enough for everything to change, for the process, the mutation, to complete itself. However, to use her own words: '. . . but some things changed and have never reverted.'

The Mother died in 1973. For UG the 'Calamity' occurred in 1967. It was a full-blown mutation of the body, enabling the human being to become fully human. It was not a mystical experience, nor a Kundalini experience (though the Kundalini experience could just be the beginning, almost elementary). And it has nothing to do with the spiritual goal (as opposed to the material, the body) that the spiritual traditions of the world with their band of teachers have been proclaiming for centuries.

Evidently, this biological mutation, or 'Natural state' as UG would call it, or 'cellular revolution' as the Mother would put it, is not entirely unprecedented. But now we have someone, in the shape of UG, to tell us, in clear physical, physiological and material terms, what it is all about.

The Body is Immortal

The Bhagavad Gita, the approximately 2000-year-old religious text of the Hindus, is certainly not considered to be a text on the subject of the immortality of the body. Rather, it is celebrated as a quintessential discourse on the immortality of the Universal or Supreme Self. Nevertheless, Chapter XI, on what is called the Universal Form or Self tells a different story. That is the paradox, the irony of ironies that the text conceals. After a longish discourse on the different forms of Yoga, and the nature of Brahman and atman, Lord Krishna bestows on Arjuna a vision of his Universal Form. Arjuna beholds this terrific kaleidoscope of life with a borrowed 'divine eye'. And what does he see?

He beholds the whole cosmos reflected in the *body* of Krishna with multitudinous arms, stomachs, mouths and eyes. It is boundless, with neither end nor middle nor beginning. Everything, all the innumerable forms of life are there, and in the centre is Lord Brahma resting on a lotus, surrounded by all the sages and the heavenly serpents.

The Sun, the Moon, and the heavenly planets blaze along, worlds radiate within worlds in a never-ending kaleidoscope, torrents of rivers flow relentlessly into thunderous seas, and behold, the flaming mouth licking up, devouring all worlds, all creatures; it is the body, with no beginning, middle or end, swallowing, burning itself up in an endless maya of creation and destruction.

There couldn't have been a better metaphor for the body. Many scholars and commentators on the Bhagavad Gita might find it difficult to accept this interpretation. However, the text reveals that truly, within the body is the cosmic dance of life. Rather, the cosmos itself is the body, and the different, immeasurable life forms, like bacteria in the bloodstream, like fish in the ocean, are rising and dissolving continually, floating, moving back and forth, up and down, with no beginning and no end.

Scientists, however, posit a point of time for the beginning of the universe and the evolution of the human body. We do not know. It is a matter of perspective. We always think in frames, in terms of time and space, cause and effect. It is an incorrigible human habit. But in actuality, says UG, what is there is a space–time–energy continuum, which has no end.

There are, of course, scientists today who have come round, however reluctantly, to more or less or 'accepting' this hard reality, yet, if only to keep their profession alive, they like to imagine that the universe has had a beginning and consequently should have an end, too. They say that the universe could be about thirteen billion years old, the Sun and the planets about four-and-a-half billion years old. And they like to suggest that it probably took a few more billion years for the first life forms to emerge on earth, and a few more million years for Homo sapiens to arrive on this planet. We cannot be sure, of course. Still, if we were to believe, however arbitrarily, in this theory, then it logically follows that Homo sapiens, the human body, which has evolved over millions of years from the 'primordial soup', must have everything of the world and the cosmos in it.

According to Paul McLean's work at the National Institute of Mental Health's Brain Research Centre, we have three brains in our skulls.[118] All three separate structures are supposed to have developed over millions of years of evolutionary history on earth. First, there is the reptilian brain (identical to the brain found in all reptiles), which includes our spinal cord and the brain stem. Superimposed on this is the great limbic structure, inherited from the mammals; it is believed that this is our emotional-cognitive brain which handles emotional energies. Superimposed on this structure is the neocortex, which is five times bigger than the two animal brain structures and occupies almost eighty per cent of our skull. It is this neocortex, containing some ten billion neurons, which is supposed to be our thinking brain and which has made possible the so-called human progress from the stone axe to the aeroplanes to the atom bomb to quantum physics.

'Speaking allegorically of these three brains within a brain,' says McLean, with impish humour, yet with great philosophical implications, 'we might imagine that when the psychiatrist bids the patient to lie on the couch, he is asking him to stretch out alongside a horse and a crocodile.' Further: 'In the popular language today, these three brains might be thought of as biological computers, each with its own peculiar form of subjectivity and its own intelligence, its own sense of time and space and its own memory, motor and other functions.'[119]

When JK talked of the necessity of mutation in the brain to bring about a radical change in human consciousness, did he mean the transformation of the three brains, in particular the animal brains? Interestingly, that is more or less what some neurologists are saying—that religion is the 'property' of the brain, that unless there is a fundamental change in the brain, the search for God, the related religious or spiritual beliefs, and the battles over religious identities will be with us for a long time. Even UG seems to suggest the same thing when he says that religion is a serious neurological problem. But a careful reading of his utterances tells us that he does not simply mean the brain, but the whole body. The brain is only a 'reactor'. The reptilian brain, the limbic structure and the neocortex perform certain jobs or tasks, but by themselves they are passive. They have to be activated and it is the 'I', the activator, which uses them.

The traces of evolutionary history, the traces of animal traits or animal consciousness exist not merely in the brain but all over the body, in the trillions of cells of the body. To theorize further on what UG has been saying, the 'I' (the coordinator of thoughts), is a squatter; it uses the body for its own continuity, and it has superimposed itself on every cell of the body. In other words, the 'I' with its age-old memories and experiences, along with the animal consciousness, is deeply embedded in every cell of the body. That is what the Mother's report of her experience of cellular changes seems more or less to be saying as well. So then, the 'I', with all its fears and anxieties, its sense of lack and insecurity, the animal trait of aggression and even the survival instinct, has to go, has to be cleansed, if the human being has to begin truly to function as a human. The cleansing has to take place not just in the brain but in every cell of the body, on which the tremendous gravity of the psychological fear and lack in the form of the 'I' or the 'self' is superimposed.

To put it in the language of molecular biology, if mutation of cells is what caused the emergence of self-consciousness (the 'I', the neocortex), then it will be another mutation in the cells that will dissolve the 'I', which has outrun its original purpose and turned self-destructive.

That seems to be the only way out, failing which humanity seems to be doomed to destroy itself, along with the millions of other creatures living on this planet. If such a catastrophe were to occur, perhaps only the tough cockroaches will survive, mutate, and let Nature start the evolutionary cycle again, for purposes only Nature knows.

It is the stranglehold of thought, or culture, over the body— culture in the form of religious ideals, goals, political ideologies and so on—that has prevented the body from cleansing itself of these 'bad habits' to begin its natural, harmonious, non-destructive movement of existence. Just as disease-causing viruses enter the body and cause havoc, these thoughts have become parasites on the body, throwing the body out of its natural order. The body can sometimes battle the viruses and regain its balance, but it cannot do so with thoughts, for they have a stranglehold on the cells of the body. There has to be a mutation if these thoughts and their coordinator, the 'I', has to be destroyed before the body finds its freedom.

Unfortunately, this kind of mutation cannot be willed. Nor can it be genetically engineered, for the 'I' is everywhere, and in every cell. It seems that we could perhaps open up the possibilities of that happening only if we stop and achieve a state of 'do-nothing' to further strengthen the already tremendous momentum of the destructive structure of thought.

There are already enough religions, enough political ideologies, and more than enough atomic bombs to blow up the earth. It is really ridiculous to talk of peace, love and compassion and then wage wars, absurd to believe in an all-loving God and then slit each other's throats in the cause of religious identity and in the name of the very same loving God. And it is plain fraud to talk of 'development' when evidently all that 'development' or 'progress' has done is to create a few billionaires and a powerful, predatory class, while hundreds of millions are forced to live a sub-human existence.

The rot has really gone deep into the very cells of our body. It is frightening.

Actually our problems are, as UG has been saying for more than three decades now, rooted in our so-called solutions: in our gods, our religious ideals, our political goals, our very notions of justice and health. It is the macabre dance of death played out by self-protective, fascist thought. There seems to be no way out unless there is a benign, biological mutation of the human body.

The 'Calamity'

UG says that it happened to him despite his long search and sadhana, despite everything he did in all his forty-nine years before the 'Calamity'. He calls it a 'Calamity' deliberately in order to discourage us from attributing any religious or spiritual meaning and value to what happened to him.

For truly and absolutely there is no religious or spiritual content there. It is a physical process, a physiological phenomenon, brought to fruition in the way Nature works on a tiny seed to give rise to a gigantic tree. It is life finding its fulfilment. It is the completion of the journey of the 'cells' started some millions of years ago from the 'primordial soup'. It is there.

Over seven days, seven different changes took place in UG's body. It was literally an explosion of energy, and UG cannot say whether it erupted from within the body or descended from outside; actually there was no outside and inside, it came from all sides, everywhere, in waves, in spirals, like a river in spate, like a tidal wave, penetrating into and breaking through every wall, every resistance; it was energy, atomic, repairing, cleansing the body, cleansing every cell of its age-old 'habits', the 'accumulated knowledge' of the traces embedded in it over thousands of years of evolutionary history; it was the flushing out of the virus of thought, memes. The accompanying pain and terror and other sensations of extreme discomfort were the death pangs of the 'I', the 'self'.

It is of crucial importance to note here that the physical process or mutation was triggered by the dissolution of the question: 'How do I know that this is the state?' There was no answer. It was the end of all answers, all knowledge born out of the separative existence, cessation of all opposites; it was a tremendous crisis within the thought structure. It was a calamitous situation for thought, for the 'self', the build-up of a tremendous molecular pressure within the structure of the mind–body, and it could have release only in an explosion. In other words, with no answer coming, which is absolutely essential for the continuity of thought, it was as if the question itself, akin to matter, cracked and set off a series of explosions in the nuclear plant of the body, blasting every cell, every nerve and every gland. The anxieties and fears, the fantasies and wishes, the images and symbols, the ideas and concepts and world-views, all created and maintained and played out by the 'self' for its own continuity, all the sensory perceptions hitherto enslaved by the self for its own separative existence, the whole history of the body inscribed by the self on every cell, began to explode, burn and dissolve into nothingness. And thus, on the seventh day, the coordinator, the self, disappeared, and with it the body, constructed by thought, disappeared too.

It was an extremely painful process, almost like physical torture, and it took about three years for the process to complete itself and let the body fall into a new rhythm all its own, into what UG calls the 'Natural State'.

The Natural State is also the state of 'undivided consciousness', says UG. With the sense of separation gone, and even the instinct of survival dissolved, the body is extremely vulnerable to everything around it; the body is 'affected' by all natural phenomena, be it an earthquake or the eclipses of the moon and the sun, or even when someone gets physically hurt. UG calls it the true 'affection'. (It is not spiritual oneness with the world, nor what is called the

'Atman becoming one with Brahman'. There is no religious or spiritual content there. It is a purely physiological phenomenon.) With the sense of separative existence dissolved, the stranglehold of culture, the 'I', gone, the body is in tune with the cosmos.

The ductless glands, located exactly in the same spots where, according to Kundalini Yoga, the chakras or energy centres are, have taken over the function of his body, says UG. He doesn't, of course, refer to Kundalini or use any spiritual terms to explain this phenomenon. The thymus gland, which is supposed to be active through childhood until puberty and then becomes dormant, is reactivated, and it is there that the physical (not emotional) oneness is felt or experienced. It is not, UG emphasizes, what the Hindus call the atman becoming one with Brahman and all that stuff. There is no spiritual content there. It is not unity of consciousness in the sense we want to understand it. It is just the absence of thought, the past, that enables UG to be in that state of oneness, which also means that he is (physically) affected by everything that happens around him. It is the natural, physical condition of his being. In UG's words:

Sensations are felt there; you don't translate them as 'good' or 'bad'; they are just a thud. If there is a movement outside of you—a clock pendulum swinging, or a bird flying across your field of vision—that movement is also felt in the thymus. The whole of your being is that movement or vibrates with that sound; there is no separation. This does not mean that you identify yourself with that bird or whatever . . . There is no 'you' there, nor is there any object. What causes that sensation, you don't know. You do not even know that it is a sensation.

'Affection' means that you are affected by everything, not that some emotion flows from you towards something. The natural state is a state of great sensitivity—but this is a physical sensitivity of the senses, not some kind of emotional compassion or tenderness for others. There is compassion only in the sense that there are no "others" for me, and so there is no separation.

He also says that with the coordinator, the 'I', which uses the body for its own separative continuity, gone, the pituitary gland—called the 'third eye', ajna chakra (ajna meaning 'command')—is now in command over the body. With the coordinator gone, it is this ajna chakra or pituitary gland that gives the instructions to the body and enables the body to function in perfect tune with the world. Since there is nobody (no 'I') there to control or interfere with the functioning of the body, thoughts arise in response to a demand or challenge, and once the task is fulfilled, they undergo 'combustion' or burn themselves up and ionize, releasing energy. Hence, says UG, he is able to talk for hours on end and yet not feel tired or drained of energy.

But when there is no demand or challenge, no stimuli (stimulus and response being a unitary action), he is in a state of 'not knowing', a sort of 'declutched state'. There is no self talking, thinking, or daydreaming, there is nothing there. But when a question is thrown at him, the response comes quickly and effectively, from what he calls his data or memory bank; it is immediate and it is mechanical. It is like a computer switching on and responding to queries by scanning its databank and coming up with an answer. There is nothing mysterious about it. It's the past, the memory—mechanical. There is nothing else there. If there is something else, there is no way of knowing it.

In other words, when there is no demand, he is in a state of 'not knowing'. There is only sensory activity, pure and simple. Each of the senses work, independently (with no coordinator or coordination) at the peak of its capacity. Sensations are not interpreted as hard or soft, sweet or bitter, good or evil, spiritual or material. There is no difference between music and the barking of a dog, or the sound coming from the toilet. It is just sound, notes spaced out in a certain order, that is all. There is no interpretation, for there is no interpreter there.

Further, UG says that his vision is two-dimensional, flat, in frames, like a camera clicking away picture after picture, but with no linkage between these pictures. The third, fifth and tenth dimensions are figments of imagination, invented by thought, by the self for its own sake and for its own continuity.

Truly a marvellous machine, an amazing body. It is, put simply, the Natural State! This Natural State is not a spiritual state, not a state of enlightenment, asserts UG. It is not a state of bliss or perfect order. For order and chaos, cause and effect, birth and death are a simultaneous process. There is silence there, but it is like the silence of a volcano. It burns everything, leaving behind no trace. It is the movement of life, the ebb and flow of life that can never be captured by thought.

Moreover, UG's body is supposed to be hermaphroditic or androgynous: qualities of both man and woman coexist in it. A perfect union of animus–anima, man–woman in union, pictorially represented by the Indian tradition in the form of *ardhanarishwara*: one half (the right side) of the body as Shiva and the other half as Parvathi, his consort—an artistic illustration of the androgynous state! But UG rejects the comparison and simply states: 'Here (in UG) the body goes back into that stage where it is neither male nor female. It is not the androgynous thing that they talk about.' However, when he says that his left side is female and responds to women and the right side is male and responds to men, he seems to imply that there is something in the traditional image of ardhanarishwara. As physical evidence of this male–female convergence in the body, there is even a dark line over his stomach upwards, as if to demarcate the male and the female in him.

If UG's body is truly both male and female, or neither purely male nor female, then it challenges our knowledge of the human body. It also certainly goes beyond the understanding of the left and right brain as having different faculties and functions, according to the present-day neurosciences. In view of UG's experience and what he has said, it seems that it is not merely the right and left hemispheres of the brain but the entire left and right sides of the body (the two brains being only vital parts of them) that respond in different ways, with their different faculties ('intelligence' would be more appropriate) and functions.

To UG, death is a continuous phenomenon. His body is supposed to go through death almost every day, and come back to life. It is the body's way of renewing itself. He says:

This is necessary because the senses in the natural state are functioning at the peak of their sensitivity all the time. So, when the senses become tired, the body goes through death. This is real physical death, not some mental state. It can happen one or more times a day. You do not decide to go through this death; it descends upon you. It feels at first as if you have been given an anaesthetic: the senses become increasingly dull, the heartbeat slows, the feet and hands become ice cold, and the whole body becomes stiff like a corpse. Energy flows from all over the body towards some point. It happens differently every time. The whole process takes forty-eight or forty-nine minutes. During this time the stream of thoughts continues, but there is no reading of the thoughts. At the end of this period you 'conk out': the stream of thought is cut. There is no way of knowing how long that cut lasts—it is not an experience. There is nothing you can say about that time of being 'conked out'—that can never become part of your conscious existence or conscious thinking.

You don't know what brings you back from death. If you had any will at that moment, you could decide not to come back. When the 'conking out' is over, the stream of thought picks up exactly where it left off. Dullness is over; clarity is back. The body feels very stiff—slowly it begins to move of its own accord, limbering itself up. The movements are more like the Chinese T'ai Chi than like Hatha Yoga. The disciples observed the things that were happening to the teachers, probably, and embodied them and taught hundreds of postures—but they are all worthless; it is an extraordinary movement. Those who have observed my body moving say it looks like the motions of a newly born baby. This 'conking out' gives a total renewal of the senses, glands and nervous system: after it they function at the peak of their sensitivity.

In the Natural State there is no conflict, no fear, no desire, and all search of whatever kind comes to end. There is only the simple yet vibrant movement of life. It is the fulfilment of life. It is life. There is nothing supernatural about this state. UG is no superman, no God or avatar come down to save humankind. UG cannot be a model for others, and one cannot convert his utterances into a body of teaching to be followed by others. Perhaps UG's state is the end product of evolution, life at last finding itself! In UG's words: 'Nature, in its own way, throws out, from time to time, some flower, the end-product of human evolution. This cannot be used by the evolutionary process as a model for creating another.'

Now, one may ask here, how does UG know this?

'I don't know,' says UG, 'life is aware of itself, if we can put it that way—it is conscious of itself.'

The *Mundaka Upanishad* speaks of this state using the metaphor of two birds. The two birds of golden plumage, inseparable companions, the individual self and the immortal self, are perched on the same tree. The former tastes of the sweet and bitter fruits of the tree, the latter, tasting of neither, calmly observes.

The notion of the 'immortal self', a much-abused term, is misleading. Perhaps we can simply call it 'awareness', an integral part of the activity not only of all organisms but of all forms of life. It is there, functioning in a tree and the birds that perch on it, as much as in a human being. And there is nothing more one can say about it, for it cannot be conceptualized or converted into a philosophy, for it would be like trying to catch the wind in one's palm and giving it a name and form.

And so, UG says:

This consciousness (or awareness) which is functioning in me, in you, in the garden slug and earthworm outside, is the same. In me it has no frontiers; in you there are frontiers—you are enclosed in that. Probably this unlimited consciousness pushes you, I don't know. Not me; I have nothing to do with it. It is like the water finding its own level, that's all—that is its nature. That is what is happening in you: life is trying to destroy the enclosing thing, that dead structure of thought and experience, which is not of its nature. It's trying to come out, to break open. You don't want that. As soon as you see some cracks there, you bring some plaster and fill them in and block it again. It doesn't have to be a so-called self-realized man or spiritual man or God-realized man that pushes you; anything, that leaf there, teaches you just the same if only you let it do what it can. You must let that do. I have to put it that way. Although "let that do" may imply that there is some kind of volition on your part, that's not what I mean.

But we don't let things be, or 'let that do'. We theorize and build traditions around that 'awareness' and hope to achieve what cannot be achieved. For it is not something to be achieved, or willed into existence. In other words, there is no need to achieve or realize what is always already there. And so UG warns: 'Get this straight, this is your state I am describing, your natural state, not my state or the state of a God-realized man or a mutant or any such thing. This is your natural state, this is the way you, stripped of the machinations of thought, are also functioning. But what prevents what is there from expressing itself in its own way is your reaching out for something, trying to be something other than what you are.'

21

The Eternal Recurrence

Some months ago, we planted a pipal plant on the grave of our daughter. We didn't want to place any headstone there. To grow a pipal tree—the Bodhi tree, under which the Buddha is supposed to have sat and ended his search—seemed a better option. The plant has grown a few inches taller in the last few months. Shruti is in the tree. She is not dead. There is no death; only change of form.

Interestingly, in an apparent coincidence, I found the following verse quoted in a book by the late A.K. Ramanujan. It is a Vedic chant recited at funerals.

May your eye go to the sun, your life's breath to the wind. Go to the sky or to earth as is your nature; or to the waters, if that is your fate. Take root in the plants with your limbs.[120]

Giving a scientific view of the immortality of life, of body, Paul Davies, himself a noted physicist, writes in his popular book *The Origin of Life*:

Since the Earth formed, its material has not remained inert. Carbon, hydrogen, nitrogen and oxygen are continually recycled through the atmosphere and crust by geological and biological processes. When an organism dies and decays, its atoms are released back into the environment. Some of them eventually become part of other organisms. Simple statistics reveal that your body contains about one atom of carbon from every milligram of dead material more than 1000 years old. This simple fact has amazing implications. You are, for example, host to a billion or so atoms that once belonged to

Jesus Christ, or Julius Caesar, or the Buddha, or the tree that
the Buddha once sat beneath.[121]

Everything returns. Nothing goes away. Only the form changes.
Death is necessary for a new birth. In fact, death and birth are a
simultaneous process, says UG. But we cannot turn that into a
philosophy in order to seek solace, to ground ourselves in it to
overcome our fear, insecurity or lack. It is how things are. Suffering
is actually a bad habit.

And like a bad habit, UG returned to India in the month of
September 2003. After a gap of nearly twelve years, I had met him
the previous January and the idea of writing this narrative had
suggested itself. I had met him and recorded some of our
conversations when he was here again last September. Now, just
as I was completing my writing, he was back in Bangalore on 10
September 2003.

The monsoon had failed yet again in many parts of the country
and farmers continued to commit suicide. But in Bangalore, where
rains are considered a nuisance, we had plenty of rain, which
mercifully nourished the pipal plant growing on Shruti's body. She
loved rain, trees, and animals. The rains transformed the burial
ground into a beautiful landscape of lush green.

But it was a hot day when I went to see UG: the same old UG,
his long silvery hair falling over his long ears, which religious
people said looked like the ears of the Buddha as depicted in
paintings and carvings found all over the country. The 'third eye',
the ajna chakra, a dark-brown dot between his eyebrows, looked
prominent now. He was wearing chocolate-coloured cotton trousers
and a long-sleeved shirt. Just as I was making my way through
the crowd seated on mats and rugs, and even before I made my
pranams, I heard UG say, 'Hello, sir, how are you?'

How was I? I had stopped asking that question of myself. When
asked by others, I, of course, made the usual courteous response.
But now, I did not answer, I folded my hands in a namaste and
then sat down, leaning against a wall.

UG started to read from sheets of papers—what he called his
'money maxims'. A young friend had put together his now
scandalously popular proverbs on money. He flaunted these sheets

of papers as if they contained the core of his teachings. At eighty-five, his eyesight was good; he read out from the sheets, without the help of glasses:

Money is the be all and end-all of our existence . . . Unless converted into money, name and fame are not worth a tinker's damn . . . Maximize the money talk . . . Minimize the love talk . . . Better be miserable with loads of money than be without it . . . Denying yourself money is the root of all misery . . . Love not anything but money . . . Money can buy everything, Even God . . . What matters most is not monism but moneyism . . ..

He read about 106 such maxims. Some of us were familiar with these maxims and knew how little he cared for money, how he gave away millions of dollars. In fact, I know that recently he gave away a million dollars for the education of bright girls born to parents of Indian origin. Why girls? He replies, with a twinkle in his eyes, because 'actually and factually, I have found the boys to be dullards, slackards and laggards like me'. But why support girls' education in America? Because 'they (girls) are the only ones who can put some sense into the heads of those Americans to save their country from total disaster'. His answers are witty, nonsensical and even misleading. If you ask him if he is really serious, with a chuckle he replies, 'For aught I know, it is wishful thinking on my part. But, nonetheless, the fact does remain that it is the coming generation that will have to face the world and stop it from the way it is heading towards disaster.' One can clearly see that he is just trying to get rid of the money. What will I do with this money? he asks. His wants and needs are the same, very basic and simple. His luggage weighs less than five kilograms. Two or three pairs of clothes, a simple bowl of oatmeal and an occasional cup of coffee with a dose of cream thrown in is all that he needs. In comparison, even a Gandhi's lifestyle would seem extravagant! However, about one thing he is very clear—the money he comes by should never be used either to promote or perpetuate his name, memory, or 'teachings'.

Strange are the ways by which he comes upon money. He says

jokingly, 'Every time I kick Goddess Lakshmi (the goddess of wealth), she comes back tenfold.' Perhaps fearing he would reject any offer of money, people mail packets of money to his post-office box in Gstaad, or leave it on his toilet seat, in his shoes and in the chandeliers in his living room. Indeed, he does reject money, though at times, smiling mischievously, he accepts even a hundred-rupee note, chanting one of his money maxims. He is unpredictable. He has a way with money and it's always intriguing! And then, every year on New Year's Eve, Annie Besant-style, he gives away literally all that has come his way during the year, be it money or clothes or gifts. Yet, today, his reading out these maxims as if they were guidelines for good living seemed outrageous. He had turned upside down many a proverb. All religions warn against possession of wealth. *Artham an-artham* goes a Sanskrit saying, meaning 'wealth is disaster,' or 'wealth undoes a man'. The Bible declares: 'Easier indeed it is for a camel to pass through the eye of a needle than for a rich man to enter heaven.'

But UG, his eyes glinting with mischief, says: 'Make money and remain selfish.' The message is clear. One cannot be otherwise. The one who wants to be different needs no message. And such a person will never speak against money. So UG encourages, ridicules and laughs at money. The maxims are meant to deride all the profound sayings and homilies we love to pass on to others. The reading did elicit a good measure of laughter, for the maxims were truly hilarious, subversive and ridiculous. But newcomers who probably expected the 'enlightened man' to speak of the grace, beauty and power of God, of transcendental spirituality, of the tenderness of love and the healing touch of compassion, must have been scandalized.

Joseph Campbell, interestingly, calls money 'congealed energy'. Probably what he means to suggest is that money, like all symbols and concepts (frozen with fixed meanings), is a form of congealed energy. Money, like ideas and beliefs, becomes a substitute for security, happiness, higher consciousness, and freedom. One has to break them open to release the trapped energy there that is potentially liberating.

UG loves to put all the usual revered symbols and concepts (and money too) in the same basket and have a good laugh at man's illusion in worshipping them as gods, although these gods have never, and will never, deliver the promised goods.

'We should call every truth false which was not accompanied by at least one laugh,' declares Nietzsche's Zarathustra.

With UG, you can have several laughs—keep laughing, if you can—at all the 'truths' humanity holds dear to itself with the fond hope that they would eventually usher in the much-sought-after freedom and happiness without the touch of sorrow.

'Comedy' says Lee Siegel, 'challenges notions of meaning, strives to undermine all hermeneutics and epistemologies, and exposes the ambiguities inherent in any knowing and feeling. In the world of comedy, absurdity itself is the logos. The senselessness of the universe makes comic sense. Laughter expresses the comic understanding that nothing is ever really understood.'[122] In other words, *hasya* or the comic *rasa* mocks heroes and lovers, saints and sages. It delivers us from the tyranny of beauty, goodness, truth, and God.

The *nirguna* poets, the poets of non-dualism, use techniques of metaphor, oxymoron and paradox in their poetry[123] only to turn language topsy-turvy, and try to break rather than construct ideas and images. Names and forms create illusions, yet they use names and forms to demolish them. Apparently, one might think that UG too uses language in the style of these mystic–poets. But that is not so. The mystic–poets, like the deconstructionists today, deconstruct symbols, images and ideas, but they are not finished with the language, not finished with the need to express the inexpressible. There is still that agony, that sense of separation or incompleteness.

With UG, there is nothing to express, for all expressions are false, even to say something is false, is false. There is only rejection, wholly and totally, and there is laughter. There is in him the delightful giggle of Krishna, the drinker of milk, and the *attahasa* or apocalyptic laughter of Shiva, the drinker of poison.

Everything is laughed at and laughed away and at the end of it all what one is left with is emptiness! A considerable number of men and women show up every day, and keep grinning, giggling, roaring with laughter from morning till late evening. It seems they come there more in anticipation of having a good dose of laughter rather than to be instructed on the right way of living, or the path to liberation. Perhaps, to them, a dose of laughter is more liberating than a bagful of profound ideas.

Actually, profound or spiritual ideas are anathema there, to be ridiculed and laughed at. Swear words are the order of the day. One is welcomed not with grace, tenderness or compassion, but with a barrage of swear words and laughter. UG says jokingly that he learnt to use them from Sri Ramakrishna Paramahamsa. It is said that Ramakrishna often swore in his freewheeling conversations with people, and that he laughed a lot, reeling off jokes that inspired much laughter. 'Laughter was for him,' writes Lee Siegel, 'a mirthful expression of freedom-in-bondage, detachment without disinterest, and transcendence-in-being.'

'Excremental imagery abounds in comedy,' declares Lee Siegel. And true enough, UG's talk is full not only of swear words, but also disgustingly delightful references to shit, and sex too. Since we are all shitters from birth to death and are born as a result of sexual intercourse, about which we always appear to be embarrassed and ashamed, the laughter that UG inspires and provokes with his 'shit and sex talk' does truly relieve us of that embarrassment and help us realize our humanness. Pray, what else can you be?

Sometimes, UG refers to our memory, (our knowledge or data-bank) as a 'shit box', saying, 'There are ideas in your stomach . . . you eat ideas . . . it doesn't come out down there but from your mouth as oral shit . . . There is nothing more to it . . .'

One evening last September, a charming young director of a hugely successful musical film happened to be present. Somehow the talk veered towards music, and UG suddenly said, 'When we go to the toilet sometimes we make sound, there is more melody in that sound than all your music put together.'

We all laughed heartily. The film director laughed, too. But I could not say if it was a nervous reaction or one of good humour.

References to sex also pervade his talk, particularly when he picks on gods, the messiahs and famous people. The sacred becomes profane, holiness a pile of shit, the virgin birth a dirty joke. Sankara, Buddha, Christ and Mohammad are dismissed in a way that believers wouldn't want to hear, even in their dirtiest dreams. 'God is the ultimate pleasure,' he would quip. 'If sex has to go, God has to go first.' Thus, constantly it seems, he is trying to free us from the 'burden of the cultural garbage-sack, the dead refuse of the past', from the tyranny of religious values and God.

There have been occasions when we have joked and laughed at UG, too. From the heights of Kailash, as Siegel would say, everything becomes comical. What is not generally known is that Sanskrit texts, as much as folk literature, are full of subversive, comical stories and remarks that provoke laughter at everything we hold dear, at every established, dominant value or idea, at everything considered holy and divine. We laugh at the great triumvirate of Hinduism: Vishnu, Shiva, Brahma; we laugh at the sages as much as the kings, at the so-called idiots or fools as well as the wise ones. And we realize we are actually laughing at ourselves, for we are all that we laugh at, including the gods.

★

UG is variously referred to as an antidote to JK, as a Reluctant Messiah, Sage in Rage, Cosmic Naxalite, and Anti-Guru, all of which he rejects saying he cannot be put in any framework, however radical. In point of fact, there is hardly anything in history that we can refer to in our attempt to understand UG's life and

teaching. But then, as UG himself admits, what happened to him
must have happened to other persons in all ages. Nature, now and
then, does throw up these unique flowers. They do not all
necessarily speak the same language nor behave the same way. To
use UG's language, when one touches life at a point where no one
has touched it before, the person is finished with the entire past,
though his or her background would continue to express itself in
a unique way. They do not offer themselves as models to be
followed, much less want to change the world, though their
utterances and their very presence might have a great impact on
human consciousness and cause some radical shift in human
understanding.

It is culture that always builds them up as models for people
to adopt or follow and thus falsify the movement of life. It is
characteristic of all cultures to produce models, to homogenize
societies, to control, manipulate and set standards for human
existence. Take away the 'models' and cultures would fall apart.
Life is not programmed the way the cultures of the world want life
to be programmed, whether in the name of religion, or in the name
of politics, moral and spiritual values, law or social norms. To do
that is to create conflict, guilt, fear, insecurity, a battle within every
mind and society.

'When you see all this for yourself for the first time, you explode,'
says UG. 'That explosion hits life at a point that has never been
touched before. It is absolutely unique. So whatever I may be saying
cannot be true for you. The moment you see it for yourself you
make what I am saying obsolete and false. All that came before
is negated in that fire. You can't come into your own uniqueness
unless the whole of human experience is thrown out of your system.
It cannot be done through any volition or the help of anything. Then
you are on your own.'

It seems to be a continuous process, this burning away or the
negation of the past. When you touch life at a point where no one
has touched it before, when you are thrown into the 'primordial
state without primitivism' or the 'undivided state', every mental
construct is seen as false and consequently all ideas and concepts,
all symbols and images, all world-views and cosmologies, religious,
secular or scientific, are burnt up in the blaze of that undivided

state. Everything born out of thought, the self, exists in pairs of opposites feeding on each other; it is destructive yet self-protective, fascist in nature, and, therefore, it needs to be destroyed. In other words, since all frames, all reference points are arbitrary, false, and in that sense an illusion, they are negated or wiped out. What is left is not nothingness but life that cannot be captured by words. There is simply no way of knowing it, for it is not in the realm of knowing at all!

★

Three great images repeatedly emerge from the ancient myths of the world: the images of eating, copulation and destruction. All creatures, including human beings, are involved in this never-ending creative–destructive process, a simultaneous process that seems to be the movement of life itself. Astronomers tell us that, in fact, the whole of the cosmos is always involved in this terrific play: universes appear and disappear, whole galaxies are ripped apart and recreated, big stars eat up small ones; black holes, like the monster born of Shiva's third eye, gobble up everything within their reach; it all seems like some ferocious display of galactic cannibalism.

The myth of Kirtimukha can be read as a powerful metaphor of this endless cycle of destruction and creation.The myth goes like this:

Once, a rakshasa desired Shiva's consort, Parvathi. He went to Shiva and stupidly demanded that Parvathi be given to him. In sudden rage, Shiva opened his third eye and out came a monster, most fearsome. The rakshasa saw that the monster was ready to eat him up. He begged Shiva's forgiveness and fled. Now, looking up at Shiva, who in his mercy had let his prey go free, the monster asked: 'What do I do now? I am hungry, you made me hungry. What do I eat?'

There was no escape. The purpose for which the monster was created had to be somehow satisfied. So, Shiva said, 'Eat yourself.'

And behold! The hungry monster, his feral eyes rolling with inexhaustible appetite, began to devour himself! Starting with his feet, teeth nibbling and lopping away chunks of his own flesh, he came right on up the line, the jagged, sharp, greedy teeth chopping through his mammoth belly, his bristly chest and enormous neck, until all that remained was a face, terrific and still livid with hunger . . .

This is the awesome image of life living on itself. The head of Kirti is carved at the portals of temples and Buddhist shrines. The suggestion is that one has to reckon with, and accept, this supreme fact of life living on life, before one approaches that which cannot be captured in the fishbowl of the mind. The metaphor evokes what UG does to people. 'Eat yourself,' he seems to be saying to everyone who approaches him for a clue to liberation, for a hint of the way to end all suffering. But there is a strange twist in the tale here. You have to start with the head and let the body live. So his apocalyptic laughter and fiery words are directed at the head, at the *self*, in order to decapitate 'you'. The self, the 'I' has to die for the body to live and start the new movement of life in tune with the cosmos!

It's been a long night. It has been raining almost continuously for the last few days. Bangalore's weather is as unpredictable as a child's bottom. Today it is Diwali, and the skies are clear. It is the time for the celebration of light over darkness. Soon the sound of firecrackers will rise to an ear-deafening crescendo, and the dark night will be lit up with dazzling fireworks. Diwali, the lighting of lamps and bursting of firecrackers, is supposed to symbolize the triumph of good over evil. But is there such a thing as good and evil? Isn't the 'evil' born of the womb of 'good'? But then people celebrate Diwali because they want to; it is a habit they don't feel the need to give up. It's a ritual, and all rituals, as Joseph Campbell would say, are an enactment of a myth.

UG has left this land of weird and wonderful myths, of huge contradictions and great yearnings, and returned to the land of the seven hills and blue sky, the land where this great, wonderful yet terrific story began, and something utterly new and incomprehensible emerged. I do not know when he will return, and when I am likely to meet him again. I do not know what the future will be like. It's better, it seems, to let go of things, but I know it's a tricky business. Be that as it may, keep the doors and windows open and let the fresh air come in.

BOOK THREE

ANTI-TEACHING

22

Telling It Like It Is
The Voice of UG[1]

How do I know? I don't know. Life is aware of itself, if we can put it that way—it is conscious of itself.

I have no answers for any metaphysical questions because I am not thinking metaphysically. I am not thinking in concepts. You may very well ask whether it is possible to use words without concepts. I say it is possible. There is no content to these words. These are not born out of any concept. They are just words. To imagine that there is a state of non-verbal conceptualization is just a myth. The purpose of this conversation is to enable you to break free from the methods of thought as a means to understand anything.

Is There a Teaching?

There is no teaching of mine, and never shall be one. 'Teaching' is not the word for it. A teaching implies a method or a system, a technique or a new way of thinking to be applied in order to bring about a transformation in your way of life. What I am saying is outside the field of teachability; it is simply a description of the way I am functioning. It is just a description of the *Natural State* of man—this is the way you, stripped of the machinations of thought, are also functioning.

The Natural State is not the state of a self-realized, God-realized man, it is not a thing to be achieved or attained, it is not a thing to be willed into existence; it is *there*—it is the living state. This state is just the functional activity of life. By 'life', I do not mean something abstract; it is the life of the senses, functioning naturally without the interference of thought. Thought is an interloper, which thrusts itself into the affairs of the senses. It has a profit motive: Thought directs the activity of the senses to get something out of them, and uses them to give continuity to itself.

Your Natural State has no relationship whatsoever with the religious states of bliss, beatitude and ecstasy; they lie within the field of experience. Those who have led man on his search for religiousness throughout the centuries have perhaps experienced those religious states. So can you. They are thought-induced states of being, and as they come, so do they go. Krishna Consciousness, Buddha Consciousness, Christ Consciousness, or what have you, are all trips in the wrong direction: they are all within the field of time. The timeless can never be experienced, can never be grasped, contained, much less given expression to, by any man. That beaten track will lead you nowhere. There is no oasis situated yonder; you are stuck with the mirage.

I've no message to give to the world. Whatever happens to me is such that you can't share it with the world. That's the reason why I don't get up on a platform or give any lectures—it's not that I can't give lectures; I've lectured everywhere in the world—I've nothing to say. And I don't like to sit in one place, surrounded by people asking set questions. I never initiate any discussions; people come and sit round me—they can do what they like. If somebody asks me a question suddenly, I try to answer, emphasizing and pointing out that there is no answer to that question. So, I merely rephrase, restructure and throw the same question back at you. It's not game playing, because I'm not interested in winning you over to my point of view. It's not a question of offering opinions—of course, I do have my opinions on everything from disease to divinity, but they're as worthless as anybody else's.

What I say you must not take literally. So much trouble has been created by people taking it all literally. You must test every word, every phrase, and see if it bears any relation to the way you are functioning. You must test it, but you are not in a position to accept it—unfortunately this is a fact, take it or leave it. By writing it down, you will do more harm than good. You see, I am in a very difficult position: I cannot help you, whatever I say is misleading.

What I am saying has no logic. If it has a logic, it has a logic of its own—I don't know anything about it. But you have necessarily to fit me into the logical structure of your thought; otherwise the logical structure there, the rational thing, comes to an end. You see, you have to rationalize—that is what you are. But this has nothing to do with rationality, it has nothing to do with your logic—that doesn't mean that it is illogical or irrational.

On Himself or the Natural State

I am not out to liberate anybody. You have to liberate yourself, and you are unable to do that. What I have to say will not do it. I am only interested in describing this state, in clearing away the occultation and mystification in which those people in the 'holy business' have shrouded the whole thing. Maybe I can convince you not to waste a lot of time and energy, looking for a state which does not exist except in your imagination.

There is nobody here talking, giving advice, feeling pain, or experiencing anything at all. Like a ball thrown against the wall, it bounces back, that is all. My talking is the direct result of your question, I have nothing here of my own, no obvious or hidden agenda, no product to sell, no axe to grind, nothing to prove.

That silence burns everything here. All experiences are burnt. That is why talking to people doesn't exhaust me. It is energy to me. That is why I can talk for the whole day without showing any fatigue. Talking with so many people over the years has had no impact upon me. All that they or I have said is burnt here, leaving no trace. This is not, unfortunately, the case with you.

The personality does not change when you come into this state. You are, after all, a computer machine, which reacts as it has been programmed. It is in fact your present effort to change yourself that is taking you away from yourself and keeping you from functioning in the natural way. The personality will remain the same. Don't expect such a man to become free from anger or idiosyncrasies. Don't expect some kind of spiritual humility. Such a man may be the most arrogant person you have ever met, because he is touching life at a unique place where no man has touched before. It is for this reason that each person who comes into this state expresses it in a unique way, in terms relevant to his time. It is also for this reason that if two or more people are living in this state at the same time, they will never get together. They won't dance in the streets hand in hand: 'We are all self-realized men! We belong!'

Man becomes man for the first time—and that is possible *only* when he frees himself from the burden of the heritage we are talking about, the heritage of *man as a whole* (not East and West; there is no East and West). Then only does he become an individual. For the first time he becomes an individual—that is the individual I am talking about. That individual will certainly have an impact on human consciousness, because when something happens in this consciousness of man it affects (the whole), to a very microscopic extent maybe. So, this is a simile: When you throw a stone in a pool, it sets in motion circular waves. In exactly the same way, it is *very* slow, *very* slow—it is something which cannot be measured with anything.

So, maybe that's the only hope that man has—that's the first time such an individual becomes a man—otherwise he's an animal. And he has remained an animal because of the heritage, because the heritage has made it possible, from the point of view of Nature, for the unfit to remain; otherwise Nature would have rejected them a long time ago. It has become possible for the unfit to survive—not the survival of the fittest, but of those unfit to survive—and religion is responsible for that. That's my argument. You may not agree. It doesn't matter.

Is There Such a Thing as Enlightenment?

There is no such thing as enlightenment. You may say that every teacher and all the saints and saviours of mankind have been asserting for centuries upon centuries that there is enlightenment and that they are enlightened. Throw them all in one bunch into the river! I don't care. To realize that there is *no* enlightenment at all *is* enlightenment.

But actually, an enlightened man or a free man, if there is one, is not interested in freeing or enlightening anybody. This is because he has no way of knowing that he is a free man, that he is an enlightened man. It is not something that can be shared with somebody, because it is not in the area of experience at all.

To me what does exist is a purely physical process; there is nothing mystical or spiritual about it. If I close the eyes, some light penetrates through the eyelids. If I cover the eyelids, there is still light inside. There seems to be some kind of a hole in the forehead, which doesn't show, but through which something penetrates. In India that light is golden; in Europe it is blue. There is also some kind of light penetration through the back of the neck. It's as if there is a hole running through between those spots in front and back of the skull. There is nothing inside but this light. If you cover those points, there is complete, total darkness. This light doesn't do anything or help the body to function in any way; it's just there.

This state is a state of not knowing; you really don't know what you are looking at. I may look at the clock on the wall for half an hour—still I do not read the time. I don't know it is a clock. All there is inside is wonderment: 'What is this that I am looking at?' Not that the question actually phrases itself like that in words: The whole of my being is like a single, big question mark. It is a state of wonder, of wondering, because I just do not know what I am looking at. The knowledge about it—all that I have learned— is held in the background unless there is a demand. It is in the 'declutched state'. If you ask the time, I will say 'It's a quarter past three' or whatever—it comes quickly like an arrow—then I am back in the state of not knowing, of wonder.

When I talk of 'feeling', I do not mean the same thing that you do. Actually, feeling is a physical response, a thud in the thymus. The thymus, one of the endocrine glands, is located under the breastbone. The doctors tell us that it is active through childhood until puberty and then becomes dormant. When you come into your Natural State, this gland is re-activated. Sensations are felt there; you don't translate them as 'good' or 'bad'; they are just a thud.

If there is a movement outside of you—a clock pendulum swinging, or a bird flying across your field of vision—that movement is also felt in the thymus. The whole of your being is that movement or vibrates with that sound; there is no separation. This does not mean that you identify yourself with that bird or whatever—'I am that flying bird.' There is no 'you' there, nor is there any object. What causes that sensation, you don't know. You do not even know that it is a sensation.

'Affection' means that you are affected by everything, not that some emotion flows from you towards something. The Natural State is a state of great sensitivity—but this is a physical sensitivity of the senses, not some kind of emotional compassion or tenderness for others. There is compassion only in the sense that there are no 'others' for me, and so there is no separation.

The Body

My body exists for other people; it does not exist for me; there are only isolated points of contact, impulses of touch which are not tied together by thought. So the body is not different from the objects around it; it is a set of sensations like any others. Your body does not belong to you.

Perhaps I can give you the 'feel' of this. I sleep four hours at night, no matter what time I go to bed. Then I lie in bed until morning fully awake. I don't know what is lying there in the bed; I don't know whether I'm lying on my left side or my right side— for hours and hours I lie like this. If there is any noise outside— a bird or something—it just echoes in me. I listen to the 'flub-dub-flub-dub' of my heart and don't know what it is. There is no body between the two sheets—the form of the body is not there. If the question is asked, 'What is in there?' there is only an awareness of the points of contact, where the body is in contact with the bed and the sheets, and where it is in contact with itself, at the crossing of the legs, for example. There are only the sensations of touch from these points of contact, and the rest of the body is not there. There is some kind of heaviness, probably the gravitational pull, something very vague. There is nothing inside which links up these things. Even if the eyes are open and looking at the whole body, there are still only the points of contact, and they have no connection with what I am looking at. If I want to try to link up these points of contact into the shape of my own body, probably I will succeed, but by the time it is completed the body is back in the same situation of different points of contact. The linkage cannot stay. It is the same sort of thing when I'm sitting or standing. There is no body.

In the Natural State there is no entity who is coordinating the messages from the different senses. Each sense is functioning independently in its own way. When there is a demand from outside which makes it necessary to coordinate one or two or all of the senses and come up with a response, still there is no coordinator, but there is a temporary state of coordination. There is no continuity; when the demand has been met, again there is only the uncoordinated, disconnected, disjointed functioning of the senses. This is always the case. Once the continuity is blown apart—not that it was ever there; but the illusory continuity—it's finished once and for all.

God Is Irrelevant

Is there a beyond? Because you are not interested in the everyday things and the happenings around you, you have invented a thing called the 'beyond', or 'timelessness', or 'God', 'Truth', 'Reality', 'Brahman', 'enlightenment', or whatever, and you search for that. There may not be any beyond. You don't know a thing about that beyond; whatever you know is what you have been told, the knowledge you have about that. So you are projecting that knowledge. What you call 'beyond' is created by the knowledge you have about that beyond; and whatever knowledge you have about a beyond is exactly what you will experience. The knowledge creates the experience, and the experience then strengthens the knowledge. What you know can never be the beyond. Whatever you experience is not the beyond. If there is any beyond, this movement of 'you' is absent. The absence of this movement probably is the beyond, but the beyond can never be experienced by you; it is when the 'you' is not there. Why are you trying to experience a thing that cannot be experienced?

Man has to be saved from God—that is very essential. I don't mean God in the sense in which you use the word 'God'; I mean all that 'God' stands for, not only God, but all that is associated with that concept of God—even karma, reincarnation, rebirth, life after death, the *whole* thing, the whole business of what you call the 'great heritage of India'—all that, you see. Man has to be saved from the heritage of India. Not only the people; the country has to be saved from that heritage. (Not by revolution, not the way they have done it in the communist countries—that's not the way. I don't know why; you see, this is a very *tricky* subject.) Otherwise, there is no hope for the individual and no hope for the country.

That messy thing called the mind has created many destructive things, and by far the most destructive of them all is God. To me the question of God is irrelevant and immaterial. We have no use for God. More people have been killed in the name of God than in the two world wars put together. In Japan, millions of people died in the name of the sacred Buddha. Christians and Muslims have done the same. Even in India, 5000 Jains were massacred in a single day. Yours is not a peaceful nation. Read your own history—it's full of violence from the beginning to the?. Man is merely a biological being. There is no spiritual side to his nature. There is no such thing . . . All the virtues, principles, beliefs, ideas and spiritual values are mere affectations. They haven't succeeded in changing anything in you. You're still the brute that you have always been. When will you begin to see the truth that the philosophy of 'Love thy neighbour as thyself' is not what stops you from killing indiscriminately but it's the terror of the fact that if you kill your neighbour you too will also be destroyed along with him that stops you from killing.

God is the ultimate pleasure, uninterrupted happiness. No such thing exists. Your wanting something that does not exist is the root of your problem. Transformation, moksha, liberation, and all that stuff are just variations on the same theme: permanent happiness.

Religion Is a Neurological Problem

Religion is not a contractual arrangement, either public or private. It has nothing to do with the social structure or its management. Religious authority wants to continue its hold on the people, but religion is entirely an individual affair. The saints and saviours have only succeeded in setting you adrift in life with pain and misery and the restless feeling that there must be something more meaningful or interesting to do with one's life.

'Religion', 'God', 'Soul', 'Beatitudes', 'moksha', are all just words, ideas used to keep your psychological continuity intact. When these thoughts are not there, what is left is the simple, harmonious physical functioning of the organism.

Love, compassion, ahimsa, understanding, bliss, all these things which religion and psychology have placed before man, are only adding to the strain of the body. *All* cultures, whether of the Orient or of the Occident, have created this lopsided situation for mankind and turned man into a neurotic individual.

Man has already messed up his life, and religion has made it worse. It is religion that really made a mess of man's life.

You cannot exonerate the founders and leaders of religions. The teachings of all those teachers and saviours of mankind have resulted in only violence. Everybody talked of peace and love, while their followers practised violence.

Holy Men and Holy Business

We have been brainwashed for centuries by holy men that we must control our thoughts. Without thinking, you would become a corpse. Without thinking, the holy men wouldn't have any means of telling us to control our thoughts. They would go broke. They have become rich telling others to control their thoughts.

The whole religious business is nothing but moral codes of conduct: You must be generous, compassionate, loving, while all the time you remain greedy and callous. Codes of conduct are set by society in its own interests, sacred or profane. There is nothing religious about it. The religious man puts the priest, the censor, inside you. Now the policeman has been institutionalized and placed outside you. Religious codes and strictures are no longer necessary; it is all in the civil and criminal codes. You needn't bother with these religious people any more; they are obsolete. But they don't want to lose their hold over people. It is their business; their livelihood is at stake. There is no difference between the policeman and the religious man. It is a little more difficult with the policeman, for, unlike the inner authority sponsored by the holy men, he lies outside you and must be bribed. The secular leaders tell you one way, the holy men another way. It makes no difference: As long as you are searching for peace of mind, you will have a tormented mind. If you try not to search, or if you continue to search, you will remain the same. You have to *stop*.

Understanding yourself is one of the greatest jokes, perpetrated on the gullible and credulous people everywhere, not only by the purveyors of ancient wisdom—the holy men—but also by the modern scientists. The psychologists love to talk about self-knowledge, self-actualization, living from moment to moment, and such rot. These absurd ideas are thrown at us as if they are something new.

You have been brainwashed by all those holy men, gurus, teachers and the so-called enlightened people that the past should die, should come to an end. 'If you attain this, life would be hunky-dory—full of sweetness.' You have fallen for all that romantic stuff. If you try to suppress the past and try to be in the present, it will drive you crazy. You are trying to control something which is beyond your control.

It is not only your past. It's the entire past, entire existence of every human being and every form of life. It is not such an easy thing. It is like trying to stop this flow of the river through all those artificial means. It will inundate the whole thing.

They talk very lightly of money as if it has no importance for them, when in fact it is one of the most important things in their lives. These holy men are greedy, jealous, and vindictive bastards, just like everybody else. You want to live through your work, and through your children. These people want to live through their religious institutions.

What these gurus in the marketplace do is to sell you some ice packs and provide you with some comforters.

Meditation Is Warfare

Meditation is a self-centred activity. It is strengthening the very self you want to be free from. What are you meditating for? You want to be free from something. What are you to meditate on? All right, thought is a noise, sound. What is sound? You look at this and you say 'This is a tape recorder,' so thought is sound. There is a continuous flow of thoughts, and you are linking up all these thoughts all the time, and this is the noise you can't stand. Why can't you stand that noise? So, by repeating mantras, you create a louder noise, and you submerge the noise of thought, and then you are at peace with yourself. You think that something marvellous is happening to you. But all meditation is a self-centred activity.

You have also been told that through meditation you can bring selfishness to an end. Actually, you are not meditating at all, just thinking about selflessness, and doing nothing to be selfless. I have taken that as an example, but all other examples are variations of the same thing. All activity along these lines is exactly the same. You must accept the simple fact that you do not want to be free from selfishness.

Meditation is warfare. You sit for meditation while there is a battle raging within you. The result is violent, evil thoughts welling up inside you. Next, you try to control or direct these brutal thoughts, making more effort and violence for yourself in the process.

Consciousness

Krishna Consciousness, Buddha Consciousness, Christ Consciousness, or what have you, are all trips in the wrong direction: they are all within the field of time. The timeless can never be experienced, can never be grasped, contained, much less given expression to, by any man.

This consciousness which is functioning in me, in you, in the garden slug and earthworm outside, is the same. In me it has no frontiers; in you there are frontiers—you are enclosed in that. Where is the seat of human consciousness?

You have no way at all of finding out for yourself the seat of human consciousness, because it is all over, and you are not separate from that consciousness. Even with all the experiments that the brain physiologists and psychologists are doing, wasting millions and millions of dollars just to find out the seat of human consciousness, they will never be able to find it out at all.

Culture is part of this human consciousness, so everything that man has experienced and felt before you is part of that consciousness.

It is really a mystery. All the experiences—not necessarily just your experiences during your span of thirty, forty or fifty years, but the animal consciousness, the plant consciousness, the bird consciousness—all that is part of this consciousness.

Consciousness is a very powerful factor in experiencing things, but it is not possible for anybody to find out the content of the whole thing—it is too vast. The genetic is only part of it. It is much more than the genetic.

Whatever you experience, however profound that experience may be, is the result of the knowledge that is part of your consciousness. Somebody must have, *somewhere* along the line, experienced the bliss, beatitude—call it 'ecstasy', call it by *whatever* name you like, but *somebody somewhere* along the line— not necessarily you—must have experienced that, and that experience is part of your consciousness. You have to come to a point where there is no such thing as a *new* experience at all: somebody has experienced it before, so it is not yours.

The consciousness of the body does not exist. There is no such thing as consciousness at all. The one thing that helps us to become conscious of the non-existing body, for all practical purposes, is the knowledge that is given to us. Without that knowledge you have no way of creating your own body and experiencing it. I am questioning the very idea of consciousness, let alone the subconscious, the unconscious, the different levels of consciousness, and higher states of consciousness. I don't see that there is any such thing as consciousness. I become conscious of this (touching the arm of the chair) only through the knowledge that I have of it. The touch does not tell me anything except when I translate it within the framework of knowledge. Otherwise I have no way of experiencing that touch at all. The way these senses are operating here is quite different from the way we are made to believe. The eye is looking at the movement of your hand, and is not saying anything about that activity, except observing what is going on there.

Awareness

I am not particularly fond of the word 'awareness'. It is misused. It is a rubbed coin, and everybody uses it to justify some of his actions, instead of admitting that he did something wrong. Sometimes you say, 'I was not aware of what was going on there.' But awareness is an integral part of the activity of this human organism. This activity is not only specifically in the human organism but in all forms of life—the pig and the dog. The cat just looks at you, and is in a state of choiceless awareness. To turn that awareness into an instrument which you can use to bring about a change is to falsify that. Awareness is an integral part of the activity of the living organism.

There Is No Self, No Soul

The belief that there is a centre here, that there is a spirit here, that there is a soul here, is what is responsible for that belief that there must be something beyond.

Is there any such thing as soul? Is there any such thing as the 'I'? Is there any such thing as the psyche? Whatever you see there, whatever you experience there, is created only by the knowledge you have of that self.

There is no self, there is no I, there is no spirit, there is no soul, and there is no mind. That knocks off the whole list, and you have no way of finding out what you are left with.

Ideas of soul and life after death are born out of the demand for permanence. That's the basis of man's religious thinking. All religious thinking is born out of the demand for permanence.

The Mind Is a Myth

There is no such thing as an unconditioned mind; the mind *is* conditioned. If there is a mind, it is bound to be conditioned. There is no such thing as an open mind.

To me there is no such thing as mind; mind is a myth. Since there is no such thing as mind, the 'mutation of mind' that J. Krishnamurti is talking about has no meaning. There is nothing there to be transformed, radically or otherwise. There is no self to be realized. The whole religious structure that has been built on this foundation collapses because there is nothing there to realize.

The whole Buddhist philosophy is built on the foundation of that 'no mind'. Yet they have created tremendous techniques of freeing themselves from the mind. All the Zen techniques of meditation try to free you from the mind. But the very instrument that we are using to free ourselves from the thing called 'mind' *is* the mind. Mind is nothing other than what you are doing to free yourself from the mind. But when it once dawns on you, by some strange chance or miracle, that the instrument that you are using to understand everything is not the instrument, and that there is no other instrument, it hits you like a jolt of lightning.

Thought Is Bourgeois

Thought in its birth, in its origin, in its content, in its expression, and in its action is very fascist. When I use the word 'fascist' I use it not in the political sense but to mean that thought controls and shapes our thinking and our actions. So it is a very protective mechanism. It has no doubt helped us to be what we are today. It has helped us to create our high-tech gadgets and technology. It has made our life very comfortable. It has also made it possible for us to discover the laws of Nature. But thought is a very protective mechanism and is interested in its own survival. At the same time, thought is opposed fundamentally to the functioning of this living organism.

It is thought that has invented the ideas of cause and effect. There may not be any such thing as a cause at all. Every event is an individual and independent event. We link up all these events and try to create a story of our lives. But actually every event is an independent event. If we accept the fact that every event is an independent event in our lives, it creates a tremendous problem of maintaining what we call identity. And identity is the most important factor in our lives. We are able to maintain this identity through the constant use of memory, which is also thought. This constant use of memory or identity, or whatever you call it, is consuming a tremendous amount of energy, and it leaves us with no energy to deal with the problems of our living. Is there any way that we can free ourselves from the identity? As I said, thought can only create problems; it cannot help us to solve them. Through dialectical thinking about thinking itself we are only sharpening that instrument. All philosophies help us only to sharpen this instrument.

Thought is very essential for us to survive in this world. But it cannot help us in achieving the goals that we have placed before ourselves. The goals are unachievable through the help of thought. The quest for happiness, as you mentioned, is impossible because there is no such thing as permanent happiness. There are moments of happiness, and there are moments of unhappiness. But the demand to be in a permanent state of happiness is the enemy of this body. This body is interested in maintaining its sensitivity of the sensory perceptions and also the sensitivity of the nervous system. That is very essential for the survival of this body. If we use that instrument of thought for trying to achieve the impossible goal of permanent happiness, the sensitivity of this body is destroyed. Therefore, the body is rejecting all that we are interested in—permanent happiness and permanent pleasure. So, we are not going to succeed in that attempt to be in a permanent state of happiness.

Thought to me is matter. Therefore, all our spiritual goals are materialistic in their value. And this is the conflict that is going on there. In this process, the totality of man's experiences created what we call a separate identity and a separate mind. But actually if you want to experience anything, be it your own body, or your own experiences, you have no way of experiencing them without the use of the knowledge that is passed on to us.

All the problems are artificially created by the various structures created by human thinking. There is some sort of (I can't make a definitive statement) neurological problem in the human body. Human thinking is born out of this neurological defect in the human species. Anything that is born out of human thinking is destructive. Thought is destructive. Thought is a protective mechanism. It draws frontiers around itself, and it wants to protect itself. It is for the same reason that we also draw lines on this planet and extend them as far as we can. Do you think these frontiers are going to disappear? They are not. Those who have entrenched themselves, those who have had the monopoly of all the world's resources so far and for so long, if they are threatened to be dislodged, what they would do is anybody's guess. All the destructive weapons that we have today are here only to protect that monopoly.

But actually, 'Is there a thought?' The question is born out of the assumption that there is a thought there. But what you will find there is all *about* thought and *not* thought. All *about* thought is what is put in there by culture. That is put in by the people who are telling us that it is very essential for you to free yourself from whatever you are trying to free yourself from through that instrument. My interest is to emphasize that that is not the instrument, and there is no other instrument. And when once this hits you, dawns upon you that thought is not the instrument, and that there is no other instrument, then there is no need for you to find out if any other instrument is necessary. No need for any other instrument. This very same structure that we are using, the instrument which we are using, has in a very ingenious way invented all kinds of things like intuition, right insight, right this, that, and the other. And to say that through this very insight we have come to understand something is the stumbling block. All insights, however extraordinary they may be, are worthless, because it is thought that has created what we call insight, and through that it is maintaining its continuity and status quo.

Where does thought come from? Is it from inside, or outside? Where is the seat of human consciousness? So, for purposes of communication, or just to give a feel about it, I say there is a 'thought sphere'. In that 'thought sphere' we are all functioning, and each of us probably has an 'antenna', or what you call an 'aerial' or something, which is the creation of the culture into which we are born. That is what is picking up these particular thoughts. You have no way at all of finding out for yourself the seat of human consciousness, because it is all over, and you are not separate from that consciousness. Even with all the experiments that the brain researchers are doing, wasting millions and millions of dollars just to find out the seat of human consciousness, they will never be able to find it out at all. I am not making a dogmatic statement or any such thing.

Thought can never capture the movement of life, it is much too slow. It is like lightning and thunder. They occur simultaneously, but sound, travelling slower than light, reaches you later, creating the illusion of two separate events. It is only the natural physiological sensations and perceptions that can move with the flow of life.

There is no such thing as looking at something without the interference of knowledge. To look you need space, and thought creates that space. So space itself, as a dimension, exists only as a creation of thought. Thought has also tried to theorize about the space it has created, inventing the 'time-space continuum'. Time is an independent reference or frame. There is no necessary continuity between it and space. Thought has also invented the opposite of time, the 'now', the 'eternal now'. The present exists only as an idea. The moment you attempt to look at the present, it has already been brought into the framework of the past. Thought will use any trick under the sun to give momentum to its own continuity. Its essential technique is to repeat the same thing over and over again; this gives it an illusion of permanency. This permanency is shattered the moment the falseness of the past-present-future continuum is seen. The future can be nothing but the modified continuity of the past.

Feeling too is Thought

Feeling is also thought. We want to feel that feelings are more important than thoughts, but there is no way you can experience a feeling without translating that within the framework of the knowledge that you have. Take for example that you tell yourself that you are happy. You don't even know that the sensation that is there is happiness. But you capture that sensation within the framework of the knowledge you have of what you call a state of happiness, and the other state, that of unhappiness. What I am trying to say is that it is the knowledge that you have about yourself which has created the self there and helps you to experience yourself as an entity there.

Knowledge and Experience

Whatever you experience—peace, bliss, silence, beatitude, ecstasy, joy, God knows what—will be old, second-hand. You already have knowledge about all of these things. The fact that you are in a blissful state or in a state of tremendous silence means that you know about it. You must know a thing in order to experience it. That knowledge is nothing marvellous or metaphysical; 'bench', 'bag', 'red bag', is the knowledge. Knowledge is something which is put into you by somebody else, and he got that from somebody else; it is not yours. Can you experience a simple thing like that bench that is sitting across from you? No, you only experience the knowledge you have about it. And the knowledge has come from some outside agency, always. You think the thoughts of your society, feel the feelings of your society and experience the experiences of your society; there is no new experience.

Knowledge is not something mysterious or mystical. You know .

that you are happy, and you have theories about the working of the fan, the light—this is the knowledge we are talking about. You introduce another knowledge, 'spiritual knowledge', but—spiritual knowledge, sensual knowledge—what is the difference? We give the names to them. Fantasies about God are acceptable, but fantasies about sex are called 'sensual', 'physical'. There is no difference between the two; one is socially acceptable, the other is not. You are limiting knowledge to a particular area of experience, so then it becomes 'sensual', and the other becomes 'spiritual'? Everything is sensual.

You cannot communicate what you cannot experience. I don't want to use those words, because 'inexpressible' and 'incommunicable' imply that there is something which cannot be communicated, which cannot be expressed. I don't know. There is an assumption that there is something there which cannot be expressed, which cannot be communicated. There is nothing there. I don't want to say there is nothing there, because you will catch me—you will call it 'emptiness', 'void' and all that sort of thing.

Whatever is experienced is thought-induced. Without knowledge you can't experience. And experience strengthens the knowledge. It is a vicious circle: the dog chasing its own tail.

Where, you ask, is this knowledge, the past? Is it in your brain? Where is it? It is all over your body. It is in every cell of your body.

Is There Any Meaning and Purpose to Life?

'What is the meaning of life?' It is not life that we are really interested in but living. The problem of living has become a very tiring business—to live with somebody else, to live with our feelings, to live with our ideas. In other words, it is the value system that we have been thrown into. You see, the value system is false.

The heart does not for a moment know that it is pumping blood. It is not asking the question, 'Am I doing it right?' It is just functioning. It does not ask the question, 'Is there any purpose?' To me, that question has no meaning. The questions, 'Is there any meaning?', 'Is there any purpose?' take away the living quality of life. You are living in a world of ideas.

Suppose I say that this meaninglessness is all there is for you, all there can ever be for you. What will you do? The false and absurd goal you have before you is responsible for that dissatisfaction and meaninglessness in you. Do you think life has any meaning? Obviously you don't. You have been told that there *is* meaning, that there *must* be a meaning to life. Your notion of the 'meaningful' keeps you from facing this issue, and makes you feel that life has no meaning. If the idea of the meaningful is dropped, then you will see meaning in whatever you are doing in daily life.

Why should life have any meaning? Why should there be any purpose to living? Living itself is all that is there. Your search for spiritual meaning has made a problem out of living. You have been fed all this rubbish about the ideal, perfect, peaceful, purposeful way of life, and you devote your energies to thinking about that rather than living fully. In any case you are living, no matter what you are thinking about. Life has to go on.

Once a very old gentleman, ninety-five years old, who was considered to be a great spiritual man and who taught the great scriptures all the time to his followers, came to see me. He heard that I was there in that town. He came to me and asked me two questions. He asked me, 'What is the meaning of life? I have written hundreds of books telling people all about the meaning and purpose of life, quoting all the scriptures and interpreting them. I haven't understood the meaning of life. You are the one who can give an answer to me.' I told him, 'Look, you are ninety-five years old and you haven't understood the meaning of life. When are you going to understand the meaning of life? There may not be any meaning to life at all.' The next question he asked me was, 'I have lived ninety-five years and I am going to die one of these days. I want to know what will happen after my death.' I said, 'You may not live long enough to know anything about death. You have to die now. Are you ready to die?' As long as you are asking the question, 'What is death?' or 'What is there after death?' you are already dead. These are all dead questions. A living man would never ask those questions.

Is There Such a Thing as Truth?

Truth is a movement. You can't capture it, contain it, give expression to it, or use it to advance your interests. The moment you capture it, it ceases to be the truth. What is the truth for me is something that cannot, under any circumstances, be communicated to you. The certainty here cannot be transmitted to another. For this reason the whole guru business is absolute nonsense. This has always been the case, not just now. Your self-denial is to enrich the priests. You deny yourself your basic needs while that man travels in a Rolls-Royce car, eating like a king, and being treated like a potentate. He, and the others in the holy business, thrive on the stupidity and credulity of others. The politicians, similarly, thrive on the gullibility of man. It is the same everywhere.

Is There Freedom?

I maintain that man has no freedom of action. I don't mean the fatalism that the Indians have practised and still are practising: When I say that man has no freedom of action it is in relation to changing himself, to freeing himself from the burden of the past. It means that you have no way of acting except through the help of the knowledge that is passed on to you. It is in that sense, I said, no action is possible without thought.

So what is necessary is that the individual should free himself from the burden of the past, the great heritage you are talking about. Unless the individual frees himself from the burden of the past, he cannot come up with new solutions for the problems; he repeats the same old . . . So it is up to the individual. He has to free himself from the *entire* past, the heritage which you are talking about—that is to say he has to break away from the cumulative wisdom of the ages—only then is it possible for him to come out with the solutions for the problems with which man is confronted today.

But that is not in his hands; there is nothing that he can do to free himself from the burden of the past. It is in that sense that I say he has no freedom of action. You have freedom to come here or not to come here, to study or teach economics or philosophy or something else—*there* you have a limited freedom. But you have no freedom to control the events of the world or shape the events of the world—*nobody* has that power, no nation has that power.

Man Is Memory

The mind is (not that I am giving a new definition) the totality of man's experiences, thoughts, and feelings. There is no such thing as your mind or my mind. I have no objection if you want to call that totality of man's thoughts, feelings, and experiences by the name 'mind'. But how they are transmitted to us from generation to generation is the question. Is it through the medium of knowledge or is there any other way by which they are transmitted from generation to generation, say for example, through the genes? We don't have the answers yet. Then we come to the idea of memory. What is man? Man is memory. What is that memory? Is it something more than just to remember, to recall a specific thing at a specific time? To all this we have to have some more answers. How do the neurons operate in the brain? Is it all in one area? The other day I was talking to a neurosurgeon, a very young and bright fellow. He said that memory, or rather the neurons containing memory, are not in one area. The eye, the ear, the nose, all the five sensory organs in your body have a different sort of memory. But they don't yet know for sure. So we have to get more answers.

There is always a space between perception and memory. Memory is like sound. Sound is very slow, whereas light travels faster. All these sensory activities or perceptions are like light. They are very fast. But for some reason we have lost the capacity to kick that (memory) into the background and allow these things to move as fast as they occur in nature. Thought comes, captures it (the sensory perception), and says that it is this or that. That is what you call recognition, or naming, or whatever you want to call it.

The moment you recognize this as the tape recorder, the name 'tape recorder' also is there. So recognition and naming are not two different things.

We maintain the separation and keep up a non-existing identity. That is the reason why you have to constantly use your memory, which is nothing but the neurons, to maintain your identity.

'Who am I?', 'What is the meaning of life?', 'Does God exist?' or 'Is there an afterlife?' all these questions spring only from memory. That is why I ask whether you have a question of your own.

What you call the 'act of knowing' is nothing other than this accumulated memory.

Can you become conscious of anything except through the medium of memory and thought? Memory is knowledge. Even your feelings are memory.

To attempt to be free from memory is withdrawal, and withdrawal is death.

You Are Not There

You don't exist. There is no individual there at all. Culture, society, or whatever you want to call it, has created 'you' and 'me' for the sole purpose of maintaining its own continuity. But, at the same time, we are made to believe that you have to become an individual. These two things have created this neurotic situation for us. There is no such thing as an individual, and there is no such thing as freedom of action. I am not talking of a fatalistic philosophy or any such thing. It is this fact that is frustrating us. The demand to fit ourselves into that value system is using a tremendous amount of energy, and there is nothing we can do to deal with the living problems here. All the energy is being consumed by the demands of the culture or society, or whatever you want to call it, to fit you into the framework of that value system. In the process, we are not left with any energy to deal with the other problems. But these problems, that is, the living problems, are very simple.

Relationship Is Division

The problem is a problem of relationship. It is just not possible to establish any relationship with anything around you, including your near and dear ones, except on the level of what you can get out of the relationship. You see, the whole thing springs from this separation or isolation that human beings live in today. We are isolated from the rest of creation, the rest of life around us. We all live in individual frames. We try to establish a relationship at the level of 'What do I get out of that relationship?' We use others to try and fill this void that is created as a result of our isolation.

We always want to fill this emptiness, this void, with all kinds of relationships with people around us. That is really the problem. We have to use everything—an idea, a person, anything we can get hold of, to establish relationships with others. Without relationships we are lost, and we don't see any meaning; we don't see any purpose.

But that relationship is already there. So, what separates you from me, and me from you, is the knowledge we have.

Love Is Fascist

What an amount of energy we are putting into making our relationship into a loving thing! It is a battle, it is a war. It is like preparing yourself all the time for war hoping that there will be peace, eternal peace, or this or that. You are tired of this battle, and you even settle for that horrible, non-loving relationship. And you hope and dream one day it will be nothing but love. 'Love thy neighbour as thyself'—in the name of that how many millions of people have been killed? More than all the recent wars put together. How can you love thy neighbour as thyself? It is just not possible.

Love implies division, separation. As long as there is division, as long as there is a separation within you, so long do you maintain that separation around you. When everything fails, you use the last

card, the trump in the pack of cards, and call it love . . . We say:
I love my country, I love my dog, I love my wife, and what else.
What happens? You love your country, I love my country, and there
is war.

It is not going to help us, and it has not helped us at all. Even
religion has failed to free man from violence and from ten other
different things that it is trying to free us from. You see, it is not
a question of trying to find new concepts, new ideas, new thoughts,
and new beliefs.

What, after all, is the world? The world is the relationship
between two individuals. But that relationship is based on the
foundation of 'What do I get out of a relationship?' Mutual
gratification is the basis of all relationships. If you don't get what
you want out of a relationship, it goes sour. What there is in the
place of what you call a 'loving relationship' is hate.

The whole music of our age is all around that song, 'Love, Love,
Love . . .' But love is fascist in its nature, in its birth, in its
expression and in its action. It cannot do us any good. We may
talk of love but it doesn't mean anything.

Sex Is Thought

Sexuality, if it is left to itself, as it is in the case of other species,
other forms of life, is merely a biological need, because the living
organism has this object to survive and produce one like itself.
Anything you superimpose on that is totally unrelated to the living
organism. But we have turned that, what you call sexual activity,
which is biological in its nature, into a pleasure movement.

It is a very simple functioning of the living organism. The
religious man has turned that into something big, and concentrated
on the control of sex. After that the psychologists have turned that
into something extraordinary. All commercialism is related to sex.
How do you think it will fall into its proper place?

You may ask: Is not sex a basic human requirement? Sex is
dependent upon thought; the body itself has no sex. Only the
genitals and perhaps the hormone balances differ between male and

female. It is thought that says 'I am a man, and that is a woman, an attractive woman.' It is thought that translates sex feelings in the body and says 'These are sexual feelings.' And it is thought that provides the build-up without which no sex is possible: 'It would be more pleasurable to hold that woman's hand than just to look at her. It would be more pleasurable to kiss her than just to embrace her,' and so on. In the Natural State there is no build-up of thought. Without that build-up, sex is impossible. And sex is tremendously violent to the body. The body normally is a very peaceful organism, and then you subject it to this tremendous tension and release, which feels pleasurable to you. Actually it is painful to the body.

But through suppression, or attempts at sublimation of sex, you will never come into this state. As long as you think of God, you will have thoughts of sex. Ask any religious seeker you may know, who practises celibacy, whether he doesn't dream of women at night.

The peak of the sex experience is the one thing in life you have that comes close to being a first-hand experience; all of the rest of your experiences are second-hand, somebody else's. Why do you weave so many taboos and ideas around this? Why do you destroy the joy of sex? Not that I am advocating indulgence or promiscuity; but through abstinence and continence you will never achieve a thing.

Marriage Is Possessiveness

The institution of marriage is not going to disappear. As long as we demand relationships, it will continue in some form or other. Basically, it is a question of possessiveness.

The institution of marriage will somehow continue because it is not just the relationship between the two, but children and property are involved. And we use property and children as a pretext to give continuity to the institution of marriage. The problem is so complex and so complicated. It is not so easy for anybody to come up with answers to the age-old institution of marriage.

Desire and Selfishness

Man is *always* selfish, and he will remain selfish as long as he practises selflessness as a virtue. I have nothing against selfish people. I don't want to talk about selflessness—it has no basis at all. You say 'I will be a selfless man tomorrow. Tomorrow I will be a marvellous man'—but until tomorrow arrives (or the day after tomorrow, or the next life) you will remain selfish. What do you mean by 'selflessness'? You tell everybody to be selfless. What is the point? I have never said to anybody 'Don't be selfish.' Be selfish, stay selfish!—that is my message. Wanting enlightenment is selfishness. The rich man's distributing charity is also selfishness: he will be remembered as a generous man; you will put up a statue of him there.

You have been told that you should practise desirelessness. You have practised desirelessness for thirty or forty years, but still desires are there. So something must be wrong somewhere. Nothing can be wrong with desire; something must be wrong with the one who has told you to practise desirelessness. This (desire) is a reality; that (desirelessness) is false—it is falsifying you. Desire is there. Desire as such can't be wrong, can't be false, because it is there.

Don't you see that it is the very thinking that has turned this into a problem? Anger is energy, desire is energy—all the energy you want is already in operation there.

You hope that you will be able to resolve the problem of desire through thinking, because of that model of a saint who you think has controlled or eliminated desire. If that man has no desire as you imagine, he is a corpse. Don't believe that man at all! Such a man builds some organization, and lives in luxury, which you pay for. You are maintaining him. He is doing it for his livelihood. There is always a fool in the world who falls for him. Once in a while he allows you to prostrate before him. You will be surprised if you live with him. You will get the shock of your life if you see him there. That is why they are all aloof—because they are afraid you will catch them some time or the other. The rich man is always afraid that you will touch him for money. So too the religious man—he never, never comes in contact with you. Seeing him is far more difficult than seeing the President of your country—that is a lot easier than seeing a holy man. He is not what he says he is, not what he claims he is.

As long as there is a living body, there will be desire. It is natural. Thought has interfered and tried to suppress, control, and moralize about desire, to the detriment of mankind. We are trying to solve the 'problem' of desire through thought. It is thinking that has created the problem. You somehow continue to hope and believe that the same instrument can solve your other problems as well. You hope against hope that thought will pull you through, but you will die in hope just as you have lived in hope. That is the refrain of my doom song.

Politics

All the political ideologies, even your legal structures, are the warty outgrowth of the religious thinking of man. It is not so easy to flush out the whole series of experiences which have been accumulated through centuries, and which are based upon the religious thinking of man. There is a tendency to replace one belief with another belief, one illusion with another illusion. That is all we can do.

Revolution Is Only Revaluation of the Old

The human being modelled after the perfect being has totally failed. The model has not touched anything there. Your value system is the one that is responsible for the human malady, the human tragedy, forcing everybody to fit into that model. So, what do we do? You cannot do anything by destroying the value system, because you replace one value system with another. Even those who rebelled against religion, like those in the communist countries, have themselves created another kind of value system. So, revolution does not mean the end of anything. It is only a revaluation of our value system. So, that needs another revolution, and so on and so on. There is no way.

Every human being is different. That is all I am saying. There is nobody like you anywhere in this world. I tell you, nobody! I am talking physiologically, you know. But we ignore that, and try to put everybody in a common mould and create what we call the greatest common factor. All the time you are trying to educate them and fit them into the value system. If that value system does not work, naturally revolutions take place. The whole idea of restructuring is nothing but a revaluation of the old value system. Revolution only means revaluation of our value system. It is the same thing. After a while things settle down, and then they go at it again. There is no improvement again. Or there is a slight improvement. But it is basically a modified continuity of the same. In that process what horrors we have committed, you know! Is it really worth all that? But you seem to think that it is. After killing so many people you go back to the same system, the same technique. What is the point?

Fear and Death

The balance of energy in Nature has to be maintained for some reason. I don't know why. So death occurs only when there is a need for the atoms to maintain the balance of energy in the universe. It is nothing but a reshuffling of atoms. This organism has no way of finding out that it was born at a particular point of time and is going to die at another point of time, and also that it is living at this moment and not dead.

You shall not taste of death, for there is no death for you: you cannot experience your own death. Are you born? Life and death cannot be separated; you have no chance whatever of knowing for yourself where one begins and the other ends. You can experience the death of another, but not your own. The only death is physical death; there is no psychological death.

Why are you so afraid of death?

Your experiencing structure cannot conceive of any event that it will not experience. It even expects to preside over its own dissolution, and so it wonders what death will feel like—it tries to project the feeling of what it will be like not to feel. But in order to anticipate a future experience, your structure needs knowledge, a similar past experience it can call upon for reference. You cannot remember what it felt like not to exist before you were born, and you cannot remember your own birth, so you have no basis for projecting your future non-existence. As long as you have known life, you have known yourself, you have been there, so, to you, you have a feeling of eternity. To justify this feeling of eternity, your structure begins to convince itself that there will be a life after death for you—heaven, reincarnation, transmigration of souls, or whatever. What is it that you think reincarnates? Where is that soul of yours? Can you taste it, touch it, show it to me? What is there inside of you that goes to heaven? What is there? There is nothing inside of you but fear.

Is there Anything to Vegetarianism?

Vegetarianism for what? For some spiritual goals? One form of life lives off another. That's a fact, whether you like it or not. He (the questioner) says his cat is a vegetarian cat, it doesn't kill a fly. Because of its association with vegetarians it has become vegetarian. For health reasons maybe one should. I don't know, I don't see any adequate reason why one should be a vegetarian. Your body is not going to be any more pure than the meat-eating body. You go to India, those that have been vegetarians, they are not kind, they are not peaceful. You will be surprised. Vegetarians can be more aggressive than meat-eaters. Read the history of India—it is full of bloodshed, massacres, and assassinations—all in the name of religion. So it has nothing to do with spirituality—what you put in there (the stomach) is not really the problem.

What Is Life?

You will *never* know what life is. *Nobody* can say anything about life. You can give definitions, but those definitions have no meaning.

You can theorize about life, but that is a thing which is not of any value to you—it cannot help you to understand anything. So you don't ask questions like 'What is life?', you know. 'What is life?'—there is no answer to that question, so the question cannot stay there any longer. You really don't know, so the question disappears. You don't let that happen there, because you think there must be an answer. If you don't know the answer, you think there may be somebody in this world who can give an answer to that question. 'What is life?'—*nobody* can give an answer to that question—we really don't know. So the question cannot stay there; the question burns itself out, you see. The question is born out of thought, so when it burns itself out, what is there is energy. There's a combustion: Thought burns itself out and gives physical energy. In the same way, when the question is burnt, along with it goes the questioner also. The question and the questioner are not two different things. When the question burns itself out, what is there is energy. You can't say anything about that energy—it is already manifesting itself, expressing itself in a boundless way; it has no limitations, no boundaries. It is not yours, not mine; it belongs to everybody. You are part of that. You are an expression of that. Just as the flower is an expression of life, you are another expression of life.

Life is one unitary movement, not two different movements. It's moving, it's a continuous flux, but you cannot look at that flux and say 'that is a flux, . . .' This is just a pure and simple physiological functioning of the organism. Because there is life, there is a response. The response and the stimulus are not two different movements: you cannot separate the response from the stimulus. (The moment you separate the response from the stimulus, there is a division, it is a divisive consciousness that is in operation.) So, it is one movement.

There Are Only Answers, No Questions

Try and formulate a question which you can call your own. This you will discover: they are not your questions at all.

Questions are there because you have a *vague* answer for the question.

Your problems continue because of the false solutions you have invented. If the answers are not there, the questions cannot be there. They are interdependent; your problems and solutions go together. Because you want to use certain answers to end your problems, those problems continue. The numerous solutions offered by all these holy people, the psychologists, the politicians, are not really solutions at all. That is obvious. If there were legitimate answers, there would be no problems. They can only exhort you to try harder, practise more meditation, cultivate humility, stand on your head, and more and more of the same. That is all they can do. The teacher, guru, or leader who offers solutions is also false, along with his so-called answers. He is not doing any honest work, only selling a cheap, shoddy commodity in the marketplace. If you brushed aside your hope, fear, and naiveté, and treated these fellows like businessmen, you would see that they do not deliver the goods, and never will. But you go on and on buying these bogus wares offered up by the experts.

What Is Maya?

Not that the world is an illusion. All the Vedanta philosophers in India, particularly the students of Sankara, indulge in such frivolous, absolute nonsense. The world is not an illusion, but anything you experience in relationship to this point, which itself is illusory, is bound to be an illusion, that's all. The Sanskrit word 'maya' does not mean illusion in the same sense in which the English word is used. 'Maya' means to measure. You cannot measure anything unless you have a point. So, if the centre is absent, there is no circumference at all. That is pure and simple basic arithmetic.

Silence

The peace there, is not this inane dead silence you experience. It's like a volcano erupting all the time. That is the silence; that is

peace. The blood is flowing through your veins like a river. If you
tried to magnify the sound of the flow of your blood you will be
surprised—it's like the roar of the ocean. If you put yourself in a
soundproof room you will not survive even for five minutes. You
will go crazy, because you can't bear the noises that are there in
you. The sound of the beat of your heart is something which you
cannot take. You love to surround yourself with all these sounds
and then you create some funny experience called the 'experience
of the silent mind', which is ridiculous. Absurd. That is the silence
that is there—the roar—the roar of an ocean. Like the roaring of
the flow of blood.

The Body Is Immortal

It is the body which is immortal. It only changes its form after
clinical death, remaining within the flow of life in new shapes. The
body is not concerned with 'the afterlife' or any kind of permanency.
It struggles to survive and multiply now. The fictitious 'beyond',
created by thought, out of fear, is really the demand for more of
the same, in modified form. This demand for repetition of the same
thing over and over again is the demand for permanence. Such
permanence is foreign to the body. Thought's demand for permanence
is choking the body and distorting perception. Thought sees itself
as not just the protector of its own continuity, but also of the body's
continuity. Both are utterly false.

The moment you die, the body begins to decay, returning back
to other, differently organized forms of life, putting an end to
nothing. Life has no beginning and no end. A dead and dying body
feeds the hungry ants there in the grave, and rotting corpses give
off soil-enriching chemicals, which in turn nourish other life forms.
You cannot put an end to your life, it is impossible. The body is
immortal and never asks silly questions like 'Is there immortality?'
It knows that it will come to an end in that particular form, only
to continue on in others. Questions about life after death are always
asked out of fear.

This body has not fundamentally changed for hundreds of

thousands of years. Its propensity to follow leaders, to avoid solitude, to wage war, to join groups—all such traits are in the genetic make-up of mankind, part of his biological inheritance.

The human body, when broken into its constituent elements, is no different from the tree out there or the mosquito that is sucking your blood. Basically, it is exactly the same. The proportions of the elements may be higher in one case and lesser in the case of others. You have eighty per cent of water in the body, and there is eighty per cent of water in the trees and eighty per cent on this planet. So that is the reason why I maintain that we are nothing but a fortuitous concourse of atoms. If and when death takes place, the body is reshuffled, and then these atoms are used to maintain the energy levels in the universe. Other than that, there is no such thing as death to this body.

Thought is only a response to stimuli. The brain is not really a creator; it is just a container. The function of the brain in this body is only to take care of the needs of the physical organism and to maintain its sensitivity, whereas thought, through its constant interference with sensory activity, is destroying the sensitivity of the body. That is where the conflict is. The conflict is between the need of the body to maintain its sensitivity and the demand of thought to translate every sensation within the framework of the sensual activity. I am not condemning sensual activity. Mind, or whatever you want to call it, is born out of this sensuality. So all activities of the mind are sensual in their nature, whereas the activity of the body is to respond to the stimuli around it. That is really the basic conflict between what you call the mind and the body.

You Are a Cheat

You are a cheat. Your religious ambitions are just like the businessman's there. If you can't cheat there is something wrong. How do you think the rich man there got his great wealth? Through lectures about non-greed and selflessness? Not at all. He got it by cheating somebody. Society, which is immoral to begin with, says that cheating is immoral, and that non-cheating is moral. I don't see the difference. If you get caught they put you in jail. So your food and shelter are provided for. Why worry? It is the guilt you have that compels you to talk of non-greed while you continue on with your greedy life. Your non-greed is invented by thought to keep you from facing the fact that greed is all that is there. But you are not satisfied with what is so. If there were nothing more than that, what would you do? That is all that is there. You just have to live with it. You can't escape. All thought can do is repeat itself over and over again. That is all it can do. And anything repetitive is senile.

There Is No Such Thing as Spirituality

Separating things, dividing things into material life, and spiritual life. There is only one life. This is a material life, and that other has no relevance. Wanting to change your material life into that so-called religious pattern given to you, placed before you by these religious people, is destroying the possibility of your living in harmony and accepting the reality of this material world exactly the way it is. That is responsible for your pain, for your suffering, for your sorrow.

Stop It

You can stop it in you. Free yourself from that social structure that is operating in you without becoming anti-social, without becoming a reformer, without becoming anti-this, anti-that. You can throw the whole thing out of your system and free yourself from the burden of this culture, for yourself and by yourself. Whether it has any usefulness for society or not is not your concern. If there is one individual who walks free, you don't have any more the choking feeling of what this horrible culture has done to you. It's neither East nor West, it's all the same. Human nature is exactly the same— there's no difference.

You Are Unique

By using the models of Jesus, Buddha, or Krishna we have destroyed the possibility of nature throwing up unique individuals. Those who recommend that you forget your own natural uniqueness and be like someone else, no matter how saintly that person may be, is putting you on the wrong track. It is like the blind leading the blind.

When dealing with these yogis and holy men, the first wrong turn you take is in trying to relate the way they are functioning with the way you are functioning. What they are describing may not be related to the way you are functioning at all. Uniqueness is not something which can be turned out in a factory. Society is interested only in the status quo and has provided all these so-called special individuals so that you'll have models to follow. You want to be like that fellow—the saint, the saviour, or the revolutionary— but it is an impossibility. Your society, which is only interested in turning out copies of acceptable models, is threatened by real individuality because it (individuality) threatens its continuity. A truly unique person, having no cultural reference point, would never know that he is unique.

What nature has created in the form of the human species is something extraordinary. It is an unparalleled creation. But culture is interested in fitting the actions of all human beings into a common mould. That is because it is interested in maintaining the status quo, its value system. That is where the real conflict is.

Man cannot become man so long as he follows somebody. What is responsible for man remaining an animal is that culture—the top dog, following somebody—that has not helped you at all. You want to be a cheap imitation of Sankara or Buddha; you don't want to be yourself. What for? I tell you, you are far more unique and extraordinary than all those saints and saviours of mankind put together. Why do you want to be a cheap imitation of that fellow? That is one of the myths. Forget it.

Sages

You cannot become a sage through any sadhana (spiritual practice); it is not in your hands. A sage cannot have a disciple, a sage cannot have a follower, because it is not an experience that can be shared. The sages and seers are original and unique because they have freed themselves from the entire past. (Even the mystic experience is part of the past.) Not that the past goes for such a man; but for him the past has no emotional content—it is not continually operative, colouring the actions.

The Real Problem Is the Solution

The real problem is the solution. Your problems continue because of the false solutions you have invented. If the answers are not there, the questions cannot be there. They are interdependent; your problems and solutions go together. Because you want to use certain answers to end your problems, those problems continue. The numerous solutions offered by all these holy people, the psychologists, the politicians, are not really solutions at all. That is obvious. They can only exhort you to try harder, practise more meditations, cultivate humility, stand on your head, and more and more of the same. That is all they can do. If you brushed aside your hope, fear, and naiveté, and treated these fellows like businessmen, you would see that they do not deliver the goods, and never will. But you go on and on buying these bogus wares offered up by the experts.

Actually there are no problems, there are only solutions. But we don't even have the guts to say that they don't work. Even if you have discovered that they don't work, sentimentality comes into the picture. The feeling, 'That man in whom I have placed my confidence and belief cannot con himself and con everyone else,' comes in the way of throwing the whole thing out of the window, down the drain. The solutions are still a problem. Actually there is no problem there. The only problem is to find out the inadequacy or uselessness of all the solutions that have been offered to us. The questions naturally are born out of the assumptions and answers that we have taken for granted as real answers. But we really don't want any answers to the questions, because an answer to the questions is the end of the answers. If one answer ends, all the other answers also go.

No Power Outside of You

Psychic powers, clairvoyance, clairaudience—they are all human instincts. And they are necessary because there are two things that the human organism is interested in. One: its survival at any cost. Why should it survive? I don't know; it is a foolish question to ask. That is one of the most important things: it has a survival mechanism of its own, which is quite different from the survival mechanism of the movement of thought. The second thing is: to reproduce itself. It has to reproduce. These are the two fundamental characteristics of the human organism, the living organism.

I can tell you that there is no power outside of you—no power. This does not mean that you have all the attributes that you read about of the super-duper gods; but there is no power outside of you. If there is any power in this universe, it is in you.

Courage to Stand Alone

Man has to be saved from the saviours of mankind! The religious people—they kidded themselves and fooled the whole of mankind. Throw them out! That is courage itself, because of the courage there; not the courage you practise.

Fearlessness is not freedom from all phobias. The phobias are essential for the survival of the organism. You must have the fear of heights and the fear of depths—if that is not there, there is a danger of your falling. But you want to teach courage to man to fight on the battlefield. Why do you want to teach him courage? To kill others and get killed himself—that is your culture. Crossing the Atlantic in a balloon or the Pacific on a raft—anybody can do that—that is not courage. Fearlessness is not a silly thing like that.

Courage is to brush aside everything that man has experienced and felt before you. You are the only one, greater than all those things. Everything is finished, the whole tradition is finished, however sacred and holy it may be—then only can you be yourself—that is individuality. For the first time you become an individual.

What Is

We are not created for any grander purpose than the ants that are there or the flies that are hovering around us or the mosquitoes that are sucking our blood.

★

We are no more purposeful or meaningful than any other thing on this planet.

★

The plain fact is that if you don't have a problem, you create one. If you don't have a problem you don't feel that you are living.

★

When you are no longer caught up in the dichotomy of right and wrong or good and bad, you can never do anything wrong. As long as you are caught up in this duality, the danger is that you will always do wrong.

★

In Nature there is no death or destruction at all. What occurs is the reshuffling of atoms. If there is a need or necessity to maintain the balance of 'energy' in this universe, death occurs.

★

An artist is a craftsman like any other. He uses that tool to express himself. All art is a pleasure movement.

★

There is more life in a chorus of barking dogs than in the music or singing of your famous musicians and singers.

★

A Messiah is the one who leaves a mess behind him in this world.

★

Religions have promised roses but you end up with only thorns.

★

It is terror—not love, not brotherhood—that will help us to live together.

★

Meditation itself is evil. That is why you get evil thoughts when you start meditating.

★

Anything you want to be free from for whatever reason is the very thing that can free you.

★

Atmospheric pollution is most harmless when compared to the spiritual and religious pollution that has plagued the world.

★

Going to the pub or the temple is exactly the same; it is a quick fix.

★

The body has no independent existence. You are a squatter there.

★

God and sex go together. If God goes, sex goes too.

★

When you know nothing, you say a lot. When you know something, there is nothing to say.

★

You have to touch life at a point where nobody has touched it before. Nobody can teach you that.

★

Until you have the courage to blast me, all that I am saying—and all gurus—you will remain a cultist with photographs, rituals, birthday celebrations and the like.

★

All I can guarantee you is that as long as you are searching for happiness, you will remain unhappy.

★

Understanding yourself is one of the greatest jokes perpetrated not only by the purveyors of ancient wisdom—the holy men—but also the modern scientists. The psychologists love to talk about self-knowledge, self-actualization, living from moment to moment, and such rot.

★

The more you know about yourself the more impossible it becomes to be humble and sensitive. How can there be humility as long as you know something?

★

It is mortality that creates immortality. It is the known that creates the unknown. It is time that has created the timeless. It is thought that has created the thoughtless.

★

You actually have no way of looking at the sunset because you are not separated from the sunset. The moment you separate your self from the sunset, the poet in you comes out. Out of that separation poets and painters have tried to express themselves, to share their experiences with others. All that is culture.

★

The feminist movement will not succeed as long as the woman depends on the man for her sexual needs.

★

All experiences, however extraordinary they may be, are in the area of sensuality.

★

Humility is an art that one practises. There is no such thing as humility. As long as you know, there is no humility. The known and humility cannot coexist.

★

Man cannot be anything other than what he is. Whatever he is, he will create a society that mirrors him.

★

Inspiration is a meaningless thing. Lost, desperate people create a market for inspiration. All inspired action will eventually destroy you and your kind.

★

Love and hate are not opposite ends of the same spectrum; they are one and the same thing. They are much closer than kissing cousins.

★

It is a terrible thing to use somebody to get pleasure. Whatever you use, an idea, a concept, a drug, or a person, or anything else, you cannot have pleasure without using something.

★

Hinduism is not a religion in the usual sense. It is a combination and confusion of many things. It is like a street with hundreds of shops.

★

Gurus play a social role, so do prostitutes.

★

Society, which has created all these sociopaths, has invented morality to protect itself from them. Society has created the 'saints' and 'sinners'. I don't accept them as such.

★

By using the models of Jesus, Buddha, or Krishna we have destroyed the possibility of Nature throwing up unique individuals.

★

As long as you are doing something to be selfless, you will be a self-centred individual.

★

The subject does not exist there. It is the object that creates the subject. This runs counter to the whole philosophical thinking of India.

★

When thought is not there all the time, what is there is living from moment to moment. It's all in frames, millions and millions and millions of frames, to put it in the language of film.

★

The man who spoke of 'love thy neighbour as thyself' is responsible for this horror in the world today. Don't exonerate those teachers.

★

Life has to be described in pure and simple physical and physiological terms. It must be demystified and depsychologized.

★

Society is built on a foundation of conflict, and you are society. Therefore you must always be in conflict with society.

★

You know the story of *Alice in Wonderland*. The red queen has to run faster and faster to keep still where she is. That is exactly what you are all doing. Running faster and faster. But you are not moving anywhere.

★

The appreciation of music, poetry and language is all culturally determined and is the product of thought. It is acquired taste that tells you that Beethoven's Ninth Symphony is more beautiful than a chorus of cats screaming; both produce equally valid sensations.

★

The peak of sex experience is the one thing in life you have that comes close to being a first-hand experience; all the rest of your experiences are second-hand, somebody else's.

★

The problem with language is, no matter how we try to express ourselves, we are caught up in the structure of words. There is no point in creating a new language, a new lingo, to express anything. There is nothing there to be expressed except to free yourself from the stranglehold of thought.

★

What you call 'yourself' is fear. The 'you' is born out of fear; it lives in fear, functions in fear and dies in fear.

★

It would be more interesting to learn from children, than try to teach them how to behave, how to live and how to function.

★

Food, clothing and shelter—these are the basic needs. Beyond that, if you want anything, it is the beginning of self-deception.

Knock Off

My interest is not to knock off what others have said (that is too easy), but to knock off what *I* am saying. More precisely, I am trying to stop what you are making out of what I am saying. This is why my talking sounds contradictory to others. I am forced by the nature of your listening to always negate the first statement with another statement. Then the second statement is negated by a third, and so on. My aim is not some comfy dialectical thesis, but the total negation of everything that can be expressed. Anything you try to make out of my statements is not it.

23

Notes

BOOK ONE

1. *Digambara*: Naked, sky-clad or one clothed in the directions of the sky. I use the term here simply to mean one oblivious to the world around.
2. *Confessions of a Sanyasi*, Mukunda Rao, Atlantic Publishers, New Delhi, 1988.
3. One who has no teaching, no disciples, and no fixed abode.
4. *Zen Flesh Zen Bones*, Compiled by Paul Reps, Penguin Books, England, 2000.
5. *The Sage and the Housewife*, Shanta Kelker, Sowmya Publishers, Bangalore, 1990, p. 99.
6. *UG Krishnamurti—A Life*, Mahesh Bhatt, Penguin Books India, New Delhi 1992, p.70.
7. *Rama Revisited & Other Stories*, Mukunda Rao, Writers Workshop, Calcutta, 2001.
8. Commentaries on Living: Third Series, from The Notebooks of J. Krishnamurti, Edited by D. Rajagopal, B.I. Publications, 1984.
9. *The Power of Myth*, Joseph Campbell in conversation with Bill Moyers, Anchor Books, A Division of Random House Inc., New York, 1991.
10. From the speech "The Dissolution of the Order of the Star" compiled in *Total Freedom* by J. Krishnamurti, © 1996 Krishnamurti Foundation of America and Krishnamurti Foundation Trust, Ltd.
11. *JK, Early Writings*, Chetana, Bombay, 1971, Vol.4.
12. *The Mystique of Enlightenment—The Unrational Ideas of a Man called U G*, Edited by Rodney Arms, Published by Dinesh Vaghela, Goa, India, 1982, p. 8.
13. *Star in the East—Krishnamurti, the Invention of a Messiah*, Roland Vernon, Penguin Books India, 2002, p. 208.
14. UG Archives in National Archives, Government of India, New Delhi.
15. Quoted from *Shiva—The Erotic Ascetic*, Wendy Flaherty, Oxford University Press.

16. Quoted from *Poems from Sanskrit*, Translated by John Brough, Penguin Books, England, 1977, p. 165.

17. UG Archives in National Archives, Government of India, New Delhi.

18. *Mahatma—Life of Mohandas Karamchand Gandhi*, by D. G. Tendulkar, Publication Division, Government of India, 1953, reprinted 1969, Vol VII, p. 85.

19. UG Archives, Government of India, New Delhi.

20. Quoted from *UG Krishnamurti—A Life*, Mahesh Bhatt, Penguin Books India, 1992, pp. 32–33.

21. Quoted from *Krishnamurti: The Years of Fulfilment*, Mary Lutyens, Avon Books, New York, 1983, pp. 204–5. Reproduced with permission from Krishnamurti Foundation Trust, Brockwood Park, Bramdean, Hampshire, S0240LQ England.

22. *Speaking of Siva*, A.K. Ramanujan, Penguin Books, New Delhi 1973.

23. Ibid.

24. Quoted from *The Collected Works of J. Krishnamurti*, Vol. VIII: 1953–55, KFA, 1991, Madras talks, 13 December 1953.

25. Refer *Ramana Maharshi and the Path of Self-knowledge* by Arthur Osborne, published by Sri Ramanasramam, 1970.

26. *Life of Sri Ramakrishna*, Published by Advaita Ashram, Calcutta, 1977, p. 44.

27. *The Kitchen Chronicles—1001 Lunches with J. Krishnamurti*, Michael Krohnen, Penguin Books, India, 1997, p. 296.

28. Ibid.

29. Extracted from *The Collected Works of J. Krishnamurti*, Vol. VIII: 1953–55, KFA, 1991, Madras talks, 13 December 1953.

30. Refer *Life and Death of Krishnamurti*, Mary Lutyens, John Murray Limited, Great Britain, 1990, and Srishti Publishers & Distributors, New Delhi, 1999.

31. For the debate between Sankara and Mandana Mishra, and Ubhaya Bharati, refer to *Sankara Digvijaya*, Madhava-Vidyaranya, Translated into English by Swami Tapasyananda, Published by Sri Ramakrishna Math, Madras, India, 1980.

32. Rohit Mehta's Foreword in *The Intuitive Philosophy—Krishnamurti's Approach to Life*, Chetana, Bombay, 1950.

33. UG Archives.

34. Ibid.

35. Ibid.

36. The Vachanas of Allama are quoted from *Speaking Of Siva*, A.K. Ramanujan, Penguin Books, 1973.

37. UG Archives.

38. Ibid.

39. Ibid.
40. Quoted from K. Chandrashekar's notes. I owe a lot to him for making his notes accessible and for the many discussions we have had on UG and Valentine.
41. Read the texts on Kundalini Yoga, in particular, *Kundalini—Path to Higher Consciousness*, Pandit Gopi Krishna, Orient Paperbacks, Delhi, 1976. Many of the texts on Kundalini Yoga seem almost elementary when contrasted with UG's 'Calamity' or physiological changes.
42. For the details of this incredible biological mutation, in UG's own words, see *The Mystique of Enlightenment—The Unrational Ideas of a Man called U G*, Edited by Rodney Arms, Published by Dinesh Vaghela, Goa, 1982.
43. Quoted from *U.G. Krishnamurti—A Life*, Mahesh Bhatt, Penguin Books India, 1992.
44. *The Mystique of Enlightenment—The Unrational Ideas of a Man called UG.*
45. Ibid.
46. U.G. *Krishnamurti—A Life*, Mahesh Bhatt, Penguin Books India, 1992.
47. K. Chandrashekar's unpublished Notes.
48. U.G. *Krishnamurti—A Life*, Mahesh Bhatt, Penguin Books India, 1992.
49. UG Archives.

BOOK TWO

50. *A History of God—From Abraham to the Present: the 4000-year Quest for God*, Karen Armstrong, Vintage, 1999.
51. For a critique of patriarchal philosophy, religion and politics, see *A Reader in Feminist Knowledge*, Edited by Sneja Gunew, Routledge, London & New York, 1991.
52. Ibid.
53. *Brihadaranyaka Upanishad* 1.4.1-5. Quoted from Joseph Campbell, *Oriental Mythology*, A Condor Book, Souvenir Press, London, 2000, pp. 9–10.
54. Ibid. p. 11.
55. Ibid.
56. *Janus: A Summing Up*, Arthur Koestler, Picador, 1979.
57. K. Chandrashekar's unpublished Notes.
58. Extracted from *The Collected Works of J. Krishnamurti*, Vol. XVIII, pp 174-1-75 © 1992 Krishnamurti Foundation of America.

59. *Mysticism & Religious Traditions*, Edited by Steven T. Katz, OUP, 1983.
60. The 'Conservative Character of Mystical Experience', by Steven T. Katz in *Mysticism & Religious Traditions*, Edited by Steven T. Katz, OUP, 1983.
61. See *The Light at the Centre—Context and Pretext of Modern Mysticism*, Agehananda Bharati, Bell Books, Vikas Publishing House, 1977, p.28.
62. *Mysticism & Religious Traditions* Edited by Steven T. Katz, p. 79, OUP, 1983.
63. Ibid.
64. *The Light at the Centre—Context and Pretext of Modern Mysticism*, Agehananda Bharati, Bell Books, Vikas Publishing House, 1977.
65. Ibid.
66. *Cows, Pigs, Wars and Witches—The Riddles of Culture*, Marvin Harris, Fontana Books, 1978.
67. *The Power of Myth*, Joseph Campbell with Bill Moyers, Anchor Books, 1991.
68. *A History of God*, Karen Armstrong, Vintage, 1999.
69. Marvin Harris.
70. *Oriental Mythology*, Joseph Campbell.
71. Ibid.
72. Ibid.
73. *The Power of Myth*, Joseph Campbell.
74. Quoted in *Post Modernity*, David Lyon, Viva Books, 2002.
75. Quoted in *Interrupting Derrida*, Geoffrey Bennington, Routledge, London & New York, 2000, p. 21.
76. *The Poverty of Historicism, The Open Society and its Enemies*, Vols. I & II, Karl Popper, Routledge and Kegan Paul, 1977.
77. 'Love's Labour Lost—Marxism & Feminism,' Mea Campioni & Elizabeth Grosz, in *A Reader in Feminist Knowledge*, Edited by Sneza Gunew, Routledge, London, 1991.
78. *Janus: A Summing Up*, Arthur Koestler.
79. *The Foucault Reader*, Edited by Paul Rabinow, Penguin Books, London, 1991.
80. Quoted in *Janus: A Summing Up*, p. 8.
81. *The Barbarian Temperament—Toward A Postmodern Critical Theory*, Stjepan G. Mestrovic, Routledge, London, 1993, p. 63.
82. Ibid. p. 47.
83. *Janus: A Summing Up*, Arthur Koestler, Picador, 1979.
84. *The Year Of The Phoenix—Not A Novel*, T.K. Mahadevan, Arnold-Heinemann, 1982.
85. *Intellectuals*, Paul Johnson, HarperCollins, New York, 1990.

86. Quoted in *Intellectuals*, Paul Johnson.

87. Ibid.

88. *Gyn/Ecology—The Metaethics of Radical Feminism*, Mary Daly, The Women's Press, Great Britain, 1987.

89. Refer online article *Osho, Bhagwan Rajneesh, and the Lost Truth*. Web Page of Christopher Calder.

90. *Lives in the Shadow with J. Krishnamurti*, by Radha Rajagopal Sloss, Bloomsbury, 1991.

91. From *The Gay Science* (1882), in the introduction to *Thus Spake Zarathustra*, Translated by R.J. Hollingdale, Penguin Classics, 1961.

92. *Friedrich Nietzsche*: Selected Writings, Stephen Metcalf, Srishti Publishers & Distributors, 2001.

93. Ibid.

94. *The Supramental Manifestation & Other Writings*, Aurobindo, Sri Aurobindo Ashram, Pondicherry, 1971.

95. Quoted in *Sri Aurobindo or The Adventure of Consciousness*, Satprem, Sri Aurobindo Ashram, 1973.

96. *The Serpent and the Rope* by Raja Rao, Orient Paperbacks, New Delhi, 1970.

97. *Total Freedom, The Essential Krishnamurti*, Krishnamurti Foundation India, Chennai, 2002.

98. Quoted in *Life and Death of Krishnamurti* by Mary Lutyens, Srishti Publishers & Distributors, 1990.

99. *God Men, Con Men*, by Robert Carr, Smriti Books, New Delhi, 2003.

100. *The Hermeneutics of Postmodernity—Figures & Themes*, G. B. Madison, Midland Book Edition, 1990.

101. Ibid.

102. Ibid.

103. *The Selfish Gene*, Richard Dawkins, Oxford University Press, New York, 1999.

104. Ibid.

105. See the Notes in his *A Theory of Everything—An Integral Vision for Business, Politics, Science & Spirituality*, Gateway, 2001.

106. *The Meme Machine*, Susan Blackmore, Oxford University Press, 1999.

107. Ibid.

108. Quoted in *The Hidden Connection*, Fritjof Capra, Flamingo, 2003.

109. Ibid.

110. For interesting insights into the body–mind problem and related issues, see Jeffrey Mishlove's discussions with Fritjof Capra, Rupert Sheldrake, Saul-Paul Sirag, Julian Isaacs, Karl Pribram, U

G. Krishnamurti and others, in *Thinking Allowed*, Council Oak Books, 1992.

111. See Vilayanur S. Ramachandran's Reith Lectures on 'The Emerging Mind' available online at http://www.bbc.couk/radio4/reith2003.
112. *The Hidden Connection*, Fritjof Capra.
113. *Thinking Allowed*, Jeffrey Mishlove.
114. *Oriental Mythology*, Joseph Campbell.
115. Julian Isaac in conversation with Jeffrey Mishlove in *Thinking Allowed*.
116. *Eastern Religions and Western Thought*, S. Radhakrishnan, Oxford University Press, 1977, pp. 26–27.
117. This quotation and all the other quotations from the Mother in this chapter are from *The Mind of the Cells—or Willed Mutation of Our Species*, Edited by Satprem, Institute for Evolutionary Research, New York, 1982.
118. *Thinking Allowed*, p. 270.
119. Quoted by Arthur Koestler in *Janus: A Summing Up*.
120. Quoted in *The Collected Essays of A.K. Ramanujan*, Edited by Vinay Dharwadkar, Oxford University Press, 2001.
121. *The Origin of Life*, Paul Davies, Penguin Books, 2000.
122. *Laughing Matters—Comic Tradition in India*, Lee Siegel, Motilal Banarasidass, 1989.
123. *The Collected Essays of A.K. Ramanujan*, Edited by Vinay Dharwadkar.

BOOK THREE

1. *Telling It Like It Is*, UG's anti-teaching, has been collated from my conversations with him over the years and from the following books:

a. *The Mystique of Enlightenment—The Unrational Ideas of a Man called UG*, Edited by Rodney Arms, Published by Dinesh Vaghela, Goa, India, 1982.
b. *Mind is a Myth (Disquieting Conversations with the Man called UG)*, Edited by Terry Newland, Dinesh Publications, 1988.
c. *The Sage and the Housewife*, Shanta Kelker, Sowmya Publishers, Bangalore, 1990.
d. *No Way Out* (Conversations with U.G. Krishnamurti), edited by, J.S.R.L. Narayana Moorty, Antony Paul Frank Noronha, Sunita Pant Bansal, Smriti Books, New Delhi, 2002.
e. *Thought Is Your Enemy* (Conversations with U.G. Krishnamurti), Smriti Books, New Delhi, 2002.